Unsettled

Unsettled

A RECKONING ON THE GREAT PLAINS

DAWN MORGAN

 University of Regina Press

COVER PHOTO: "Evening view of an old fence in Grasslands National Park, Saskatchewan, Canada" by jkgabbert/ Adobestock.

MAP: Weldon Hiebert. Contains information licensed under the Open Government License (Canada) and from the United States Geological Survey.

COVER AND BOOK DESIGN: Duncan Campbell, University of Regina Press
COPY EDITOR: Dallas Harrison
PROOFREADER: Nancy Mackenzie

Library and Archives Canada Cataloguing in Publication

TITLE: Unsettled : a reckoning on the Great Plains / Dawn Morgan.

NAMES: Morgan, Dawn, 1957- author.

DESCRIPTION: Includes bibliographical references.

IDENTIFIERS: Canadiana (print) 20210367407 | Canadiana (ebook) 20210367482 | ISBN 9780889778573 (softcover) | ISBN 9780889778603 (hardcover) | ISBN 9780889778580 (pdf) | ISBN 9780889778597 (EPUB)

SUBJECTS: LCSH: Morgan, Dawn, 1957- | LCSH: Morgan, Dawn, 1957-,—Family. | LCSH: Great Plains,—Race relations,—History. | LCSH: Great Plains,—Ethnic relations,—History. | LCSH: Frontier and pioneer life,—Great Plains. | LCSH: Indigenous peoples,—Great Plains,—History,—20th century. | LCSH: Great Plains,—Social conditions,—20th century. | LCGFT: Autobiographies. | LCGFT: Creative nonfiction.

CLASSIFICATION: LCC PS8626.O7447 U57 2022 | DDC C814/.6,—dc23

University of Regina Press, University of Regina
Regina, Saskatchewan, Canada, s4s 0A2
TEL: (306) 585-4758 FAX: (306) 585-4699
WEB: www.uofrpress.ca

We acknowledge the support of the Canada Council for the Arts for our publishing program. We acknowledge the financial support of the Government of Canada. / Nous reconnaissons l'appui financier du gouvernement du Canada. This publication was made possible with support from Creative Saskatchewan's Book Publishing Production Grant Program.

Dedicated to the memory of my parents,

Bern Maxwell Morgan,
born 1923 Cabri, Saskatchewan,
died 1979 Cantuar, Saskatchewan,

and

Nona Grace Morgan Lucas
(née McLeod),
born 1927 Cabri, Saskatchewan,
died 2013 Assiniboia, Saskatchewan,

and my brother,

Curtis Ralph Morgan,
born 1952 Cabri, Saskatchewan,
died 2003 on the Morgan homestead near Cabri

To weep into stones are fables.

—THOMAS BROWNE, *Urn Burial* (1658)

Contents

CONTENTS
(annotated)

"This is two fools, they are all three"
—Rodeo clowns distract the enraged bulls
—The undertaker calls back—Approximation
of the grave

I followed, tailgates we ate from—Chuckwagon
races—A memorable pen in Selden, Kansas—
Contrails connect parents to their children—
Art Bell on late-night radio—Coordinates,
constellations—Taxidermy stills the faces of
contradiction—Joe Fafard's *The Evil Moon
Guides the* Santa Maria *to the New World*—
Buffalo Commons—The Ring of Fire—
A selective history of branding—*Grievous Angel:
The Legend of Gram Parsons*—Suicide Notes

Dodge City, Kansas—The Nature Theatre of
Oklahoma—Social climbing and falling, angels
and ladders—Reunion of parents and children
—Karl May, western pulp fiction fabulist—
Three corralled horses at Madrid, Nebraska—
Chase, a cowboy in Nashville—Dwight Yoakam
alone on a barstool— Heartaches by the number
—I take up the pen—"Now That I Been to Nashville"
—Western or Denver? The sandwich—North
or south? —"In my hour of darkness"—On
the road with William Walker—Where
to sever the Americas—Sandinista final
offensive, spring 1979—Water for my horses—
Madrid Farmer, Hunter, Coyote, the trio at odds
—Missing sandal, lost footing—Buffalo Bill
Cody's Wild West Show—Death of Sitting Bull—
Loss of territory at the touch of the pen

The word *cowboy* an insult—Dutch Henry—
The Big Muddy, Station One of the outlaw
trail—Butch Cassidy and the Sundance
Kid—Sarmiento's *Facundo*, story of an

Argentine gaucho—Severing of ties, children from parents, settlers from Europe—The *Martín Fierro*, cowboy masterpiece in any language—A manual for how to shape the truth—The word *cowboy* a compliment—Roosevelt "In Cowboy Land"—Corral and cowpen, Spanish and English exchange glances in a mirror—"The Bullfight as Mirror"—At my mother's deathbed—Outline of my life—Stirring of the Buffalo God

A NOTE ON VOCABULARY

Indigenous peoples and communities are identified in this work by the names used at the times and places depicted. Assiniboine, Sioux, Blackfoot, Cree, Ojibway, Stoney, Blood, and Peigan are referred to and named primarily from my perspective as a descendant of settlers.

The name Assiniboine in particular is retained throughout because it is the source of the place name Assiniboia, my birthplace, a central reference point in the narrative that commemorates on maps the Indigenous people displaced from the townsite and its environs to make way for European settlement on the territory later covered by Treaty 4, signed in 1874.

The terms "Indian" and "Aboriginal" are used in some instances to refer to Indigenous people in keeping with the setting or context of narrated events, as long as that usage is not derogatory. The term "Indigenous" is capitalized where adopted, which is consistent with the standard capitalization of equivalent terms, such as "English," "British," and "European."

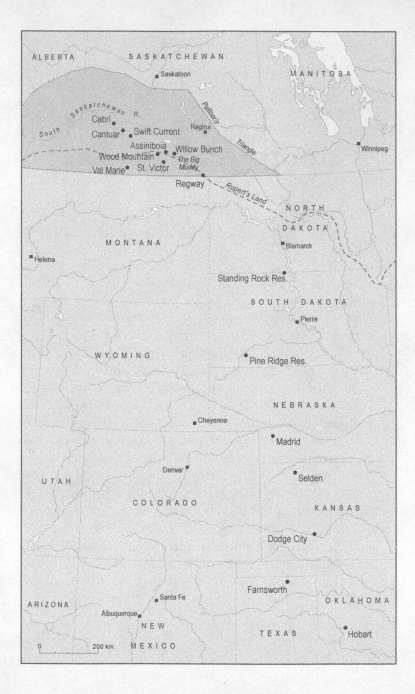

Unsettled

Insert #2

CORRAL

What I've been able to piece together is that Dad was then living on Johnny Bradley's ranch near Cantuar, already a ghost town, now just a community hall and freight stop on the Great Sandhills Railway, northwest of Swift Current. Dad was taken on as the hired man, ranch hand, and wrangler to help with the buffalo that Bradley, an old bachelor rumoured to be fairly well-to-do, was breeding and reintroducing to the area, prairie ranchlands dotted with see-sawing oil pump jacks and, to the west, drifting sand dunes, land marginal for farming anyway. Bradley's rescue of my dad from homelessness and despair was probably motivated by the same spirit that moved the rancher to shelter the buffalo, the once majestic beasts of the Great Plains chased and hunted nearly to extinction with pioneer fervour and even murderous glee in the demarcation of homesteads around piles of their bones on land fenced for proving up and taking possession as private property. With the same kindliness that Bradley showed the buffalo, he gave my dad a refuge when all was wrecked and torn asunder by the forces that tossed him about ever since surrendering his own farm, what had been his dad's, Pop Morgan's homestead, in the very year that I was born.

How sorry and lonesome Dad must have been when Johnny took him in. How lucky to run into Johnny one day, likely at the Healy Hotel in Swift Current. Whether Dad left or was forced out of our house of nine kids and my mom and rode out of Assiniboia—the town named for the people wiped out there to make room for the settlers, a town that had nothing but menial, piecemeal labour for him and less and less of that the more that he took solace in drink—is a matter of some dispute. However it was, Dad made his way back to Swift Current, the commercial centre for Bradley's ranch and the farms all around there where my parents grew up, the Morgan place by then farmed by Willard Colpitts, the best man at their wedding. That whole territory—Cabri, Cantuar, Swift Current, Assiniboia, Wood Mountain, Cypress Hills—was the booty of Treaty 4, though no one talked about it that way at the time. I heard that Dad got irregular work as a stonemason at first, the trade other than farming he was most interested in but seemed to be another cause of dissension with my mom. Why that was so I was never able to fathom.

Johnny laid out one condition: no drinking on the ranch. "I don't care what you do anywhere else, Bern," Johnny might have said, "but there's no drinking once you cross that Texas gate," the metal grille flush with the ground that cattle will not cross for fear of a hoof slipping through. Johnny needed an extra hand, or maybe he did, to handle an especially ornery buffalo bull, his star breeder King, sire of most of the calves that spring, eight in all, though one, a twin, didn't make it, and Johnny found it frozen to death not far from the barn but not close enough to have found it in time. By all accounts, he had grown attached to King and loved to show him off to neighbours and stock buyers whenever they came by the ranch. But something had gone wrong. King was jumpy and easily annoyed, and the vet said that it was likely because of his age. He'd gone partly blind, and maybe he'd just had enough. He would lower his massive curly head and ram his thick pointed horns into the fence boards of the corral with no apparent provocation, even stamping and snorting with menace at Johnny when he came to open the gate so King could roam free in the pasture. The King had had his day. When Johnny took Dad on, likely the abattoir and taxidermist had already been notified and a date set for early March to load King onto a truck and take him to meet his final fate. It would be quite a job to get the old beast loaded onto the truck. My dad's help was sorely needed.

Time passed until the raw early weeks of spring arrived. The ground softened. They said my dad worked hard on the ranch, but in the spring, once the calving is done, there is always a lull in the work, so I suppose he thought he could spare some time in town before things got busy again. Dad worked hard most of the time and had his room and board in Johnny's ranch house. But maybe he was jumpy and disturbed, too, during King's last days. Prevailing northwest winds blew down in a duel between the steaming ground and slow melt of the snow under the fledgling sun at the end of February, beginning of March. However it was, Dad went to town one day in an old half-ton, either his or one that Johnny gave him for work on the ranch. Dad would have angled in alongside all the other trucks parked in front of the Healy Hotel, farmers, ranchers, road crews, construction workers, all restless for the final thaw and the season's work to begin. In a time-lapse video, I imagine all of the trucks—driven by leather-skinned men in John Deere or Roughrider caps, the odd oversized cowboy hat—pulling up to the bar, backing out, each truck soon replaced by an identical truck, driver, and cap pulling in. Over two or three days or so, a couple of nights, only my dad's truck would not move in that video. Dad was on a bender and unable to go back to the ranch for all the reasons that more and more drinks would never be enough. Finally, though, like always, Dad would emerge, a small man with bright brown eyes, alert and laughing, but with sorrow flickering, always slight shadows, at the corners. When he was sober, there was no one brighter than my dad, although on that day he might have been moving a bit less sprightly, sobered up just enough that morning to drive to the ranch after downing a raw egg in tomato juice at the coffee shop counter. He gets into his truck not exactly sure of how much time has passed since he pulled in, but anyway, heads back to the ranch.

Dad might have met the ambulance on the road out of town, or maybe, alarmingly, it was still parked with lights flashing in the yard beside the cattle truck with its loading ramp extended down to what was left of the gate to the corral. "What the hell?" he thinks. "Did Johnny have a heart attack? An accident? Fool didn't try loading King without me?" Maybe Dad slowly realized the date as he tried to calculate, on the way out to the ranch, exactly how long he'd been in town. He pauses a moment behind the wheel, his mouth gone dry, the taste of ashes and dread moving up his throat. Maybe he sees the finality of things even before he slowly opens the door, engine left idling, and steps onto the softening and slippery ground. The corral fence is smashed where the truck and ramp are backed up to it, wooden planks and poles splintered and scattered about like trash. The truck driver, cradling a still warm rifle in his arms, chin sinking to the ground, glances sideways as Dad moves in beside him. King lies still, dead, near the ramp in a huge bloody heap, blood trickling from his smashed head. That much could have been expected. But the once powerful body of Johnny Bradley also lies still a few feet away where paramedics bend over him, and probably the coroner tramps about looking at the situation from all angles. There seems to be more than one piece of Johnny, and my dad's face crumples, his skull pressing into his jaw and his teeth locking down.

"Gored him," says the truck driver in a low voice. "Got him in the front and back before his nephew, the kid there, could get the gun and shoot the son of a bitch. I nearly seen the whole thing. It's like he's thinking, 'If I have to go, you're coming with me.'" The trucker means King, as if he saw what happened from the bull's point of view and is thinking its thoughts. "It's like he's got a plan for as soon as we lower the ramp and unlock the gate to nudge him through the chute. He's bucking and stamping and ramming his head. He isn't going anywhere."

My dad's heart—I mean all reason for showing up for work, all gratitude toward Johnny, any recollection he might have had of his nine kids, estranged wife, whom he once loved like crazy, the lost farm—collapsed and burned, lodging a charred stone in his chest in place of any alibi for living, let alone showing up for work on time. The ambulance attendants would be covering Johnny's mangled body parts, his stubby legs sheathed in chaps that ended in tooled and polished but now muddied cowboy boots, the whole a twisted mess of leather and flesh, his corpse mostly severed at the midsection, belly and legs all but ripped apart from his once powerful, bighearted chest. When the cover was pulled all the way over his head, his last facial expression probably would not be visible because of the unnatural turn of his neck away from King and outside the corral. Looking in that direction, Dad would have seen Johnny's nephew, still a kid, talking to the ambulance driver, one hand raised to his face, tears streaming down. The smell of shot mixed with blood in the air, all of it pounding in my dad's head, closing in.

Like the truck driver, Dad probably couldn't prevent Johnny's point of view from invading his own and Johnny's from bleeding into the bull's. Johnny would have been reluctant to cancel the truck even without anyone to help load King because, for a single head, and a troublesome one at that, he had to take the truck whenever it had room and was coming by. He had to load the animal when the truck showed up or pay for it anyway. He probably wondered where the hell Bern was, when he might show up. "Quite a few days this time," Johnny might have thought, "though there's been nothing else to do here." So he called on his nephew, knowing that he wouldn't be much help, skinny and as jumpy as King. Dad would have known how to calm and not spook the bull, how to distract and lure him away like a rodeo clown would do at any sign of danger.

The truth is, it occurred to Dad, Johnny had a special bond with King or thought he did. The paunchy old rancher probably let himself believe, if only for an instant, that the feeling of affection went both ways, the way we do with animals, though we know better. Maybe Johnny allowed himself to think they understood each other and had a shared interest in what was best for the ranch, the open prairie, cycles of lives. And perhaps there was a bond, but for King it was shattered by the sound of the rattling ramp as it was lowered from the idling truck and backed slowly toward the corral, the ramp that clanged and seemed to move of its own accord under the gate. The old bull was instantly enraged. Johnny lowered himself into the corral from the fence and approached him slowly, crooning a kind of country and western cattle call with his deep voice, one arm outstretched as if to embrace an old friend. King bolted in a sudden charge, and the abyss opened wide, as Dad would have imagined it, between Johnny's outstretched arm and King's fury, the ground falling away in the instant that Johnny saw, too late, that for King things had changed. He would not be calmed.

Johnny would have turned his upper body in a flash, back toward the fence, maybe one leg already climbing up before he reached it, and he never reached it, because King's horn punctured Johnny's back, lifted his whole cowboy body on that one curled horn, and threw Johnny down with a snarling nod of his enormous head. If Johnny then moved, attempted to get to his feet, unaware they were barely still connected to the rest of him, or tried to pull himself away in the mud with his forearms, and King—snorting and turning, his nose steaming—charged a second time, and a third, horns spearing Johnny's flesh, thrashing his body this way and that until finally it went limp and did not move. King paused and slowly stepped backward, then sideways, this way and that, over the stilled body, his nose and mouth streaming mucous and saliva and blood, about to amble away when a mechanical click off to one side distracted his attention. He turned toward the sound

THE CORONERS ACT
(Form B, Sec. 7 (1))

DECLARATION OF CORONER UNDER OATH

WHEN INQUEST NOT NECESSARY

CANADA:

Province of Saskatchewan,

TO WIT:

I, *JACK MAY*

of the *SWIFT CURRENT* of *CITY*

in the Province of Saskatchewan, a Coroner in and for Saskatchewan, do hereby declare
under oath that from information received by me I am of the opinion that

JOHN BRADLEY

deceased did not come to h *IS* death
under circumstances requiring investigation by a coroner's inquest; and after viewing
the body of the deceased, and having made such further inquiries as I deemed necessary, I have come to the conclusion that an inquest is unnecessary, the deceased having
in my judgment come to h *IS* death from

BEEING GORED BY A BULL

and I have in consequence issued my warrant to bury the body of the said

Sworn before me at the *City*

of *Swift Current* in the

Province of Saskatchewan, this *11*

day of *June* A.D. 19 *79*

Coroner.

A Commissioner for Oaths in and the Peace
the Province of Saskatchewan.
My Appointment expires Dec. 31, 19 *79*

of the rifle, pausing to focus his weak eyes on the dark shape
poised on the corral fence. The shot fired in almost the same
instant the rifleman leapt back to safe ground outside the car-
nage-strewn corral, just in case his shot only maimed and further angered the bull. My dad saw all of this in the crumpled

carcass of the bull, stilled and still bleeding, as Johnny's body was carried to the waiting ambulance and driven slowly out of the yard.

It's pretty certain that my dad's heart collapsed, as I've already said, and that his own perspective was obliterated, at least momentarily, although understandably no one has been able to fill in the details of precisely what took place over the next three weeks. The coroner, Jack May, would have been there for some time that morning. There must have been a funeral in the following days. Johnny was well known and well loved all through the area from Swift Current to Cabri, the Sand Hills, Sceptre, and beyond. Dad surely would have gone to the funeral of his last friend. Did the mourners see him as Johnny's betrayer, or was it only my dad who saw it that way? Or is it only me? I wouldn't know who to ask and might not want to know anyway. Guilt, remorse, shame, and finally defeat are generally assumed to be what moved him at the end of those three weeks, on the 1st of April, to load a .22, maybe the same one that killed King if it had the fire power, and sit down at Johnny's desk just off the kitchen of the ranch house. Dad might have downed a couple of stiff drinks to keep his resolve or make up his mind about what to do. Many years later I got a copy of the second coroner's report, sworn under oath:

> I, d'Arcy H. Morrice, a Coroner in and for the Province of Saskatchewan hereby declare under oath that after an inquiry by me, I am of the opinion that *Bernard Maxwell* MORGAN (Born: *October 3, 1923*) of *Swift Current* in the province of *Saskatchewan* came to his death on the *1st* day of *April 1979* at the *District* of *Cantuar* in the Province of Saskatchewan under the following circumstances:

> At 6:45 A.M., on April 2, 1979, I received a call from the RCMP Rural Detachment, Swift Current,

Corral

THE CORONERS ACT
Form B

Declaration of Coroner

[WHEN INQUEST NOT NECESSARY]

I, _____ d'Arcy H. MORRICE _____ , a Coroner in and for the Province of

Saskatchewan hereby declare under oath that after an inquiry by me, I am of the opinion that

_____ Bernard Maxwell MORGAN _____ (Born: October 3, 1923)

of ____ Swift Current _____ in the Province of _____ Saskatchewan

came to h is ___ death on the 1st ___ day of April _____ 19 79 at

the ____ District ____ of ____ Cantuar ____ in the Province of

Saskatchewan under the following circumstances: (set out brief circumstances and cause)

At 6:45 A.M. on April 2, 1979 I received a call from RCMP Rural Detachment, Swift Current, Sask. requesting my attendance at a farm home 1 mile east and 4 miles north of Junction of Highway 332 and 32. I attended at the farm where I found Bernard Maxwell MORGAN deceased in a chair in a farm home office. The subject had obviously been dead for some time. From my investigation it was learned that a young lad looking after this farm for his deceased Uncle had been at the home the evening previous and knew that the deceased was in the office, when he departed to visit friends at approximately 7:30 P.M. When the young lad returned to the farm home he observed MORGAN sitting in the chair in the office only this time with his head lying back on the desk. He thought nothing of this position because MORGAN was quite a heavy drinker and he just assumed that he has consumed a large amount of alcohol and had passed out. Just prior to my receiving the telephone call in the early A.M. April 2, this young lad had looked into the office more closely and in daylight observed a .22 calibre rifle sitting between the knees and clutched in the left hand of the deceased.

It might be of interest to know that this is the farm home of John BRADLEY who died approximately 1 month before by being gorged by a bull and the nephew is looking after the farm for the estate. MORGAN prior to the demise of BRADLEY had been helping with the farm work on and off and had been given a room in the home to stay when he was working around the place. His presence was not unusual nor was his state of intoxication, which I spoke of above.

I ordered an autopsy by Dr. R.S. SMITH, Pathologist who confirmed that death was due to a gun shot wound to the head, the missile entering the head in the centre of the forehead with no exit. A sample of blood was analyzed with a reading of 240 milligrams of alcohol in 100 millilitres of blood.

and that as a result of my inquiry, I consider an inquest unnecessary, and I have therefore issued my

warrant to bury the body of the said ___ Bernard Maxwell MORGAN

SWORN before me at the

of

Province of Saskatchewan, this

day of _____ A.D. 19

_____
d'Arcy H. MORRICE   Coroner.

_____
A Commissioner for Oaths, Justice of
the Peace or Notary Public.

9

Sask. requesting my attendance at a farm home 1 mile east and 4 miles north of Junction of Highway 332 and 32. I attended at the farm where I found Bernard Maxwell MORGAN deceased in a chair in a farm home office. The subject had obviously been dead for some time. From my investigation it was learned that a young lad looking after this farm for his deceased Uncle had been at the home the evening previous and knew that the deceased was in the office, when he departed to visit friends at approximately 7:30 P.M. When the young lad returned to the farm home he observed MORGAN sitting in the chair in the office only this time with his head lying back on the desk. He thought nothing of this position because MORGAN was quite a heavy drinker and he just assumed that he has consumed a large amount of alcohol and had passed out. Just prior to my receiving the telephone call in the early A.M. April 2, this young lad had looked into the office more closely and in daylight observed a .22 calibre rifle sitting between the knees and clutched in the left hand of the deceased.

It might be of interest to know that this is the farm home of John Bradley who died approximately 1 month before by being gorged by a bull and the nephew is looking after the farm for the estate. MORGAN prior to the demise of Bradley had been helping with the farm work on and off and had been given a room in the home to stay when he was working around the place. His presence was not unusual nor was his state of intoxication, which I spoke of above.

I ordered an autopsy by Dr. R.S. Smith, Pathologist who confirmed that death was due to a gun shot wound to the head, the missile entering the

head in the centre of the forehead with no exit.
A sample of blood was analyzed with a reading
of 240 milligrams of alcohol in 100 millilitres of
blood. . . .

As a result of my inquiry, I consider an inquest
unnecessary, and I have therefore issued my warrant to bury the body of the said *Bernard Maxwell*
MORGAN.

The pathologist who performed the autopsy described my
dad's body in cold but somehow reassuring detail:

The body is received clothed in a shirt, t-shirt,
green trousers and belt, long underwear, sock[s],
and shoes. The deceased is a middle-aged man
of average build, well-nourished, appearing consistent with the stated age measuring 187 cms in
length. Rigor mortis is present, and there is considerable post-mortem lividity of the back of the
head, neck, and trunk. The eyes are brown with
equal pupils. There are no upper teeth or den-
ture[s], but the lower teeth are natural. Blood
is issuing from the mouth and nostrils. On the
forehead there is a circular bullet wound 0.5 cms.
in diameter, 1 cm. to the left of the midline and 3
cms. above the left inner canthus. The edges are
covered with a thick layer of encrusted blood, as is
the right side of the forehead and face. The neck is
bent over to the right side. There is a well marked
bilateral circumorbital hematoma present. No
other recent injuries are noted, and there are no
old surgical scars or other external abnormalities.

The internal examination began with the central nervous
system, of course, with the brain, the wound, and the bullet
still lodged inside. "The skull reveals a bony defect," Dr. Smith

writes, "in the left frontal bone 1 cm. from the midline below the skin wound noted."

> From this point, fracture lines radiate into the left and right ethmoid and sphenoid bones. A lateral fracture line also runs from the bony defect to the left through the frontal, parietal, and squamous temporal bones. This ends 5 cms. anterior to the occiput. The meninges are bulging and the cerebrospinal fluid is heavily blood stained. The brain (1460 gms.) shows a cylindrical track of disorganization corresponding to the track of the bullet extending from the anterior pole of the left frontal lobe backwards about 1 cm. to the midline and 1 cm. above the lower surface of the hemisphere. The track has disorganized the white matter and basal nuclei on the left side. The track ends 3 cms. from the posterior pole of the occipital lobe, at which point the partly mushroomed projectile is found. Bleeding has occurred into the ventricular system on both sides, apart from which the right hemisphere, brain stem, and cerebellum . . . are unremarkable.

Next Dr. Smith carefully examined Dad's respiratory, cardiovascular, alimentary, genito-urinary, endocrine, and recto-endothelial systems, finding nothing remarkable other than the bullet and its path through part of his brain in the central nervous system. There was no food, only ten millilitres of "turbid grey fluid," in his stomach. Remarkably, Smith found no damage to the liver or kidneys that one might expect in such a drinker, though perhaps Dad allowed sufficient time for recovery between benders, preserving his otherwise robust health through it all until firing the gun that day. The blood-alcohol content was confirmed at 0.24 percent, and the time of death, calculated from the potassium content of the ocular vitreous humour, was estimated at eight o'clock in the evening on April 1, 1979.

The blood-alcohol content is a lot in what was overall a shocking tabulation of the facts. The coroner's restrained prose sympathizes with the living witness, Johnny Bradley's nephew, referred to three times as the "young lad" who belatedly discovered the corpse of the hired man in his uncle's office off the kitchen. Coroner Morrice errs in writing that Bradley was "gorged" by a bull, when he should have written "gored," as Johnny's coroner, Jack May, correctly and bluntly put the cause of death in his report, and both coroners failed to record that it was an extremely large and old buffalo bull, not just any kind of bull, that gored Johnny to death. I have no reason to suspect that these errors were anything more than hasty or distracted slips of the mind or pen, such as might be understandable in any writer confronted with a gory scene, and from a coroner's point of view, of course, one bull is like another in causing death, which was the main concern, so it might be expecting too much for a coroner to specify that it was a buffalo that killed Johnny. But that fact it was a buffalo bull makes quite a difference.

The novelty, attraction, and even romance of keeping buffalo at that time, as I recall from childhood visits with Dad to Johnny's ranch, were that except for the loading chutes and corrals to move stock to and from the ranch, you didn't have the bother or expense of fencing, and the elimination of fencing had the sublime effect of restoring the prairie to the condition it was in when buffalo roamed free. Or that's what I thought Johnny was talking about one time when he led Dad and some of us kids piled in the car beyond the corral and some distance around the perimeter of the huge pasture where the buffalo grazed, lazily looking our way when we stopped. Johnny had old telephone poles laid down end to end as far as we could see in both directions, and that was the only barrier between us and the fearsome animals. Johnny swept one arm toward the western horizon and looked right into my dad's eyes, Dad just as intently looking back. "This is what it must have looked like before the fencing," Johnny said, "when there were enormous herds, millions stampeding through to the summer grazing lands." He got a huge kick out of our fear and surprise at the lack of stand-up fencing, relishing the explanation—which I since learned was probably a joke and not true—that, because a buffalo's front legs are so short, especially in relation to the bulk and weight of its head and front of its body, it cannot raise its front hooves high enough to step over the poles. I remember how amazed Dad was, or was he winking too? And how he looked at us to make sure that we were registering this astonishing fact, its elimination of the need for fencing, the most onerous, tedious, and expensive part of keeping livestock, besides the sheer amount of land needed for grazing, though I remember that Dad didn't let us get out of the car. Back at the house, the men drank small glasses of whiskey while we skipped and played on the bare wood bachelor floor around a giant stuffed buffalo head in the middle of Johnny's sparsely furnished living room. Johnny told Dad how he was waiting for a carpenter to come and reinforce the wall so he could hang the trophy head, and they both laughed when Dad said, "Why hang it up when it's about the perfect height for an ashtray?" The heavy glass was nestled right in there among the curls. "And there's even a place to hang our hats," Dad said, as he took off his and dangled it from a polished horn handily curving upward.

The violent death of his uncle Johnny and his later maturity as a livestock producer and businessman, rather than nostalgia for the open range or sentimentality about buffalo, were perhaps behind the nephew Dennis's contrasting emphasis on building big and even reinforced fences, as quoted in a Swift Current *Sun* article nearly ten years later, on April 27, 1988. Pictured standing beside a corral of wood planks, Dennis tells the reporter how stronger fences are needed for buffalo because they are so much stronger than cattle. The reporter goes on to describe how the younger Bradley installed a triple barbed-wire fence with an additional smooth top wire electrified to keep the buffalo in. Bradley, the reporter writes, says that the corral system must also be heavier for sorting and loading buffalo. He doesn't give the example of a buffalo goring his uncle Johnny to death, and over the years I finally figured out it was not Dennis but his brother who was the "young lad" of the coroner's report. His brother was "the nephew" who found Johnny and might have shot King and then later found my dad in the office off the kitchen. But Dennis was the Bradley nephew who took over the ranch and invested in tall, strong fences for his buffalo stock, and to the *Sun* reporter he gave the example of another buffalo, not King, so nervous as they loaded and unloaded that he was spooked just by seeing a shaft of light through a crack between the fence boards and then knocked out by the current running through the top wire when he thrashed his head against it. Dennis speaks of respect for buffalo but does not mention how his uncle was killed or any other reason for that respect. It's hard not to hear a tone of protest, or maybe defensiveness, in his emphasis on the need for tall and rigid fencing in his interview with the *Sun* reporter. "They're not so much dangerous," he is quoted as saying about buffalo, "but they have a strong sense of self-preservation." However it was with the Bradley operation and fences by then, Dennis reportedly raised buffalo mostly for meat, which he marketed along with open range nostalgia products such as ornamental gunpowder cases made from the horns, moccasins made from the hides, fur coats, and even a novelty necktie made from the hairy tail, carded and knitted, and sometimes made into mittens and scarves.

As for the date my dad chose to end his guilt and suffering by departing this world, it undermines the tragedy of it all with the comedy of taking place on April Fool's Day. The nephew realized that my dad was dead and not just drunk and called the RCMP before 6:45 a.m. on April 2nd. The coroner reported that Dad had obviously been dead for some time. Then the medical examiner, Dr. Smith, calculated the time of death from the potassium content of Dad's eyes and set the time of death at approximately 8 p.m. the previous evening. Technically, as all school children know, the licence to play jokes and expose April Fools ends at noon, after which "April Fool's is gone and past, / And you're the biggest fool at last!" as we would squeal at anyone who violated the noontime cut-off for jokes and pranks. Still, when inquiries were made about my dad, and how he died, and when exactly, we have to say it was suicide, the gunshot to the head. At this, the horrified inquirer can only reluctantly press on while thinking wildly about how to change the subject by asking when, to which the answer, especially in the proximate aftermath, is April 1st, the date's social significance being April Fool's Day. So either we can just say April 1st and let the absurdity sink in for the sympathetic inquirer, as it did for me, like a snake slithering behind the eyes, or we can own up to the folly and announce the date as April Fool's Day, which risks the brutal facts and all of the pain being presented and diminished as some kind of sick and disrespectful joke. Either way, the date of death undoes the moment of condolence, let alone commemoration, even for me, and I am piqued, not to say tortured, by speculation to this day about whether or not Dad selected the date for just that reason—to soften the blow by complicating it with doubt or ambivalence. I mean to an even greater degree than normal with suicide, when you never really know the reasons or intentions, only the grisly effects, and in this case the surrounding story of an acutely suffering man whose last friend was gored and torn apart by an enraged buffalo bull in a surprise rodeo apocalypse while his wrangler tarried too long in town.

But then again, I would think, how aware could Dad have been of the date, or the trigger for that matter, when he pulled it with a 0.24 percent blood-alcohol level? Was he drinking and turning it over in his mind all that day? In 1979, there would have been a wall calendar in Johnny's office visible from a sitting position at the desk, and isn't it reasonable to expect that Dad glanced up at it? He had 20/20 vision. It would have been a calendar with a picture of a mountain lake, a Wheat Pool map of RMs, or some equipment dealer. I've mulled over those three hollow weeks between Johnny's death in the corral and Dad's firing of the gun in the ranch office. According to my research, wheat prices were up, and there would have been big talk by the farmers in the Healy Hotel about how many acres should be seeded, how Johnny's nephew would be a fool to keep all that grazing land out of production as Johnny had intended. They would have heard on the news that China-U.S. relations were quietly being normalized that spring, to Moscow's annoyance, perhaps mere static and inconsequential stirrings of the lingering Cold War, and some would have ventured opinions, over coffee or beer, on what it all would mean for grain prices. Were the powers that be really that close to toppling, or does it always just seem that way? The Shah of Iran should have been jittery at the warm welcome received by the Ayatollah Khomeini that spring, hundreds of thousands turning out for his return from exile to his home city of Qomby, though probably even the Shah didn't suspect that he'd be uncrowned entirely by the end of the year. The Sandinistas of Nicaragua must have sensed the support of the entire countryside about that time, and already set their sights on Managua, though Somoza probably hadn't yet packed a bag or suspected that he'd be forced to flee by July 19th. Minority white rule ended in Rhodesia, just like that, or so it seemed, and the upstart Margaret Thatcher, cunning dog, was already sniffing her election victory in May. I myself was running magazine copy about the rising and falling of markets and companies, ruthless dictators and armed rebellions, up and down Front Street in Toronto, back and forth between editors and typesetters, thinking about how I could overcome such unlikely beginnings, how to get onto the merry-go-round, or even if I wanted to, the world tormented and writhing, now buckling under, now throwing off shackles, and then I wonder how likely it is that Dad thought about killing himself on, say, March 17th, then think, "Naw, that's St. Patrick's Day," and then again on the 29th, and then thinking, "No, I'll wait until the 1st, April Fool's Day, like I'm winking from the great beyond to cheer everyone up with assurance I had everything planned, just in case they are overwhelmed by the shock and the sorrow and the shame."

Or did Dad hesitate, thinking the date might just as well confirm his damnation for cruelty to others not sorry about his death? Or did that quiet Sunday morning coming down— the 1st of April was a Sunday that year—did that whole long day, the bars closed and everyone else at home with their families, the rigidity and numbness that he had felt since Johnny's death beginning to loosen and leave his body, make Dad begin to feel his losses? The family he thought he had lost, or did lose for a while, but who all that time might have been longing to rejoin or be reclaimed by him? And then Johnny, and where else to go, all of it rattling around in his mind, all the scenarios that could have taken place in the corral before he arrived that morning, the hollowness of that big empty house, just the young lad coming and going from time to time, reminding Dad of his own four sons, five daughters, all not there, his six brothers, seven sisters; he was used to houses filled with people and food and laughter, always a mewling in the crib, an old man in the corner with a pipe, women making supper or washing up; all this he exhaled like smoke become ghosts wafting up to the rafters and dissipating, drifting away. It might have become impossible to imagine that day in the still house ending any other way. It could have been May 13th or November 7th for all he knew. He was probably in some other time frame, gone in his mind. I know it. I just don't see it. More easily, I see a quivering finger on the trigger, hesitating, the gun, the day, the whole damned situation then blowing him and all of us to kingdom come.

Still, April 1st is the date we have, at least in time as we mark it, as all the documents prove. It's the date I have to get on with. I've supposed that the fact of the date is what the Greeks called Fate, the unexplained given that they animated with the names of the gods to personify it, Zeus sometimes taking exactly the form of the bull, as when he seduced Europa and she clambered lovingly onto his back and he stole her away. But then it occurs to me that the idea of a plan at work—a story of the founding of Europe or anywhere else or the Fates as three sisters weaving each and every life story, and one of them one day snipping a thread selected at random, while dreamily envisioning the tapestry as a whole, enjoying her work without any special attachment to the individual threads that make it up—is not so far from the opposite of fate, the idea of the absurd, that there is no plan, there are no sisters, no spinning or embroidery or pattern, no organizing principle to any of it.

For even to say, as I have, that Dad killed himself on April Fool's Day in time as we mark it, is to loosen the event from a date that is both doubtful and suggestive of significance. This is the uncertainty that my dad and his death shot into the world, scattering all before us as he made his exit. The calendar date is that fanciful name tacked onto time, geological, biological, universal, if such exists. Who knows the actual date or any exact time? And once that bull is out, the idea that time doesn't exist in the way that we mark it, once that thought is thought and rages around the corral of my mind, then begins the reign of disorder and misrule. By design or by chance, Johnny's sentimentality in reaching out to and naming his prize buffalo King, and Dad's selection, by design or by chance, of April Fool's as his day to die, the two things together upend all order and solemnity. Enter the Fool, who disputes certainties of time and space, casts all to the four strong winds, the flimsy body of any cowboy tossed into the air, all boundaries, fences, corrals, calendars a mockery, and that's how I began to consider Dad as a rodeo clown, the role he was supposed to play on that fateful day and so took it up on April Fool's instead, antic and gun and motley mustered to distract the stampeding, enraged buffalo away from Johnny and onto the truck by the loading ramp. On April 1st, Dad steps into the ring with mock heroism, only a little late for work, streaks of colourful rags masking his serious role of distracting the bull, enhancing life in the delay and defiance of death. Goading and taunting the bulls of fate by darting and cartwheeling, slipping and falling, the Fool never fails to get back on his feet, dust off his bum with exaggerated disdain, and stride around the ring, arms akimbo in a victorious embrace of the crowd that goes wild, the cheering chorale affirming that at every moment, through his folly, death is averted and life recomposed. The Fool personifies laughter and regeneration, antidote to death, condition of life.

Thus my thoughts and dreams have rioted and died down, flickering like rogue flames, tracing the fractures, lateral, horizontal, that spread to make way for the bullet to the brain, my own big bang that exploded the grounds of coherence, dispersed all my vital spirits along cylindrical tracks of disorganization, corral and rodeo, sentence, syntax, and circus ring. Histology, according to Dr. Smith's autopsy report, confirms that the wound on my dad's forehead was the entry wound, caused by a gun fired at close range. Examination of the brain and radiographs taken before the post-mortem indicate that the bullet track was slightly to the left of, and parallel with, the midline, and in the horizontal plane, parallel with the lower border of the cerebral hemispheres. Thus were we blasted, all nine of Dad's children, scattered to the four corners, blown apart, muted and thrown into nine separate solitudes by events resistant to words or sense. We got out of Dodge nine different ways, each shaking off the horror like horses shuddering and shaking their manes on crossing a river of blood. Speaking only for myself, I followed any old band of players heading out, my eyes poring over maps, books, roilings of words tracked to sources, and while I wandered I was mysteriously steadied, sometimes, by gravitational forces that held me to a predictable orbit around something like the partly mushroomed projectile, the lead shot stuck in the brain, lodged there during the earliest dews of April, that moisture revered by alchemists because it was supposed to be the semen of God, the *materia prima*, first ingredient for the alembic in the transmutation of lead into gold. Of all that has value. Many have perished in the work.

"In all mourning there is a tendency to silence," writes Walter Benjamin, "and this infinitely more than the inability or reluctance to communicate. The mournful has the feeling that it is known comprehensively by something unknowable, by the unknowable. To be named—even if the name giver is godlike or saintly—perhaps always brings with it a presentiment of mourning." For who calls you your name? Our names are like mere calendar dates, more or less fanciful patterns impressed like stencils on swirling eddies, the tugging currents of matter and time that coalesce us briefly, our infant foreheads touched as with a parent's kiss or the baptismal palm. I was imprinted with the old English name Dawn, or Dawn-before-Daylight, as Pop Morgan called me, and for rhythm, I guess, it was combined with the most French-sounding of names, Lynette. This must have been why the first story I recall making up out of thin air for my young friends when they came over to play dolls, none of us yet in school, was that I had not just one Barbie doll but dozens of them, which my French grandmother had sent to me, each wearing a gorgeous tiny gown or sports outfit and even lace underwear that Grandma had lovingly sewn with the very tips of her fingers. The dolls were too good to play with, I said gravely, but I reached up on tiptoes to pull open the door of the linen closet in the upstairs hall and pointed to the unreachable top shelf, where they were stored in a special decorated box just out of our five-year-old sight. My second name, I explained, was after that very grandmother, and it was the reason she dressed the dolls and gave them just to me. Even as I surprised myself at the effortless weaving of this fabulous tale, all the while monitoring my friends' faces for signs of skepticism or outright disbelief, I remember thinking that there must be some such explanation for my French second name and its musical complementarity to my English first name. So I kept that story inside my mind and began from that moment to harbour a secret French story, or a not-English one, though of course there were no Barbies on the top shelf of the linen closet or anywhere else in the house. No gowns or ski suits or tiny sets of lingerie, and most of all no French grandmother, but even in my tender years I knew that my story was not about any of that anyway, and I felt myself borne on an awesome power that until that moment I had not suspected could exist.

I had always assumed that my first name signified my nature as a morning person, like my mother, since it matched our temperament and metabolism, the best part of our day being always before noon, or up to two o'clock in the afternoon at the latest. But then I realized, with some embarrassment at having missed it, after Dad died and I began to have trouble in my sleep, that the morning of my name was only a homonym for mourning, what I was fated to live, what really shaped my days, the blasted dispersal of the whole world at my dad's unspeakable death. Then I rushed to the hope that the French of my middle name maybe rescued and rejoined his life with his death, for Dad was a sportsman who until that day shot only ducks, and he loved to visit his sister Myrtle to go fishing in Meadow Lake. And the happiest image I have of him, holding up his catch on that northern shore, bears as its only adequate caption the French expression for the April Fool, *Poisson d'avril*, literally "the fish of April," as I jokingly translate it for myself.

Did Dad know my name? He must have, but he called me Li'l Punk, one of many nicknames reported and repeated, and I named him Punky Daddy in return when he and Mom came to visit me in the hospital with my little leg in traction because of a dislocated hip between age one and two. But back in the house crammed with nine kids, no one, not even the so-named, could keep all of our names straight in the flux and turmoil of things, so Dad, about to ask me to polish his shoes on a Saturday night, on the pretense that he needed them to shine for church on Sunday, which he rarely attended, would say after supper as the hockey game was starting, "Heh-La-Von-Lor-Da," going through the first syllables of my sisters' names in descending order by age, until he would give up with a laugh and say, "Sister, can I give you a quarter to shine my shoes?" I loved being called Sister, and that's what all of us, the girls, were actually called, the name of our bond, the snug sound of our belonging and connection to each other and to our family. The names of the boys stuck better, but there were only four of them, and all of us had nicknames too, tormenting or belittling or affectionate. Mine began as a taunt and expulsion, Gypsy, when my sister said I'd been left on the doorstep as a baby by Gypsies, which meant I didn't quite fit in, as she said, and I was different in some fateful way, an outcast no one else had wanted until my family took pity and carried me inside the house, despite already having so many other kids. I pretended to take it as a joke for a while but, teased and teased, eventually screamed and cried until Mom made her stop. But still she whispered "Gypsy!" when Mom was out of earshot, for years it seemed, and eventually I stiffened and adopted the name, thinking how excellent it might be if I were an orphan, good riddance to them all anyway, *bon débarras*. I was a mysterious foundling, and my royal blood would be discovered one day, and then they'd be sorry and come begging, and I'd cast pearls into the slop and mud at their feet, toss them a gold coin on days I felt like it, on others not.

The actual Roma, as far as I know, did not venture so far onto the northern plains, but I recognized even then the tentativeness of their place wherever they ended up, their persistence even though they had no territory of their own, how they held out the possibility of an elsewhere, their very nickname embodying freedom from borders and constraint. My nickname so liberated me for wandering, I thought, perhaps even endowed me with wanderlust, for searching and seeking, I never knew for what exactly, but it supplied me with certainty, however wrong-headed, that I would know when I found it. Thus the names multiplied, were tacked on or adopted, or came unstuck from earliest times, more promptings to explore than set terms attached in any fixed or essential way. Even my common first name was a sprightly allegory of the break of day, a time, an idea, a feeling, and, even if I was sometimes mistaken for a boy or accused of masquerading as one behind its androgynous sound, my name made me laugh to think of the morning itself getting up to walk around and rearrange the furniture, move away, come back, pick a fight with my sisters.

The "trembling moment of dawn, when those who are dreaming the world are few," wrote the young Jorge Luis Borges, toying in 1917 with the conjecture of philosophers that the world is a mere "activity of the mind," and daybreak marks "the brink of danger and disorder," when

> . . . the persistent dream of life
> is in danger of breaking down,
> the hour in which God might easily
> destroy all his work!
>
> But once more the world comes to its own rescue.
> The light streaks in inventing dirty colors
> and with a tremor of remorse
> for my complicity in the daily rebirth
> I seek my house,
> amazed and icelike in the white glare,
> while a songbird holds the silence back.

But why remorse, Borges, at recreating such a miracle as a new day? It's only so long since, after so many revolutions around the sun, so many years that I know the remorse, certain misfortune, is due to the hazards, the likelihood of reconceiving a world not so different from the one we lie down to sleep in. No actual new world when it is cobbled, as it must be, out of the shards and shreds, debris of the day before, damned as it is, the only materials ready to hand. Asleep and awake, I labour under the burden of those shreds wrapping the corpses I carry, the bodies as they were even then piling up. Johnny Bradley,

King, my dad, they unbalance me and put unbearable pressure
on speaking words such as those that can be exhaled in sighs
between breaths, their dead weight on my back, sometimes
dragging out my sentences when I forget how and where they
began, reluctant to come to a full stop amid the torn torsos,
flayed limbs, disorganized brain matter, my horse spooked,
my foot caught in the stirrup, head bumping along the ground,
all of it bearing down on the commas, buckling conjunctions,
enforcing reliance for carrying on in letting the voice go in
moans, murmurs, sighs, sometimes recovered in chants, rec-
itations, quotations, ventriloquism, chorales, repetitions and
lists, interminable lists that themselves waver and list, echo,
trail off, then come around again like the haunting refrain of
an old ballad without end. I am that poor wayfaring stranger,
graced and wracked by barely grasped poems, speculations,
snatched and excerpted lives, croonings, insistent flash visions
of angry horned bulls, steaming nostrils, stamping on barren
ground, prods and jabs, triggers pulled, scrapes of shovels,
sunken graves, discounted or misbegotten corpses, blind and
ill-conceived pursuits, digressions hither and yon, and this
is my *saeta*, broken song of the country and western world,
of the perennially unsettled, and no going back, there is no
remedy, *no hay remedio*. Follow all the thrown multitudes,
wayward and displaced, aching and torn, just enough blood
in the tongue to remake another day, splattered and streaked,
the splayed guts, riders of the outraged bulls of fate we hold
onto for dear life, feeling only a few times the motions of a
seeming grace, pleasure in the loins, mounted, as we all are, on
the backs of beasts mightier than ourselves.

GRAVEYARD

The terror in King's eyes, stench of diesel and blood, smashed corral, mangled bodies, idling of the truck, all of it reassembled from hearsay, offhand comments, overheard conjecture, surmise, voices lowered and muffled into collars around kicked tires, the ground pawed, heads hung all through that country. The details no sooner gathered up than scattered again at the repeat of the gunshot in the still ranch house three weeks later, final dispersal, what makes listening and gathering my unending task, to figure out what happened, a recomposition with the disadvantage of dismemberment, of not only the story but also my own mind, where are all the bits, what goes where, in what order, lining things up, rearranging, endlessly, years of failed attempts to put the whole thing together in just the way that remains true to its deshaping power, paradox of promise, taste at the back of the throat metallic, lead shot that I tasted often— terror, dissolution, the limit of things, where all this is headed.

By the time I found out what happened in the corral, and then in the office off the farmhouse kitchen, it was close to the middle of April. From my basement apartment in Toronto, I was feeling the distance I had put between myself and all things country and western, corrals, kitchens, all the while wishing I hadn't, or didn't feel the need to, and could somehow go back and find a way to live there. Sundays I usually called any one of my sisters, a different one each week, so even then I knew my hanger-on expendable status outside of marriage to a farmer and having children to reproduce all the sorrow, though I couldn't have put it into so many words at the time. I rotated my calls among sisters so I wouldn't be bothersome, as I imagined I was in hearkening back to the failed original family all the while they were making their own new ones with apparent certainty and optimism I could not share. They were always busy cooking, cleaning, changing jobs, moving house, putting up curtains, and the sister I called that second or third Sunday in April said she'd just seen some cousins in Swift Current. I got the idea there'd been some occasion I'd missed or hadn't even known about, and in the course of her telling me about it, this and that, she mentioned where they'd gone after the funeral, and the phrase stood out for me, but I didn't want to interrupt her, so I listened to the whole tale, which to this day I have lost all recollection of, before asking, "Whose funeral were you at?"

Imagine our disarray, my sister's, where and how to begin, as she realized no one had thought to call me, and I had no idea Dad had died, let alone the gruesome details of why or how. In all the grief and conflagration, no one had noticed I wasn't at the funeral or anywhere else to be seen. My sister recounted the news haltingly, the bare bones, no details like dates, just days of the week, the funeral last Thursday. All was awash, a blank whiteness, eventually making out the sound of a gunshot, firing, shattering the bones in my face that then collapsed like scaffolding, jaw crushed, skull splintering and crashing down into it, mouth full of broken sharp sticks, flesh giving way to ribs jabbing into stomach, hips pressing inward, all formal integrity gone. Throat lined with chalk that was clotted with shame. I should have got a call at work so the shock could be public and shared, and I wouldn't have to explain why but would be shepherded out with the sympathy and solemnity of the lowered gaze. As it was, over the few days following the call, I gave my notice without much explanation or consequence, having forgotten completely why I had picked up and abandoned the West in the first place.

I met up with a brother-in-law's transport truck just then leaving Toronto after delivering a load of cattle to stockyards on the outskirts. The truck still stank like the shit of their terror, and the driver was from somewhere near Moose Jaw. I thought we were deadheading back West, the trailer empty, but at the last minute he got a call to head over to the Ontario Rubber Company, so we swung by and hitched up a trailer filled with foam rubber that didn't smell so bad. From there we pretty much drove straight through, me in the passenger seat and Garnet taking a few winks in the sleeper a few hours at a time. In Moose Jaw, he left me at a warehouse that was closed, my bags piled around me on the curb near a payphone, and he couldn't keep from taunting me as he drove off that probably no one was coming to pick me up, ever, and with that cruel raillery touched the sore spot of my profound lack of consequence, my easy disposability even worse than his low-status drudgery and need to follow orders, pick up or drop off whatever and whoever, wherever, whenever the bosses ordered.

Garnet was dead right that no one expected me in Moose Jaw. How could they? And then there was the last leg home through the Coteau Hills and past Old Wives Lake to Assiniboia, and I can't remember how that worked out, but when I got back and asked around I found no one inclined to talk about Dad, or Johnny Bradley either, no one exactly sorry I had not been contacted. Not callousness, I hoped, just pain beyond all speaking, though my mother's matrimonial allegiances had moved on, and news of Dad's death seemed not hers to tell, and slipped through the cracks, like I did, nowhere to be found. In all my surprised annihilation, my thoughts, if you can call them that, pulsated outward along cylindrical tracks of disorganization, disbelief, the sorrow of it all, until finally I went quiet, too, falling in with the social paralysis, muted and stone-faced, as though nothing had happened, and no one asked why I had suddenly quit my job to come back West after barely a year of chasing what I thought were my dreams.

Meanwhile, they worked away on me, the dreams. Startled awake in the middle of the night wherever I lay my head, a sister's attic or basement fold-out couch, I'd catch a glimpse of the instant of daylight. Unaware I was dreaming, I watched a thin line of brilliance seep in beneath the darkened horizon to outline the slope rising gently from where I stood in a field of soft furrows and thin stubble. A gleaming, a shimmering glow, and then light, like a realization, glares over the edge, flooding the scene, just as footsteps approach out of the darkened distance, shuffling and hesitant, burdened and strained. A procession of workmen, small darkened figures, emerges into the coming light, though still quite far away from me in the shadows of the slope. They don't see me as I move toward them. There is no sense of danger or foreboding, only curiosity. The joy of anticipation, a new day. What's going on? But it's a struggle to walk in the soft soil, bristling stubble, and takes me forever to get close enough to see that one of the men holds a shovel. I make out a darkened object, a box, a coffin they are carrying, and I see they've come to bury someone. They set the coffin down, and the gravedigger with the shovel bends to pitch the blade into the ground. The sound of metal hitting dirt and then the heaving of the load to the side becomes rhythmical, goes on for some time as I continue my approach, on and on, in the way of dreams. Suddenly, the shovel blade hits something with a thud, not a rock but wood that muffles the sound and stops the rhythm of the digging. It's always at the sound of the shovel obstructed, hitting against something that resists, the rhythm interrupted, when I remember I've been here before. Or I've had this dream. Maybe I've had it every night forever since I talked on the phone with my sister. Stretched out on my bed, I fill slowly with dread, like water flooding my grave. I know what happens next and don't want to hear it but cannot ever fully wake up until the gravedigger says, "We can't bury him here. This is Bern Morgan's grave."

That's when I wake up crushed and ashamed, and every day is April 1st, and Dad's dead body occupies every inch of ground not marked. Everywhere Dad is about to be unearthed, anywhere you might think to dig. All this flutters into the shadows as the gravedigger lays his shovel on top of the coffin, the cue to the pallbearers to lift while they turn, slowly, to shuffle off along the slope with their other corpse, unburied, a kind of ceremonial closing to my dream that disperses in the light.

Around that time, a historian at the University of Vermont was writing about how individual memories survive for only about thirty years without general repetition and social commemoration at a gravestone or cenotaph or other memorial site. Particular griefs wear away, and our losses persist only as private touchstones for publicly shared memories, the social and sanctioned openings for our grief to pour forth. Professor Hutton drew from studies written between the world wars by the scholar Maurice Halbwachs, who found that whether or not a memory endures depends, too, on the social power of the group that mourns. My thirty-year allotment of time has long since passed to commemorate the loss of my dad, the old cowboy, his loss of Johnny Bradley and King, the bull turning on them, along with Johnny's cowboy dream of restoring the free-roaming buffalo, along with the migrant Assiniboine who had followed and hunted the buffalo on foot, later on horseback, and then all the cowboys, pioneers, settlers-become-Indians, Indigenized of the Americas, all tossed in the mainstreams of misrecognition, those stories long since gone and now far beyond the reach of correction or redress. To locate myself there seems both urgent and futile now. I broke away from those lost plains just as I thought they were slipping over the edge of the world, their falling away pointing in the direction opposite to run, ride off, move on, save yourself.

How many days and nights, years, how many April the 1sts, count my attempts to fix that death in stone and regain unhaunted ground? I gathered all the evidence in documents, declarations, the autopsy reports, news clippings, obituaries, which I hoarded, packed, unpacked, here and there, labelling and filing, reporting, travelling in what became my habitually unsettled life, stoking fires and then smothering flames, killing thoughts while propping up corpses, more and more draft versions of the story in tow, claiming then denying, pitching in, giving up, and only in retrospect betraying a dogged pursuit that all the while felt wayward and hesitant, the meandering well known to the downwardly mobile, no place to go, the unattached and professionally undefined, barmaid, chamber maid, crew cook, traveller, vagabond, thin-coated browser of stacks in regional and then university libraries, taunted by exacting librarians demanding effective keywords for chasing faint notions, restless and driven, hopeless and sunken, ecstasies of angels touching on the miseries of scholars.

That corral and its breach eventually takes the shape of a story, my dad's, the story that survives, persists, in my refusal, later inability, to let go of the corpses, where they are not buried and where they might be, the corral and the ranch house office where they perished, attaches not only to me, my flesh, but also to the romance of the buffalo, what Johnny saw and raised his arms wide open to, and my dad, the cowboy clown who could have distracted the bull and played the fool anyway by the day he picked to die. I lug the dead weight of this unrecounted tragedy, having attached myself to it in the first place to gain my balance, then later out of loyalty, then stubbornness, and finally because of the atrophy of my own limbs, lacking the strength to stand without them. I hung on so long their dead hands and horns and hooves clutch and pierce me back, continuing to grow into me, grafting onto flesh like grotesque appendages, body and life deformed by long accommodation of ungainly burdens. "But what am I hanging on to?" I would sometimes have the wherewithal to ask myself. Two old cowboys, killed in a rodeo not rigged or rigged in the most deviously indirect way. Two cowboys not on the stopwatch but on the real clock at the end of time. Lucinda sings such a song of grief about her friend at Lake Charles, her song that makes me long to leave an offering of my own at the corral, high altar of the country and western world, the place that remains, no matter how far away I run, sole destination and ground of all the stories that have never been told.

It's pretty certain I would have walked past Andrew Suknaski many times without knowing it at Wood Mountain, whose rodeo was on the circuit for bull and bronc riders, clowns and wranglers, from the more famous but not older Calgary Stampede. I would have been at Camp Woodboia, the summer camp that joined the Wood of Wood Mountain to the boia of Assiniboia, Wood Mountain being the nearest site of recorded history, as opposed to the obliterated history of Assiniboia, Wood Mountain having been a North West Mounted Police post from the days of the fur trade, those days of the scattering or rounding up of the Indians whose absence is marked by the name Assiniboia, to make way for railways and farms, livestock and grain. We knew about all that, history recorded and unrecorded, or thought we did. The rodeo ring and grandstands were at the Old Post just south of Wood Mountain village, where Suknaski grew up in a shack, his little cot behind the wood stove that was the only source of heat. Even as a kid, I noticed quite a few of the cowboys in the rodeo were Indians, Buffy Sainte-Marie's "Starwalker" and "Indian Cowboy of the Rodeo." At Wood Mountain, they were either Métis or descendants of the Stone or Dakota Sioux that went by the name Assiniboine, the Goodtracks, Gaudrys, Lethbridges, and Ogles, Roy and his brothers, children of Lizzie, more or less directly descended from Chief Sitting Bull it was said, a fact that turned out to be only somewhere near the truth. Lizzie made the most sought-after moccasins with intricate beadwork, and we had no difficulty celebrating her artistry and buying up all she could make while at the same time remaining studiously oblivious to the cruel irony of our own descent from the people who had reduced her, elderly by then, to that way of making a living on the edge of the rodeo grounds. What I later learned to call imperial nostalgia—the melancholy pleasure of longing for what colonial settlement has destroyed and displaced—we drank in our mother's milk.

In his poem "Letter to Harold Ogle," Suknaski writes to Roy's brother, long gone and wandering all through the West like a cowboy who never felt more like singing the blues, who brought Lizzie a silver and turquoise ring from somewhere in Arizona one time, dreaming of writing some way-out novel just like Kerouac's *On the Road*, but who broke his arm twice, the same arm, two years in a row, falling both times from his horse into the Bow River upstream from Calgary, the river he was sure had something against him. Stories like that swirled about and populated Wood Mountain with people like Harold and Lizzie and Roy, and all the south country shone briefly in the light of Suknaski's poetry and recognition, the literature and films they spawned that then vanish, over and over again, in the shadows of time. Roy led trail rides on the retired rodeo horses, and that's where I learned to ride. He later sold us an old Appaloosa, tall and particular, descended, I imagined, from the straggling herds of the Nez Percé fleeing the settlers then arriving and flooding the banks of the Palouse River in Washington state, the river that gave those speckled horses their New World name. She probably descended from those rustled in Montana that were then confiscated from Wood Mountain milkmaid and horse thief Jenny Sallet, who worked with the outlaw everyone knew as Dutch Henry. My horse came from the Ogles already named Princess, since Appaloosas, like buffalo, were considered the royalty of beasts. Princess held her head high when she ran, not hunched or pulled back or tucked down. Like all Appaloosas, she was especially graceful, regal, even stuck up. We knew she was too good for us. We never used the cruel curved bit with her, just the gentler straight one, but still Princess kicked ferociously at the jingling approach of halter and bit, so I never could saddle her up by myself. Once mounted, and in spite of her resistance, I easily imagined she enjoyed riding the trails through the coulees and around buttes on the lookout for who knows what around Wood Mountain.

But I never really liked the rodeo. All too cruel, cinches cranked, burrs or rivets placed to drive the animals wild, and I couldn't understand what it was about except to show off some kind of absurd bravery long after all the beasts and people have been domesticated and defeated, subdued, land enclosed, fences secured, what more do you want? Lassoing the little calves and hearing them squeal, they'd go flying, half-strangled at the end of the rope. Some were strangled, their necks broken, in what was treated as sport. I did like to walk the rodeo grounds, though, especially to see the horses running in their corrals connected by narrow fenced passageways, labyrinths of chutes and channels leading to various entrances to the barns and the rodeo ring at one end, pasture and open range at the other. Sloppy fearless clowns perched on the rails ready to leap out and distract the raging bulls, while the cowboys, usually quite thin, all wind-burned and bow-legged, tough yet polite, with overly proper manners, like they were sorry for living, hung back, talking or drinking themselves into the next ride. Suknaski wouldn't have been one of the cowboys since he didn't come from a farm with livestock beyond what was needed for work or food, but he might well have hung on the gates, spotting for clowns and ready to open and close the way for them and for the bulls and horses bursting into the ring in high spirits, or shepherding them back into the barns once spent.

It would not be entirely surprising, then, that I soon ran into Suknaski on getting back from Toronto, and we even teamed up together for a while. He'd become a little famous for writing his poems out of the words of ranchers and farmers and just the way people talk around Wood Mountain, Assiniboia, Killdeer, Val Marie. Poetry so everyday, "How could it be poetry?" we thought, and I even feared it exposed a poverty of significance, but Suknaski made it something haunting and profound, ingenious, and it was even going to our heads since the publication of his book *Wood Mountain Poems* to wide acclaim some few years earlier. As soon as Suknaski heard about the trouble I was having in my sleep, intrusions of the gravediggers, night after night, he knew exactly what to do. He stepped into the role of what he called the Holy Fool, a fast talker, like an Electrolux or Fuller Brush salesman eager to get a foot in the door by showing the housewife how to get a bloody stain out of the rug right there on the front step. Blood stains, haunted dreams, irresolutions of the dead, especially those by suicide, were his stock in trade. Those were the stories of Wood Mountain, too, the voices and tongues he conjured up and cultivated, like a farmer his furrowed fields. Part Holy Fool of the Eastern rite, part impersonated Dakota medicine man, and part Confucian-cum-Buddhist priest steeped in misty wisdom gleaned from descendants of the Chinese coolies, like his brother-in-law in Lethbridge, or from the Beats or the Black Mountain poets, or anyone he met on the road or whose songs he sang, Harold Ogle's, books he read, *The Icon and the Axe*, or that wayfarers read to him and told him about along the way, Suknaski was all about raising up ghosts and then laying them to rest in that "geography of blood," that phrase, where Candace Savage locates herself in her book of that title, borrowed from Suknaski. Compromised homesteaders who killed themselves out of remorse, loneliness, young Leila Hordenchuk as she lay dying, thrown from her horse, Postmaster Lee Soparlo stumbling across teepee rings in Vasile Tonita's pasture, traces of the forced wandering and exile of the Nez Percé with their proud Appaloosas, and the Teton Sioux, edged off the land around Wood Mountain and slowly finding themselves homeless, on the wrong side of a border and stranded outside newly fenced properties, already starving to death, the buffalo gone.

With the practicality of a surveyor or tradesman, Suknaski saw clearly that what was needed in my case was to find and mark my dad's grave in the ground—geologic, semantic, and psychic. He built a wooden cross out of 2x2s and painted it blue, Carpathian blue, he said, slightly darker than the blue of

Mediterranean window- and doorsills that prevent the dead from re-entering the house, his blue deepened by the Slavic gloom of his own displacement, and that would keep the dead in their place. He measured the space at the intersection of the vertical and the horizontal, then sent me to the jeweller's to have a plaque sized and engraved with Dad's name and years, 1923–1979. All this took some time, my meeting up with Suknaski, the telling of the story, his pondering and strumming of his guitar, howling at the moon, my months of sleeplessness and dread. I clung to his shabby coat, consoled by the smoke and smell of his pipe. One day, finally, he said all was ready. I was to call Reverend Kirk, the minister who presided over the funeral in Swift Current, whose name I got from the card my sister kept, even as she snarled with impatience, "What are you whining about? Good riddance," she said, meaning Dad's drunkenness embarrassed her even more than the tragedy of his death moved her to sympathy. For Dad, or for me. Or herself.

I wrote to Reverend Kirk instead of calling because I didn't think I could ask about the location of Dad's grave without losing coherence on the phone, ashamed that I needed to ask a stranger how to find the grave of my own father, which meant I didn't already know, and that was the whole problem. If he asked why I didn't know, I would have had to admit to being too insignificant to have been notified, and cast my sisters and brothers, my own mother, as letting me down or being asleep at the switch, when I didn't want them to be blamed for what was an oversight that made complete sense in a family like ours, not talking and ruled over by a well-meaning but faltering drunk on the one hand and a puritanical nose-in-the-air moralist on the other. Maybe if he heard all that, Reverend Kirk wouldn't want to be bothered with me either. So I was relieved when he called back to say he didn't know where the grave was but would find out, then called again a few days later with the number of Dad's grave, 224. The effect of getting an exact number, the specific address of a definite place, was electrifying. It verified with a jolt what up to then had seemed like shadows or hallucinations. Two-twenty-four made it official, external, acknowledged, and even before we made the trip out to the graveyard in Swift Current the gravediggers let up a little from my dreams. I still dreamed them but knew they were a dream earlier and earlier in the unfolding of events, and that diminished the shock and horror and woe. Eventually, I was able to wake myself up as soon as I heard the approaching footsteps.

Suknaski wrapped the Carpathian blue wooden cross in cloth, a piece from the rag-bag, and tied it all together with an old bandana torn into strips. He then placed the bundle in his guitar case, along with a crowbar, a hammer, and a small gardening trowel, and laid it in the trunk of the car. We drove the two hours west to Swift Current on the morning of April 1st, which fell on Good Friday that year, 1983. Quite a lot of time, four years, to have been without a decent night's sleep, when you think of it. I drove while Suknaski played his guitar and sang songs or murmured incantations in his conjured-up language that included the few Cree or Dakota words he'd picked up, the way those languages survived and circulated at that time, heard at pow-wows, in Buffy Sainte-Marie songs, refrains wafting along the Qu'Appelle Valley, Katepwa, or on travels farther west around Banff, the Kicking Horse Pass, listening around campfires along the foothills of Alberta, Canmore, or in libraries down on the Lower Mainland, at public readings, poetry happenings, he was all Canada Council by then. Toward Swift Current, the sky darkened with low blue clouds. When we checked into the motel at the edge of town, and the woman behind the desk handed over the room key, I suddenly saw Suknaski and myself through her eyes, an odd, perhaps suspicious, even mysteriously furtive pair, since Suknaski with his beard and pipe looked even older than he was, fifteen years older than me, and I with my scraggly permed hair and oversized glasses appeared younger than I was but trying to look older by wearing a second-hand fur coat and carrying, incongruously, a colourful woven sack for a purse, bought at a fundraiser for refugees of the civil war then raging in Guatemala.

There was no explaining what we were up to, which I thought proceeded like a farcical episode of *Mission Impossible* once inside the motel room. We moved about silently, as though stealthily, checking all our props and equipment for executing our plan. Suknaski opened the guitar case to inspect the illicit cross with its pointed end that he had shaped with a small axe. Then he checked the hammer and crowbar, each unwrapped and wrapped again separately. The crowbar was to start the hole in the ground below the thawed surface. We would then pound the cross down into the spot where Dad was buried. I took the roses I had brought in the cooler and set them in the guitar case alongside the cross so we would have only one thing to carry once we left the car. I wondered if they were the right kind of flowers as our eyes met briefly, Suknaski's and mine, over the lid of the guitar case, and Suknaski snapped it shut. We would seem, we thought, as unremarkable as any sentimental folksingers come to visit the grave of a loved one, sing a song over it, instead of how others might see us, as trespassers or even vandals installing an irregular marker, handmade, on a lost man's grave not otherwise marked a full four years after his burial, and still without a proper stone.

By the time we arrived at the graveyard, the glowering sky opened and let fall a flurry of large, wet flakes as the last gasps of winter swirled and ducked into puddles on the softening ground. The graveyard gate was unlatched, but there was no one around. We drove in and parked by the chapel shed since we couldn't see the grave numbers from the car. I strained to find where we were in the numbering to estimate where 224 would be. The graveyard was long from end to end, so there was quite a distance from the fence at the far end to the chapel and street entrance near the other. I didn't want to risk the car sliding off the dirt trail that wound among the graves, so we set out walking, heads down, intent on our mournful purpose. Suknaski carried the guitar case and hummed quietly under his breath. We walked for what seemed an eternity, the sound of our trudging steps melding with the boots of the gravediggers along the slopes of my dream. As we approached the far end, I could see the fence that separated the graveyard from a cement block building with an asphalt drive around it and a parking lot on the other side. The back door of the building was open in spite of the storm, and steam billowed out in puffs. The mouth of hell, I thought, one of the many inconspicuous places from where nightmares and feverish dreams arise. Suspecting nothing in the full light of day, we usually pass them by. At that very thought, a kind of hell opened up when the numbering of the graves stopped at 219 in the corner away from the road. I thought I must have missed their continuation somewhere. I darted about trying to see where they picked up, but Suknaski saw right away that the numbers resumed in the 250s in the last row across the road, now slippery with watery snow. From 250, they went up, not down, so there seemed to be no 224, only a gap where graves 220 to 249 should have been.

A kind of hysteria seeped up the back of my throat, tasting of lead, and I saw, in that moment, how doomed we were, my dad and me, what fools, not to mention the extreme eccentricity of Suknaski shambling around in the snow and mud, puffing on his pipe, the smoke entwirling our frosted breath. My glasses were splashed and smudged, with snowflakes hitting into my eyes, the phrase "hitting into your eyes" lingering from Margaret Atwood's poem "You Are Happy," the title, sadistic or not, melting against my flushed skin, the book of that title I happened to be reading in Toronto just before making the doomed call to my sister and stumbling onto the news that brought me to the graveyard. I only felt both sweating hot beneath my coat and sweaters and chilled to the bone, the flakes pricking like needles. "You are happy," the words sang, even after seeing in "the ditch a deer / carcass, no head."

The pig, the bull, the corpse all sang in those poems as the world fell apart, and now they sang of my father's corpse, his missing grave, or so it seemed, the resonance and residue of my reading. Suknaski stopped humming. He took my hand, and we walked up and down every row, checking every number of every grave, and they rose to the 700s before I noticed Suknaski giving me a sideways glance. I saw a quiver of his lip turn into a cough, but that could have been a laugh. My throat and then my stomach caved in, and at first I thought I was crying, but then I realized I was laughing, as if independent of myself, both of us breaking up and pretty soon bent double, laughing ourselves silent to the end of every laugh, just like Sancho Panza and Don Quixote when the illusion slips, even just for an instant, and they glimpse their true significance, or lack of it, the paunchy sidekick beside the skinny cowboy-knight with a book in his saddlebag, as in the Gordon Lightfoot song, and we saw our situation, raised hands treading the air, and we roared parts of words over the uncountable graves, cheeks swelled to bursting with pious blasphemies: "The dying that will not die!" Suknaski yelled into the unlistening sky. "April fool!" I shouted down to the unsettled ground.

When we could stand up straight again, Suknaski said, "Let's get the car and go over there to the other side to warm up, it looks open." The entrance to hell turned out to be a laundromat, and people were there folding and reading and barely looked up when we walked in, although one guy gawked at the guitar case that made unmusical clinking noises when Suknaski set it down. At the back near the bathrooms, there was a payphone on the wall, so I dug out the number of the funeral home Reverend Kirk had said I could call when I came to town. Someone must have got the grave number wrong. Suknaski winked when he came out of the men's and saw me already on the phone. It rang four, five, six times. Our sad merriment dissipated as my call seemed to go unanswered. Then suddenly a click on the line. A faint old man's voice spoke, and all seriousness was back. The voice said the owner wasn't in on the long weekend but gave me his home number, perhaps sensitive to an accusing tone in my voice as I described the disjointed and missing numbers of the graves. I called the second number—all this was costing just dimes—and it was answered by a slightly effeminate but kind man's voice. The man heard me out, and by this time there was another sob in my throat, though I was closer to yelling than crying, the laugh having restored my voice to a surprising volume. He apologized for the mix-up. He said he'd have to look up the records, could he phone me back? I gave him the payphone number and hung up to wait. We stepped outside the back door to where I'd noticed steam billowing from this hell when I'd looked over from the graveyard. Suknaski lit his pipe, then my cigarette, and we settled in to wait for the undertaker's call back.

The laundromat and lost grave, so far from anything holy, but Suknaski's Holy Fool lent the whole thing the dignity of the Eastern Orthodox Church, which, he said, canonizes fools, an entire order of saints, maybe among those whose icons are radiant still in the humble magnificence of the Saint Peter and Paul Church at Lakenheath near Wood Mountain. The first priest of that church was the Romanian Părinti Dionese Necifur, who collected the hard-earned tithes from struggling farmers, all speaking accented English, to pay for the painting of the icons and frescoes, not stinting on the gold leaf, by his fellow monks back on Mount Athos, and arranged to have them carried all the way down the Greek mountainside, mules stumbling among vines and crumbled altars, scattering loose rocks, detritus of wizened gods underfoot, to the harbour, and then onto the ship that carried the sacred cargo via Jerusalem or rounded the Peloponnese to steam directly west to the Strait of Gibraltar, across the north Atlantic to the mouth of the St. Lawrence, up into the outstretched arms of Our Lady of the Harbour at Montreal, through the Lachine Canal and across the Great Lakes, one after another to cross the inland sea of Superior, and finally docking at Fort William, the Lakehead, where they were transported on carts to the train yards to be loaded as rail freight, destination Moose Jaw, and there picked up by ox-drawn wagons and carried in sections southwest to

Lakenheath, arriving in the momentous autumn of 1912, the year my grandparents married just northwest of there in Swift Current, eleven years before my dad was born and thirty years before Suknaski, one hot day at the end of July when his father was away in the fields, and his mother passed out from the pain, leaving her and the world unsure to this day if the poet's birthday was the 29th, the 30th, or the 31st when finally, no other help arriving, she struggled to her feet and walked the two miles into the village to register the newborn wrapped in her arms, and the priest, who by then had replaced Părinti, wrote out a birth certificate in Cyrillic script, which served to identify Suknaski in the sea of English for the rest of his life.

Sources are careful to stress that the icons not only depict the saints but also partake of their divinity. They themselves are divine in a world where matter and spirit—paint, saint, and the wood they appear on—are not conceived as distinct from each other. Even before the arrival of the icons at Lakenheath, farmers around there had gathered the stones from their fields to build Părinti a house, situating it on a rise above the church at his insistence so he could be sure to see in advance any marauding Turks, never convincingly outrun or defeated in his mind, who might appear at any moment to attack the Orthodox anywhere on Earth they presumed to rebuild their lives and revere their saints, their church, their towns and fields. My collection of thirteen porcupine quills originates from the visit my sister and I made to the stone ruins of Părinti's house, all that remained by the 1970s. I climbed onto a wide sill, the wood frame long since rotted away, and felt the pleasant coolness of the stone on my skin as relief from the still scorching twilight of late August. My sister was not far behind, when a jostling in the tall brittle grass in the corner of what had been one of the rooms startled us, and suddenly a porcupine looked right at us from amid the thorns and fallen stones, his quills slowly rising, fanning out, while we backed away and I ran down the hill, blood in my throat, my sister laughing, knowing I'd expected a ghost, some version of the priest or his vision of the Turk who would vanquish him. I took photos from a good distance on that strange day when the sun was setting as the moon was rising, and we argued, my sister and I, about whether or not porcupines throw their quills or if that's just an expression, yet I have found the small pouch of quills among my most valued documents, the Declarations of the Coroners, and cannot say for certain they were left on the ground by the disturbed current resident of what we always called the stone ruins. I told my sister the story from Suknaski's poem, how Părinti was in a car accident in 1928 and lost his memory. The townspeople called for donations to pay for his fare back to Romania, where he might recollect himself, but before he left he was robbed of the fare raised and at the same time discovered the cheque he'd been given for the farmland surrounding the stone house was bad. Then again in Regina, where he went to catch a train east, he was robbed of his life's savings, $2,200, and finally put on a train to Montreal and then a ship back to Constanta by fellow Romanian immigrants scattered across the country from Wood Mountain to Windsor, among them many of those who dug Wascana Lake with shovels and built the graceful Saskatchewan legislative building before they were trampled into the ground and forgotten, their immigrant fortunes like Părinti's ricocheting between good and ill, like all the suffering, every settler and clown, Suknaski, my dad, to the very end. So, when Suknaski was invited, in 1978, to review Emir Rodriguez Monegal's literary biography of Jorge Luis Borges for *Brick* magazine, volume 9, he was eager to explore the Argentine writer's famous fear of mirrors, because of their intolerable multiplication of the number of people in the world, the very quality that attracted Suknaski to the double and doublings, what he said the Holy Fool means, according to the stories, the Fool Părinti embodying and pointing to alternatives that always lie on the hidden other side of things.

Commenting on the tendency of Borges to mask his fictions as book reviews or scholarship, Suknaski mirrors this special genre, his "review" occurring amid his interpretations, ruminations, and stories couched as correspondence between him and Eli Mandel, the poet with Jewish as well as prairie roots explored in his book *Out of Place*, with both poets, for the purposes of the book review, assuming nicknames that reveal hidden other sides of their characters. Suknaski is Muzhik, and Mandel is Wowk, and Muzhik's letters are crammed with quotations, scraps of verse, and reported conversations with yet other country and western poet-clowns, Rudy Wiebe, Robert Kroetsch, their gossip, tangential mutterings, the review meandering interminably—it's a book review with latitude. Even one of Suknaski's own icon-collages is reprinted, like the ones that eventually crowded us out of the small house we shared in Regina.

In the *Brick* review, Suknaski twins the Nile River of Borges's story "The Golem" with the Qu'Appelle River that cuts east-west through the Saskatchewan plains, and anchors his self, Muzhik, with Mandel, Wowk, Ukrainian for wolf, then writer-in-residence at the Regina Public Library, leaving a note on Mandel's office door promising to call again on his way back. Suknaski's Muzhik walks out of the pages of Gogol and Tolstoy, the cunning peasant, unhorsed, considered an imbecile by the landowners mounted on horseback who look down on him, the little man appearing for all the world to be obediently hard at work with rake or scythe, while under his cap he is plotting their overthrow and the freeing of the people and horses and land according to another scale of justice, a cosmic scale. Borges's double was his father, who failed to become a writer, or a successful one, whereas Muzhik fails to become a farmer like his father, instead becoming a poet-priest Holy Fool who finds out that his father became a farmer only after failing to realize his vocation as a priest because of war, famine, and flight from the Carpathian Mountains above Constanta.

Wowk, writes Muzhik, working his nimble thoughts and fingers to weave together the most far-flung threads of stories, "isn't it astonishing that, hemispheres apart, the dreamed

pampas of Borges and I should double for Mandel and me?"
And that's how Suknaski's review got its title, "borges and i;
mandel and me," doubling the short prose piece, "Borges and
I," by which Borges distances himself from his own writing
that echoes and multiplies his every word. Both pairs of writers were thrown to the Americas where they track a lost code
that criss-crosses Muzhik's meanderings, Mandel his Jewish
identity lost, maybe, in Moorish Spain, Borges and Suknaski
tracing the losses and gains of acquiring two or more languages
at once, Borges English and Spanish, Suknaski Ukrainian and
Polish and then English on top.

Muzhik notes that Borges regretted he wasn't born a
century earlier when the gauchos ruled the pampas, riding
free on Indigenous lands wrenched back from Spain, and the
poet's longing to find a way to fully occupy the new hybrid
identity of gaucho, cowboy, vaquero, but instead finding himself both celebrated and betrayed as European in his study of
literature, English and Spanish, Shakespeare and Cervantes,
and the biographer Monegal records Borges saying the chief
event of his life was not settlement of the pampas—far from
it—but inheritance of his father's library. For Borges, Buenos
Aires was a mirror in which the New and Old Worlds look
at and double for each other, the library the site of the mirror and its reflections, the major event of his life a library.
"And are Mandel and me so different?" asks Muzhik. "Don't
we dream, amidst our researches, of riding with Dumont in
the last Métis buffalo hunt? Who dreams more of hounding
the Cossacks over and beyond the steppes? The Old West now
gone," only "so many Midnight Cowboys" cruise in Mustangs
"through downtown Edmonton, Dallas. . . . Borges, they say,"
as Muzhik works up his reverie, "was scarcely ever found on
campus at the Texas university where he was a visiting resident during that one year stay as an honoured writer and guest
in fabled America. Borges, already stone blind, was instead
to be found in some old movie theatre, not the superstar of
New World or Modern Literature, but slouched in the dark

like a misplaced gaucho, breathing in still another country & western movie." And by this circuitous route, which nevertheless conveys a foreboding inevitability, Suknaski arrives at the main theme of his book review and source of credentials for ushering me through the graveyard: the suicide that was an obsession for Borges, according to Monegal, after his own father's death.

In a piece written in 1940 but not published until 1973, Borges described in the third person his consideration of suicide at the Adrogué Hotel. The poem remains unfinished but makes clear, at least to Monegal, in Suknaski's view, that Borges remained alive by becoming fascinated with the paradox of using "the same hand trained to write" for pulling the trigger instead and putting a bullet into his head. "To move from the pen to the revolver, from his life as an obscure municipal clerk to the rival of his heroic ancestors, from metaphysical speculation about death to an actual test of that speculation—in short, to move from inaction to action"—that is how, Monegal writes, suicide entertained Borges and vice versa. Suknaski takes the story from Monegal's biography but then emphasizes the opposite implication, the taking up of writing with the same hand that toys with the gun, the choice both Borges and Suknaski made in the end. Monegal goes on to interpret this and other moments as Borges's symbolic killing of his nonwriter self that was only his father's faint reflection, as in a wavy, cracked mirror, after which the poet assumed a new identity, the one the world came to know. Borges, according to the lefthanded Suknaski, finally located the lost cipher, arrived at the heart of the labyrinth, reached by making only left-hand or sinister turns, and trailing behind him the Ariadne's thread of his writing to find his way back out. When he finally entered the maze, Borges wondered about the fabled Minotaur he was about to take by the horns and wrestle to the death: "Will he be a bull or a man? Will he perhaps be a bull with the face of man? Or will he be like me?"

Suknaski sought the lost ciphers in poems, songs, draw-
ings, icon collages, the moment of choice between pen and
gun presenting itself not in the image of the Cretan bull and
its Greek destroyer but while fishing north of Lac La Ronge,
half hoping to somehow cast off the whole project of writing, its difficulties, despite offering the pretense of choice of
word or genre in all our little dramas of self-composition. Two
young Cree women drove up in a battered old car asking after
an old woman who had been seen walking that way earlier
but had not returned. Since Suknaski's mother had passed
away just the Friday before, Suknaski well suspected who it
was the women had seen and who had perhaps followed and
even brushed past him, exposing what he was up to there. He
said nothing to the Cree searchers and instead turned in the
encounter toward what then appeared to be a new and "difficult freedom." He walked back to a waiting car and headed
out of the bush and down south to Joni Mitchell's wide-open
"Paprika Plains" to finally and fully embrace the doom of the
writer, the settler-writer of divided and compounded loyalties,
recording, four months later, the similar difficulty he was in
when standing by his father's graveside. "When you are your
father's pallbearer and mirror image," he writes, "the name the
priest pronounces is also your own, and you stand there wondering who was buried, while your double descends into the
last of all labyrinths."

The icons Suknaski made with such fervour and agita-
tion and ingenious bricolage had an ungainly beauty, and, on
dismantling our household a few months or years after com-
pleting our work in the graveyard, I kept a few, until I fled
the country and western world again for what I thought was
forever and lost track of many more things than I managed to
hold on to. In the photos, the provenance of which I do not
recall, what stands out, besides the strange icons themselves,
are Suknaski's bare feet and dual-coloured harlequin cap, oversized, and in some photos he is smoking his pipe. Despite my
losing the icon mitres or sceptres, having no place or means to

keep or carry them, can't think where they've gone, I clung to Suknaski's poetry, which I thought belonged with my corpses by association. Eventually, I wrote an essay on laughter and the Fool of Wood Mountain to present at an international conference in Moscow, a paper in which I was trying and failing to get at something about him, the pen and the gun, that preoccupied me perhaps longer than was altogether healthy, all the while anticipating the thrill that would be experienced in the Russian academy when I delivered news of a western Canadian poet, major-minor, successfully trafficking in Slavic literary devices and religious influences, a poet who performed as a Holy Fool on the Great Plains and in the engulfing language of Shakespeare.

That's what I thought at the time, but now it is impossible to overstate the indifference my paper encountered, the thud of its insignificance, from blank to bored to indignant incomprehension among the ten or eleven participants in attendance at my conference session. The facial expressions I glimpsed when I glanced up from my reading made me laugh inwardly because they so resembled the stone-faced women, in kerchiefs and threadbare sweaters pulled over thin dresses, seated at ornately carved wooden tables on each floor of the hotel where the conference was held, faded European grandeur combined with the most subtle dash of the Orient, each floor of the hotel consisting of long, wide hallways, the walls covered in damask, tattered at the corners, and the floors with threadbare but once-sumptuous woven carpets. The halls led left and right from the gilded elevators to such distances as to vanish into the tiniest specks of light from high windows at the most distant tips of the hotel wings. Opposite the elevator doors, interaction was enforced between the entrants and the one or two Babushkas, as the kerchiefed women were introduced to us, leading us to understand the term as one of respect for female authority, for the experience and wisdom of older women, and not a term of derision, like "old lady," more familiar in the country and western world I had come from. The Babushkas presided over enormous thick ledgers, cloth-bound books a foot and a half wide, and about two feet long, that could only be opened by raising their hefty arms and pulling back their bodies to turn the huge pages, yellowed and stiff and filled with columns crawling with Cyrillic script, which they added to, silently, watchfully, each time a hotel guest came or went. We were all afraid of them, though they had courteously learned a few English, French, and German phrases for our benefit, and I doubt I've ever heard such aggressively growled good mornings and good evenings anywhere else on Earth, spoken with harsh declarative emphasis instead of the rhythmical pro forma salutations they function as in English. A Babushka's "Good morning" felt more like an accusation, a tone I thought must have bled over from the Russian, a language so nuanced as to differentiate, as I gathered, minute degrees of familiarity between speakers and their social ranking relative to each other.

Once the greeting was pronounced on stepping out of my room or out of the elevator, the Babushka, noting my room number and sizing me up and down, would turn pages of the ledger slowly, then crouch forward to note the departure or arrival in a seemingly quaint and cumbersome surveillance or inventory procedure. I was lodged in a room with a New York specialist on the transmission and circulation of the *Mahabharata*, an epic that itself continues to evolve in depicting the evolution of ancient Hinduism over thousands of years, the working out of moral codes in a central story of conflict and war between horse-warrior first cousins vying for the kingdom. One of the sets of opposed cousins, the sons of Pandu, are born from unions between Pandu's wife and various gods, including Krishna, enmeshing the whole series of tales in mind-boggling complexity regarding relations between the human and the divine, as I learned all through the long night before I was to present my paper, sleeping barely a wink because Lakshmi first had to call New York at a time convenient to her mother there, but not to me, about two in the morning

Moscow time, and then, having hung up the phone after an hour of loud talking that was none of my business but became so by sheer volume, felt compelled to either punish or pronounce me a worthy roommate, I suppose, by initiating me into the *Mahabharata* and to certain stories and episodes within it that she was concerned with in writing an anthropological study. Beguiled by the tales, the finely twisted strands of dilemmas of so many colourful intertwined characters, their intricate inter-generational descents, betrayals, failures, losses, yearnings for the feasting and dancing and praying that punctuated the wars, in spite of feeling, as though it were physical, my own burden of hoarded treasure, the story of the corral, hardening in my throat and then in my belly and bed, a spreading lump, Cantuar, Wood Mountain itself, the poems sinking into the ground like abandoned homesteads, ruins, lumbering icons, hectoring voices, ponderous silences, unrecounted corpses.

By the end of our first day in the Moscow hotel, various Babushkas on our floor and other floors had begun eyeing my roommate Lakshmi in a certain rather hostile way, or so we thought. In the hall and in the lobby, on seeing her, they would approach her, stand very close to her face, and say in the most harshly demanding tones, "Why don't you pay?" Lakshmi was small and very young looking, though like Suknaski she seemed older by virtue of the ancient tales she had command of, and she strained her face and neck upward, immediately entangling herself in what I thought were quite comical exchanges of misinterpretation, broken Russian to broken English, louder and louder, that left her feeling helpless and indignant at the same time, the accusing Babushka walking away in disgust with loud clicks of her tongue. I was at Lakshmi's side the first time it happened, and later that night she told me about two further confrontations over the course of the day. She was exasperated, and neither of us could fathom what it meant. The next day she skipped out of the conference sessions to spend most of the morning going between the hotel reception desk and the conference registration office,

a room some distance from the front lobby, at each place insist-
ing she had paid the hotel bill in advance when she registered.
We got a laugh out of the contrast between the giant ledgers,
meticulously marked at our every movement but seemingly
mistaken somehow in this one crucial accounting. When I
told the story to other colleagues, I began to hear more tales
of misrecognition and mistaken value that we began to call
"Why don't you pay?" Credit cards were sometimes turned
down and traveller's cheques refused, even U.S. dollars were
not accepted if they were creased or worn, so unaccustomed
was the recently post-Soviet Moscow in 1995 to the foreigners
and currencies flooding the city. I began using my tiny travel
iron to smooth out my dollars before going to the restaurant
and had no problem paying my bill with crisp currency, and
soon word got around. By the afternoon of the second day, I
had a line-up of conference delegates at my hotel room door
and even thought it possible a new column would have to be
opened for me in the ledger to record all the comings and
goings of visitors to my room. I was busy thus "money laundering," as we jokingly called it, with a dampened towel, one
or two delegates hovering around my contrived ironing board,
when suddenly Lakshmi burst in and squealed, "It's you!"
She looked at me every bit as fiercely as the Babushkas had
stared down at her repeatedly. "You haven't paid," she yelled,
real anger in her voice, and I was accused of trying to get
away without paying my hotel bill and making the Babushkas
think it was Lakshmi who had not paid. In fact, I had not paid
despite attempting to do so several times, but I was repeatedly
told I had already paid. I had even spoken to the conference
president about it, and he'd instructed me to see him on the
last day to settle up, since he was too busy while the conference was in session to deal with what he thought could not be
urgent, since I was considered to have paid. I then went to the
registration desk again and asked to see both my account and
Lakshmi's. After some time, I realized what seemed so incom-
prehensible to both of us that neither could have suspected it:

they had confused Lakshmi and me, both our names and our faces appearing so identically foreign and out of place that they could only guess which of us was which, or worse, saw no substantive difference between us. I thought of the ledger recording my movements as Lakshmi's, hers as mine. Did it matter? How had she been spending her time? What if she had done something untoward, even in innocence? I didn't know her that well. I was finally, sheepishly, allowed to pay my hotel bill, but when I explained to my roommate what I now understood of the confusion she continued to treat me warily and as though I had tried to get away with something dodgy and pin it on her. On reflection, and in the absence of another explanation of her hostility, which did not abate, I imagined she was incensed that anyone could mistake her, descendant and bearer of the *Mahabharata*, with me, cipher of insignificance, bearer of nothing of value, some lost cowboy place, Wood Mountain, the opposite of epic. That was the self-defeating and somewhat paranoid thought I had, and so indeed it was, *itihas*, to borrow the refrain of the *Mahabharata*, which has become more or less indispensable to me now, though under my breath, not out loud. So indeed it was that the fun of what became famous as my money laundering operation came to an abrupt end, and thereafter I lent out my travel iron with the electrical converter rather than iron the dollars of others in our now tense and unwelcoming hotel room.

So, when Lakshmi called her family from our room at all hours that night and spoke at full volume, not only to her mother but also to several family members, for more than two hours by the time she got through all the Russian and then European and then American operators, and then all the members of her extended family, I could not help but feel even more miserable, in retrospect, in my twin bed across the room, that she was avenging the embarrassment I had caused her, and reinforcing her evaluation of me as not worthy of the slightest consideration, putting me in a position in which I could not refuse a hearing of whatever she cared to talk about, her beloved *Mahabharata*, told to impress how much she and I were absolutely different from each other and distinct, East versus West, only cheap hotel beds artificially and mistakenly twinning us, and it was somehow a sacrifice demanded, a price I was required to pay for the gift of a thousands-year-old story, whether I wanted it or not, and at the time of her choosing, a story that entranced a continent if not the entire Eastern hemisphere, whose grandeur and significance would be the only weapons adequate to destroy me, her opponent, emphasizing my unworthiness by contrast and forcing me to acknowledge myself as bereft of any story worth telling. Or so I thought, almost losing my sense, if only momentarily, of the absurdity of the situation. The lack of sleep and my resultant confusion the following day, the epic tales enmeshing and displacing my groggy thoughts about an increasingly remote Wood Mountain, made me wretched. I was experiencing what Suknaski was up against, the fantastic energy and courage he expended, a small man powered by the audacity to circulate perspectives and voices from the unlikeliest of places, against that enormous sky, stories about the unhorsing and demise of cowboys, stampeding of buffalo in pounds, corrals, over cliffs, lands grabbed, and all this against the glorious Hindu spiritual story tradition that gained in life and energy the longer it was circulated and passed down through more and more generations. But, I thought, weren't the feuding warrior cousins of the *Mahabharata* just a couple of cowboys until the Sage Vyasa began to explore and discover and massage the many meanings their contest might hold out for the generations of listeners and retailers of epic tales in the founding and destruction of civilizations? Thus my mind smouldered with self-defensive anger and insight into my failure to get a proper repose, let alone a grip on my story and subject matter, now seeming both paltry and increasingly significant and complex, dense and intensified, as I viewed and reviewed my materials over the passages of time.

Imagine my surprise, then, to see Lakshmi in the small audience at my out-of-the-way panel session on the last morning! I thanked her afterward for coming, which I thought was big-hearted of me and of her. She hastened to say she had not come to hear my paper but that of another speaker, and didn't I agree his paper was so very interesting? Or was it fascinating? She left me a flayed bird, flesh limply falling from my bones as she turned and walked out of the room, restoring me to my pathetic solitude, in which I nearly missed receiving the collegial handshakes of two more sympathetic listeners who now approached the lectern. One was Professor Pavel Olkhov from the University of Vladivostok, who reminded me that he had travelled farther than I had to attend the conference, crossing as many time zones and equally a foreigner in Moscow, though with the advantage of speaking roughly the local language. Several months later in a letter, Pavel remarked on what he called the "unforgettable" Fool of Wood Mountain described in my paper, and he revealed the pretext of his writing to me to inquire how my students responded to finding Russian or Slavic literary tropes in English poetry. His question recalled my surprise, naive no doubt, that except for him no one in all of Russia or among the hundreds of international scholars in attendance at such a momentous conference showed the slightest interest in how the social form of the Holy Fool had survived and even flourished in what was surely the most alien and remote contexts of time and place, Suknaski's country and western poetry. I thought of poor Pârinti and recalled how fragile that survival was in Wood Mountain, how unlikely its flourishing to enliven the guitar strummings and left-handed jottings of a young man with literary inclinations stranded among roughriders and cowboys, hobbled nomadic Aboriginal tribes, their remnants, amid industrializing agriculture. My expectation that the Russians would find this amazing, as I did, and hopeful somehow, and that they would embrace Suknaski like a prodigal son, raise him up above the crowd in a great hurrah, in the process elevating me to a position of recognition, all that was obliterated in my awareness, slow I admit, as my whole body blushes with the thought and blushed at the podium, that it would never occur to Russian readers that their literature would fail to dominate wherever it travelled and was read, even to the most remote reaches of the Earth, since wherever has been the centre of an empire the assumption of supreme self-importance emanates to the meanest individual member, that sense lacking in readers from the lesser margins of history and geography.

The work of ironing dollars for spending in Moscow restaurants, humouring the Babushkas, coming and going, suffering the recitation of the *Mahabharata* through the night, in the midst of it all the delivery of my paper was only the last bit of stale air slowly seeping out of a tire. Pavel later wrote to me that it was not the unlikely survival and rejuvenation of Slavic cultural forms in Wood Mountain and in English that he found remarkable, as I suspected, but my account made him want to know how English readers responded to Suknaski's poetry, for what that might tell him, I guess, about tapping into English interest in his own writing if he could get it translated. Or that's what I thought, but then later I was not so sure. His letter was written on the back of a photocopy of a medieval woodcut that depicts two speakers talking and gesturing toward each other, a friendly exchange, as if in a tavern or similarly congenial social setting. A caption and riddle in Cyrillic script is translated in Pavel's hand: "This is two fools, they are all three." He leaves it for me to see how the dialogue between the two fools makes three in what they create by talking to each other. Pavel makes three in sending me the woodcut, our communication being the third thing, an act of creation that could lead anywhere. Subtle and powerful and these fools are the real scholars, I thought. It's winning a gamble by playing your wild card, putting the joker in play, and chance falling your way, which it has to do some of the time, those are just the odds and the counterweight to all the bad luck and ill-fatedness. When we open our mouths to speak, fools that we are, or when we take up our pens, I thought, we surrender to that third thing suggested but not shown in Pavel's riddling woodcut that ends up being an entire unending commentary on how everything turns on the exchange, words and perspectives, the roundabout and the back and forth of the story and the telling that binds the teller to the listener and makes a community right then and there, a world that does not exist until the hazards of speaking or writing are risked.

The family resemblance was unmistakable between Suknaski, his raggedy Holy Fool, kooky saint of the onion-domed church, and the rodeo clowns at Wood Mountain now commingled with the muck of the graveyard, hellish steam of the laundromat, our search for the missing grave, results of the surprise rodeo at the godforsaken corral just northwest of where we were waiting for the undertaker's call. Befriending Suknaski the way I had done was in defiance of my mother's instructions to avoid the Romanian boys at the rodeo dances, where the word *Romanian* could include Ukrainians, Poles, Serbs, Austro-Hungarians of any ilk, all the fled peoples of the wolf-infested Carpathians who, it was said, had "Russian hands and Roman fingers," a warning wrapped in xenophobic puns about Romanians, to a man deadly handsome and ethnically Slavic, Mom said, yet observant of the Latin or Catholic rite, and speaking a Latin-rooted language that sounded more like French than Ukrainian, or like Saskatchewan French with a Ukrainian accent, to our Scottish-clipped western English ears. Partly this and partly that, she waved a hand, trying to say and not say what she meant, more Eastern than Western, and besides they dance you in circles into the corners, like coyotes separating out a calf or lame heifer in order to prey on it, instead of circulating you around the dance hall in all fairness, out in the open and on the up and up, as if they might kill instead of love you.

As with the Romanians, with their dark eyes and olive skin, the Assiniboine descendants and the Métis, and everybody else from Wood Mountain, Suknaski, his very person, somehow conjured up both the Old West and the faded grandeur of gilded ballrooms of Vienna and Prague with their crusted cathedrals, war-weary Europe, yet bearing their tatters with a beleaguered dignity, brocade drapes, covered, on close inspection, with dust smelling of sagebrush, old and new worlds touching just there, as in the astounding stomping dance of couples like Nick and Bonnie Lawrick, bound in a kind of terrifying waltz combined with flourishes of tango, where every twelfth beat or so Nick's jewelled cowboy boot would come down BAM! on the wood floor, just missing his wife's delicate open-toed shoe, and all the kids and half the crowd would slow and then stop to gape in fear and amazement, suddenly aware of space in a way we had not been before, the space between us and its elimination, where we set a foot down, and how far we'd stepped from where we thought we were. That guy must be part Gypsy, they said, and we noticed his wife's foot was never grazed, let alone crushed, nor did she seem concerned or wary of danger in the least. Suknaski's poetry, even a new poem just finished, sounded that ancient, with the same hints of barely escaped violence that made all the people of Wood Mountain seem to have come from the depths of a faraway fiery past, in that moment, or in the moment of reading, like overhearing words and stories filling the room with longing and horror, a kind of muffled but terrified ecstasy behind titles of poems that were just the names of people like Nick and Bonnie Lawrick, the parents of my friend Jocelyn, people we knew or their parents, uncles, neighbours, brothers, or sisters.

Spun anecdotes, jokes, ghost stories like the "Three Coffins Dream" (circa 1850) the one great-grandfather Domich had one time foretelling deaths he couldn't otherwise have known about, a whole world of people like him, murmuring their fears, sorrows, journeys, their endless homelessness, wandering and wayfaring, hardships, losses, and once inside Suknaski's poems there are others listening who come into view, tending to the tales and commenting on them in the ongoing chain of recognition, kinship, and consolation. No thin stranded inner voice of a lone poet suffering or scheming in isolation outside the poem-village, no one sewing detached or private systems of images, nor is there the knife-like precision with words, the surgical shocks of "You Are Happy," though that poem is well muddied by the glimpse of the mutilated deer in the ditch, like a rip in the insulation of the purported happiness, letting in that blast of cold. In Suknaski, poetry is a matter of listening, not speaking or wielding a blade. He is an eavesdropper, not an originator or a solitary genius. He's losing his balance or struggling to regain it amid the accented sorrows and complaints of immigrants and exiles and orphans, the tossed and the thrown, Teton Sioux, Métis, halfbreeds, all displaced, their stories landing them in places like Wood Mountain, Val Marie, or leaving them hanging, and it's hard to say where Suknaski starts and stops, the voices fluid, his poems the overheard voices of others. Even his books are collections of compromised authorship, or, better, compounded authorship, the works introduced, mediated, moderated, edited, sometimes heavily, by other writers. Al Purdy, Dennis Lee, Dennis Cooley, John Newlove, Stephen Scobie. Lee in particular, I heard, challenged and even faulted Suknaski for undermining his own voice in attributing every word, every voice, every poem to a named speaker overheard in the Trail's End pub in Wood Mountain, or on the shores of Duck Lake after the battle of Batoche, the edge of Tonita's pasture, Lee Soparlo's post office, all the places and voices whose imminent disappearance makes them briefly audible, Suknaski a Minerva's owl swooping down at twilight toward the end of the world now slipping into darkness and oblivion.

Murmuring, muffled, disenchanted, disdained, drowned, drowning voices. The only way to speak at all is through the words of the shadowy doomed, no more safe from the enemy for being dead. To mimic the voices of others and speak through them, that's the way of the fool, the Holy Fool, who catches the eye, the ear, and stumbles, by design or by chance, onto the hidden other side of things. Suknaski sought that other way to see things, like the April Fool who picked the day to pull that trigger and with a wink shot comic relief into his own tragedy, the possibility of a happy ending in the breaching of fences, rejoining of lands with peoples and beasts—that's the comedy, the comic version of the story—the wink that reunites my dad and I, Johnny and King, the unsettled and displaced, all restored to the lands of our reckoning. Suknaski cast me in this drama as Coyote Lady, a creature who slipped down from the hills to embrace and answer him, make supper, drive the car, an allegory of companionship and care, not anybody distinct from him or the web of words, languages, voices, names threaded together in songs and poems, spoken in hindsight from a diminishing habitat, even naming his pamphlet press Three-Legged Coyote after the trapped creature whose hold on life is so strong that it gnaws off its own snared leg, leaving the severed part in the trap to escape the threat and getting along thereafter in spite of the wound with a distinctive limping gait. Suknaski's Holy Fool was my coyote mate on three legs, hobbled but, like the rodeo clowns, supremely skilled at distracting the bulls with the red rags of his poetry, drawing the horned charge yet evading the gory thrust most of the time.

Standing in our coats outside the back door of the laundromat, we look toward the graveyard through the wire fence. Our exhaled smoke curls upward to merge with the steam coiling up from the dryer vents. The laugh we shared earlier still flickers at the corners of Suknaski's eyes. In the instant before the payphone begins to ring, the undertaker getting back to me about where to find the grave, I wince at a sensation of doubt that rolls over me like a cloud. Suknaski's idea is that my nightmare about Dad's death, his remorse and suicide, my not knowing about it, or about the funeral or grave, followed by the shock of knowing all about it, or nearly all, and the crumpled bodies of man and beast in Johnny Bradley's corral, the final blast from the farmhouse kitchen office, all that could only be accommodated and dispelled by going through with the burial, the physical experience of loss and paying of respects. Suknaski told me the story of Antigone of the ancient Greek tragedy. Against all reason and the law of the land, she insists on burying her brother, giving him proper rites, more than once, despite his disgrace in betraying the powers that be, risking her own life to offer relief to her kin guilty of treason. The terrible choice between what is owed to kin and what to community did not overwhelm the Greeks when they encountered it, Suknaski said, but became the source of their literature, the flowering of their poetry, tragic and comic, enactment of loyalty to both in actual places at set times, Cantuar, Swift Current, Assiniboia, Wood Mountain.

About the third or fourth ring of the payphone, I picked up the receiver and ducked inside the back door of the laundromat to talk to the undertaker. His voice was thin and hesitant, the rumble of dryers nearly drowning it out. He said, as it turned out, the former owner of the funeral home, who I later realized was a cousin, maybe second or third, to my mother, was also a drinker. "His records are not complete, or very accurate, as far as we can tell," said the undertaker. "It says here the plot should be 224." During a long pause, I listened to him swallow, his throat gurgling a bit, and then with a new breath he said he thought the new owner, his boss, had renumbered all the plots in an effort to straighten everything out when he bought the cemetery the previous year. The agitations of the washers and hum of the dryers filled another long pause as this new information sloshed around in my mind. Renumbered the plots? Then maybe no one knows where he is. Which bodies are where. Drunks who just toss other drunks here and there. The phone receiver left my hand to dangle on its cord, hitting the cinder block wall, smashing, smashing, then dwindling to tap, tap, tap, it dangled and tapped, and I have that image in my mind and maybe a memory of saying something more, swearing, Suknaski might remember what I said, though even he has gone to his grave by the time I'm getting the word out about how it all happened. I never did thank the undertaker, so I guess he got the message of my disappointment or disgust and hung up, and the question of where my dad might be buried went unanswered. I don't think I thanked Reverend Kirk either, though I've kept a letter I might or might not have sent to him once we found not the grave but the place we decided to mark it, where we thought the grave might be, around number 294 at the time, as I recall.

Suknaski led me out to the car, saying the number was not what mattered to quiet my dreams. We bundled up against the gusts of wind that blew in from the cemetery. Large wet flakes hit our faces and melted, running down like tears as we slipped and slid among the plots and gravestones. A Three Stooges skit dashed through my mind, the grief talking, the grave darting around the graveyard underground and just ahead of us as we search for and pursue it, farther and farther away as we approach the appointed number, as if larger forces resist our every move, every scheme, dropping banana peels, swinging ladders, cracking skulls. Suknaski had the idea we should go back to plot 219 where the numbering left off. He said maybe the numbers did not continue because that was the drunken cousin's numbering. Then we counted from there, sliding along ground increasingly greasy with mud, to where 224, counting from 219, might have been. There was an old mound there but no marker. It could have been my dad's grave, though the next one on the other side was in the 250s somewhere. This one mound, at pseudo-224, had no number, but somebody had been buried there. My dad had died four years previously, so wouldn't his grave have been sunken by then, not still a raised mound? Suknaski set down his guitar case, opened it up, handed me the roses, then took out the cross and unwrapped the tools. He pulled some strands of sweetgrass from his coat pocket, cleared a space on the ground, and lit a smudge. He stabbed a hole in the mud first with the crowbar, then set the cross and hammered it in, the peg end sinking easily into the prepared ground. All this time he held his pipe between his teeth and talked a slow blue streak with a chanting intonation. "Wuh-nay-ska wiska noma add single space before the period . . . Wayyyyyyyaaa." He was talking to ghosts.

We just made it up, where the grave was, and I was worried it wouldn't work if it wasn't really the right spot, but that's just the lingering of superstition, Suknaski said, it's all made up anyway. What's not made up is the physical going through with the mourning, in time and place. The wind whipped and squealed in sharp gusts. Once the cross was set deep enough to stand upright, Suknaski cleared away more snow with his hands, and I was startled by how simple and beautiful it looked, streams of grace flooding the ground in a haunting reversal of my gravedigger dream, my accidental discovery of Dad's unmarked grave in every night's sleep, and we fixed the spot. Here is the spot, I thought, but can such a vivid and sleep-destroying nightmare be tricked away with a homemade wooden cross at an approximate grave site? I set the roses to stand leaning on the cross. Suknaski was chanting his made-up lyrics to a steady strumming of his guitar. The photos show how he did a kind of dance on the grave as he sang and how neither of us felt the damp or the cold by then. We stamped around the cross, looked out over the other graves as if from Dad's perspective, his grave, the wind and snow refreshing our eyes to see ourselves and the grave from the point of view of the more respectable or better-remembered dead, with their neat stone markings, and in the view of the new owner of the cemetery, who would find this blue cross on Monday morning and probably have it removed. I didn't care, and it didn't seem to matter. We left the graveyard and found a diner for lunch, then tooled around town, driving up and down the main street for a while, noticing how it was still lined with half-tons angle-parked at the Healy Hotel, and then went back to our motel with a kind of restless giddy satisfaction.

Some years later I heard Dad's own brothers and sisters laid a proper headstone. I could not ask anyone for the grave number, or thought I couldn't, without telling of this whole escapade, which I thought could only aggravate their loss, so I've kept it to myself until now. I don't know if the Morgans saw our wooden cross and if they did whether it embarrassed them. The photo I received from someone is dated 1999. Or 1995, it's hard to make out the numbers.

BUFFALOED

Here is the place, my father's grave, and now is the time when telling the story of the one demands telling the story of the other. Only gradually could I see how we were trapped in the story of cowboys and Indians, and how that story had begun to chafe despite its allure and familiarity. I clutched on to my dad and Johnny Bradley, their corpses and stories, yet at the same time held fast to the buffalo and Assiniboine, their decimation and displacement necessary, in my story and in history, to put Johnny in the corral with an enraged buffalo bull and Dad late for work and then in the ranch house office with his rifle. The buffalo and Assiniboine had to be cleared from those plains by the first settlers, the parents of Johnny and Dad, to make their farm fortunes there and generate enough wealth to bankroll the romance of the buffalo on land formerly inhabited by the Assiniboine. Johnny had to amass the land and money required to forgo crops, more and more each year, to be able to restore the buffalo to the plains as he set out to do. To isolate and tell only the story of those cowboy-victims, or cowboy-heroes of the corral, Johnny and Dad alone, presumed the prior destruction of the buffalo and Assiniboine that set the stage for the whole sorry culmination of our origins as the historical dead end it turned out to be. So the story of the buffalo and Assiniboine had to be told alongside the story of the corral, with the effect of holding Johnny and Dad and all their kin, including me, responsible for the deaths, displacements, decimations, and that is not entirely true or the whole story either, since all of us, including the Assiniboine, were playing our parts in the stories to which we were born. And I tried and failed to tell both the story of the corral and the story of the clearing of the land to make way for farming and Bradley's ranch without siding with one and obliterating the other. I could not, and I could not get on with any other story either, so I had no story or alibi to justify living there or grounding me anywhere else. I went on with my various jobs and paying the rent but all the while felt stymied, dishonest, and stuck, unable for the longest time even to pose the question that might have helped, of who would want to hear again the story, sorry or triumphant, of how the West was won for settlement by hunting the buffalo nearly to extinction and dispossessing the Assiniboine. To whom could I tell my sorrow about the destruction of the settler-descendant cowboys in their attempts to restore the buffalo to the lands where the Assiniboine had been at home? The very awkwardness of these sentences, these convoluted lines running on and on and around to the ends of the Earth when I try to lay it all out, only lays out the whole problem. The answer to the question of who could bear to read such a story was no one I could think of, and since I lacked standing to tell the story of the buffalo and Assiniboine on its own, and was hopelessly ensnarled trying to tell and not tell the two stories at the same time, the one choked up by the other, then what was the harm, I thought, of just letting it go and not telling a story at all and leaving it unspeakable, as I find it to be? I was pretty certain my sisters and brothers would not welcome reminders or my reimagining of events in the corral from documents, hearsay, and oral accounts, all of it, like the deaths of the buffalo and Assiniboine, now as then, too terrible to look at. So I left it at that and found I could not leave it at that, unable to live with myself or compose the story yet unable to figure out how else to answer or proceed.

Soon after I set up housekeeping with Suknaski, my mother gave me a set of seven tea towels that she had embroidered, each with a scene of little pigs doing the work to go with the days of the week along with the song she'd taught me and my sisters spelled out in hesitant but colourful threads: Wash on Monday, Iron on Tuesday, Mend on Wednesday, Visit on Thursday, Clean on Friday, Bake on Saturday, Church on Sunday. Even as I was honoured to receive such a gift from her work-worn hands, I knew the tea towels muffled a hard discussion we might have had about some poems I'd written, especially the one called "Work to Go with the Days of the Week," which now reads as harsh, maybe unduly so, about how the rhyme and reason of life faltered and then more or less fell apart after Dad left or was kicked out, calling for the composition of a new rhythm, what I was searching for and working on, and in the poem it was daughter against mother against father.

With the gift of the tea towels, my entrapment as a young woman, as I then was, in the dead-end story of cowboys and Indians without my say-so was further complicated by my mother's objections, out of loyalty to her parents and my dad's, the pioneer settlers, to any other way I might situate myself in the story or its telling except as a prime user of tea towels and keeper of the daily rhythms of homemaker and farm wife, the very role I repeatedly failed to occupy whether out of perversity or inadequacy or sheer neglect of what it takes to land that role by marrying this or that cowboy.

This Magazine published that poem and another, a kind of work song that went "Left, left / I had a good job and left / left . . ." that was also repeatedly and fatally interrupted by various events at home and in the news. Suknaski also published the two poems together as a pamphlet under his Three-Legged Coyote imprint that he created for all creatures wretched and wounded.

"What if someone reading this," Mom asked after she read my poem about the tea towels, "what if they think this is a true story? How it really was?"

"No single version could ever encompass the whole truth," I said, not without insolence. "You'll have to write your own story if you think mine is not accurate or complete."

And that's when my mother became the Writer, not only on the tea towels but also in two books of her self-published memoirs, which she suddenly announced had been her life-long dream to write yet was the first we ever heard of it.

BOOK REVIEW

My Hourglass
by Nona Morgan Lucas
Printed by Derksen Printers, Steinbach, Manitoba, 1987
ISBN 0-920739-37-7

The Dance
by Nona Morgan Lucas
Printed by Art Bookbindery, Winnipeg, Manitoba, 2007
ISBN 978-09782984-0-1

Full disclosure: both books were written by my mother. I do not here feign objectivity about their literary or histori-cal quality or significance but only point to some telling ways they inform my own memoir in which they are embedded, enmeshed, and embroiled even beyond this inserted "review," perhaps the first, though one of my brothers spotted a used copy of *My Hourglass* for sale on Amazon once. From the trunk of her well-travelled car, Mom sold every copy of the original print run she had paid for with her own money.

First, as to the spinning of stories in pursuit of one's given name: in the preface to her first book, Mom writes, "Being ninth born, given the name 'Nona' because a Scotch lady, Mrs. Harry Smith, told Dad it meant nine, having nine children of my own creates an interesting aurora." I recoil in shame at the ungrammatical lawlessness and challenged diction of this sentence, even as I blush with amazement at her unwavering belief in herself, her own story, enough to write and publish and foist it on anyone crossing her path in any parking lot. Instead of "aurora," I'm pretty sure she must have meant "aura," Aurora being my name, not hers, though presumably we both have an aura, and what's the difference or the big deal? The words *aura* and *Aurora*, and the writers, mother and daughter, obviously share roots. She was all about the number nine according to her name. She bought nine Bibles, each inscribed with the name of one of her nine children in gold lettering, the birthday gift for each of us at the end of our ninth year, which she considered the age of moral responsibility. When she travelled to Germany to visit my brother stationed at Lahr, she returned with nine Black Forest cuckoo clocks, gifts for the nine, and, whereas Dad anchored us in the space of the corral, Mom wound us in time, and I awakened in reading her book to my own not entirely distinct aura.

I did not say anything about that sentence or any other infelicity I discovered in Mom's book, partly because, in the end, her restless unsettled energy and overriding pride overwhelm any piddling errors of grammar or word choice. One of my sisters and I casually offered to copy edit and proofread her second book, assistance she accepted and acknowledged in "special thanks" to my sister in *The Dance*, explaining to her, but not to me, that my role, a professor of English by then, could not be publicly acknowledged because if people thought I was *involved* (her word) they might not believe she wrote either book herself, given her modest domestic life experience and grade ten education, which makes it all the more a wonder. Let me here attest publicly that my copy editing was very light, nothing more than insertion or removal of a few commas, rearrangement of a clause here and there, and I accepted with grace (her middle name) my lack of acknowledgement, its perversely backhanded compliment of my own presumed skill in writing.

"There will no doubt be episodes here written that another remembers but can hardly recognize as they saw or heard it differently," Mom continues in the preface to the first volume of her memoirs, *My Hourglass*. "Therefore please remember this is my story, the way I saw it and felt about it, the way I remember. I hope those near and dear to me can excuse me for anything told or colored in a way they cannot understand." This was killing me with kindness and condescension, my own words turned back on me with no small tone of triumph, since I had by then written no book of my own and would not, until now, and that's how it went and was going to go between us. Her usurpation of the role of Writer along with the gift of seven embroidered tea towels oppressed me with the force of a dowry, my fate written and unwritten at the same time in a none too subtle hint or manacle attaching me to my real work in life, modelled on hers, as recounted in her book, a matter of joyful routines of housework and child rearing (for which I am forever grateful), gardening and sharing in service to the community, each day preparing for the next in the ascent of the elect toward "Church on Sunday."

"I had a rigid routine for my housework," Mom writes in chapter 4, once she was brought up, the youngest of nine, and given the Latin name of one of three thread-snipping Fates, which significance the Scotch lady Mrs. Harry Smith seems not to have mentioned. Mom was swiftly married, more or less in a subordinate clause, and soon giving birth to her own nine children, whom she nursed through all the household epidemics of measles, mumps, chicken pox, scarlet fever. "I felt like Florence Nightingale," she says, prompting readers to see her as that heroic ancestor of all nurses, "when they had red measles so bad, their poor bodies on fire, skin bumpy and blotchy, lips cracked. They were far too sick to complain, I guess washing, cooking and caring for the sick took care of that year and a half," she writes. All children the wounding of their mothers, we found ourselves the grains of sand running down her portion of time in the hourglass.

In chapter 5, she writes again, "I had a rigid routine for my housework. I sewed almost everything the children and I wore. Baked all our own bread and buns, canned farm hens bought for $1.00 each. I sent the children clean and well-fed to school. I planned my work and enjoyed it. Each morning I made a pudding for dinner, a cake for supper, dust mopped and dusted the whole house then went on with the biggest or dirtiest jobs." Writing exactly as she spoke, she continues, "Once on Friday, which was my cleaning day, Fanny Forness and Isabelle Root came calling. I was almost finished and had just waxed the living room and dining room floors, the chairs were upside down on the table, paper rack on the chesterfield when a knock came. For a stunned moment, I was embarrassed but they soon put me at ease. I re-arranged the furniture, made tea and we made quite an inroad to becoming fast friends."

The pastoral comes to an abrupt halt, though only temporarily, in chapter 6, when "in April, 1968 Bern lost his job due to drinking and moved to Swift Current." That's the end of that, and Mom carries on seemingly unruffled: "I liked cooking, cleaning, arranging and organizing. I thought if you could run a household like ours smoothly, have time to relax with your husband [who had left or been kicked out by then] and read to your children, you could run the Bank of Canada. I remembered what I'd heard my Dad say when I was a child," she goes on. "You don't pray for the good things, pray for the strength to take what comes. What came was that I had to work outside my home." The only other time she'd been forced to work outside the home—a kind of death to her—was in 1944 when she responded dutifully to what she described as ten-foot-tall posters and the radio shouting in unison for "girls" to take over men's jobs so the men could go finish the war. Mom went to work at the Royal Bank in Cabri when Velma Cole, now Johnson, was the accountant, when "May Weston (née Trembath) was the teller and I was on ledgers. Can you imagine adding up columns one and a half feet long?" she asks suddenly. She means without a calculator or even a rudimentary adding machine. "I liked it and became good at it so that to this day when I make a purchase or buy a bus ticket I delight in having the total figure before my clerk with her computer." Tax included.

"I'm not belittling computers," she hastens to add, "but it's sure fun to use your head." As far as I know, she only left out of her memoir how that bank job included the weekly dismantling and cleaning of the heavy revolver kept under the counter to defend the bank's treasure from outlaws riding through town, a task I thought could only add to her horror at being forced to labour in a man's world, so unladylike. For whatever reason, her handling of the gun does not appear in the published version of her life story, but it was told to us in lowered tones of warning as we helped to hang out the wash or did the dishes as sisters together.

As for Fanny Forness and Isabelle Root, they are among the hundreds of characters, acquaintances, and kin who come and go in my mother's sentences, sometimes reappearing from previous chapters, but nowhere introduced, only embedded and recurring, so eventually they hold the whole thing together, as they must have her life, all the while remaining mysterious to all but one reader. Like the people, her sentences and subject matter and pronouns especially, like her embroidery threads, run together or run off in the way Mom reflects on her damaged life. "One time Barney McGuigan came to get Dad's mower and rake," she sets off. But who is Barney McGuigan? "How happy we were" when the war ended and "we" danced to Wilf Carter's song "When a Ration Book Is Just a Souvenir," and "every day someone got word that their uncle or brother or husband was on his way home. I felt sorry for Mrs. Hopton as we gathered in the back of the post office in the mornings as her son would never be coming home." But who is Mrs. Hopton, and what of her son?

Willard Colpitts is among the most frequently recurring characters, and the Healy Hotel in Swift Current the place most significant, at least to me, being where my parents spent their honeymoon on the night of October 27, 1945, the site of their conjoining situated midway between their birthplaces at Cabri and where they ended up in Assiniboia just nine days before I was born. So the only reader my mother's book could possibly have been addressed to was my dad, since he was the only one who would have known without footnotes or explanations the people Mom was talking about in the one place and in the other. Their Cabri and Swift Current people would not have known Fanny Forness or Isabelle Root from a hole in the ground, and Fanny and Isabelle, not to mention Mom's children and grandchildren later born in Assiniboia, had not a clue who Barney McGuigan was, or the myriad others from Cabri and surrounding area, unless we interrupted to ask and remembered from telling to telling, characters unreal to us unless we met them later at wedding dances or family reunions among the crowds of kin and all-but-kin. There are no footnotes, as I've said. And Mom's run-on sentences assault and even numb the senses, locked into repeated recountings of daily routines, the cleaning, comings, goings, canning, sewing, dancing, card playing, along with the naming of more and more people, everybody Mom ever met, what they ate and at what time and who prepared it, who paid, who served and on which tablecloth. Gus Trembath (perhaps the brother of Mae Weston née Trembath at the bank), Howard and Beth, Rose and Palmer, Willard and Barbara, and on and on without explanation, so we couldn't always tell the difference between who was related to us and who was not, where our families stopped and the world began, and that was her view of things as beginning with her and emanating outward in accordance with the bonds found or made with whomever she encountered, and only the most attentive listeners, with no thoughts of their own, could discern or disentangle her world of insistent, infinite kinship. Within minutes of meeting people, she would find their particular tie to her and use it to bind them closely, even if the hapless wayfarer had only shopped once at a dress shop in Gravelbourg where her cousin's daughter-in-law had worked in 1966. A family tree that never stopped growing, fertilized by continual circulation of names in preposterous sentences marked by erratic punctuation, that grammatical nicety scarcely tolerated as a nuisance and only now and then to be reluctantly indulged. If your uncle had worked at the hardware store in Silton between 1963 and 1978, well, he might have known the hotel there when it was owned by the parents of Rachel MacKinnon, my dad's ginger-haired mother, or Mom would dance with somebody in Killdeer or Rockglen who, fantastically, turned out to have previously owned and just recently sold the motel near Medicine Hat where Elsie Speir stayed during that June snowstorm in 1972 just after Jock had surgery, and on and on like that until everyone was accounted for and pinpointed in our past and on the map and all the weather and what was had for supper besides. I know it bothered Mom to no end that she couldn't place a single Assiniboine in that web of kinship. It made her frantic, perhaps, why that was, anxious to fill in all the gaps, though she never put that into so many words, and some of us might have imperceptibly adopted her ways without knowing exactly where they came from, took them in different directions, or tried to shake her influence, cultivating reticence, listening, and silent instead, going mute, only scribbling in secret all the reasons we might have for not standing up for ourselves, exploring and then telling another story that might be the death of her.

Nine Reasons (for my delay in writing the story):

1. blown to pieces
2. disbelief
3. dodging of pain a little larger than the Western Hemi-sphere

4. lack of documentation
5. lack of courage
6. lack of form, social or literary
7. deference to my mother's version, acceptance of the tea towels
8. fatigue from carrying the corpses
9. despair, indulgence of

The second volume of her memoirs, *The Dance*, chronicles her dancing in the arms of countless partners all over the Great Plains and the bordering deserts from Las Vegas to Phoenix to Manitou Beach, the resort straight north of Moose Jaw famous for mineral hot springs and a horse hair dance floor, the hair buried beneath the boards to buffet the leg muscles and prevent fatigue when dancing the night away, as Mom often did whenever three or four other widows would chip in for gas, and they would drive up together from Assiniboia. I easily imagine the Bern and Nona Dance Land at Manitou Beach, my parents swirling to the "Watch Your Step Polka" called out by kd lang, her song inspired by a dream about couples dancing around the school gym in Consort, Alberta, to a special melody composed to ensure they avoided the fresh cow pies and buffalo chips, shit strewn and steaming on the ground and threatening to grime Mom's dress hem, Dad's shined-up boots. As for my recommendation, the reviewer to the reader, both memoirs are more or less subsumed within the one you are already reading, my own memoir both blinded to and insightful of that world even now vanishing from the Great Plains forever.

After Mom read my poem "Work to Go with the Days of the Week," and questioned me on its contents and argument, I was stunned to realize what I might write was life threatening to her, since I was not accustomed to having much consequence for her or anyone else. She must have feared I would topple and tear apart everything she worked so hard to make and maintain, getting nine kids on their way in the world, body and soul, without much of the help a husband should offer after Dad left or was kicked out, and there were no words to bridge her version and mine, only then gestating. Startled, I dropped the pen and desisted, not wanting to lose both my parents just then. Thinking to outlive her, I retreated to my place in the pecking order of authority on What Happened that Mom asserted then and there, but I later noted the words *buffalo*, *Assiniboine*, *dispossession*, and *colonialism* had never crossed her tongue or landed on any of her pages. I continued with my own version in secret, often under cover of night. I assembled research materials, built up my archive of sources. I kept lists, drew up outlines, and even wrote drafts I then squirrelled away according to an obscurely coded filing system. I dreamed up titles, works, and songs but, rightly or wrongly, was more or less paralyzed as a writer from that moment to the day Mom died. Any composition of mine, in deviating from the perfect circle of hers, was tantamount to destroying both my own mother and her story. It would be matricide, that horror even occurring to me in another dream, what I could avoid only by full and unconditional surrender to her authorship, despite my sense that not to tell my own story was to put out my own eyes, there seeming something so slapdash and tentative about any place I might have in her story as just one of nine. I hasten to add I was the only one who received hand-embroidered tea towels, and then two more sets in the years following, one with kittens and one with sisters doing the work and marking the days, each more perfect than the last. My mother fully recovered her embroidery skills in making them, and I am convinced she wished for me to similarly succeed in life, except in writing that story or any other.

Although I kept quiet for the most part, what I experienced as her curse against my writing, never uttered in so many words, but so clearly enunciated by the gift of the tea towels, intensified my sense of agreeing to a fatal compromise against my will, and it made me flinty, the slightest friction, related or not to my suppressions and denials and withholdings, setting off sparks of anger. Eventually, that rage softened a little with distance and age, but the fact I had to maintain that distance to keep the peace further infuriated and defeated me when I so longed to dwell on the plains. I came to recognize that same flintiness in others and thought it was the mineral and chemical reactions, calcifications from so long a sacrifice, as Yeats would say, that turn the heart to stone and makes all the balanced and happy people wonder where on Earth does that anger come from, seeming out of all proportion, and maybe that anger and denial get mapped onto the cowboy and Indian story of the settlers and live on to be passed down through generations, the recollection of who and what had to be destroyed to make way for the thriving of the new arrivals, and that combined with memories of harrowing escapes from God knows where in the world, and the suffering entailed in settling the land, proving up and raising families and wanting to blurt it all out, but finding themselves tied up in the compromises, the same ones I experienced even without my mother's prohibition on my writing the story, and then to top it all off they watch their children flee to live out stories of their own making, but far away, reluctantly or not, contradicting their parents in the ways they find to survive and live out their lives, dust to dust.

The tea towels were made from recycled flour sacks Mom had saved from the hard times of the 1930s and '40s and commemorated the sacrifices of the war rationing that made every scrap and morsel precious. She probably kept them in the linen closet together with my imaginary Barbie dolls, keepsakes of those heroic times in the lives of the pioneers. Mom flintily claimed not to have gone out of her way to make me a gift. They were only the by-products of her reteaching herself embroidery, the skill and knowledge she'd lost when she was thrown from a horse named Tinker, hers or Opal Horne's, at about the age I then was, early twenties. Whatever the case, and despite the coarse fabric and homemade, higgledy-piggledy threads of her embroidery, the tea towels seemed bewitched and at the same time too good to use for some years because they came from her hands, while the weight of my unrecounted corpses, the stories that could not be told, bore down on my hands that would write or weave or sew. They burdened my breath that would speak, what Suknaski called my prairie reticence, which I overcame from time to time in fits and starts of courage and resolve to write for myself, but then dissipated and trailed off in my shameful obedience, cowardice, and fear.

Among the corpses I carried was a short poem called "Buffaloed," a grim exploration of my bafflement and confounding, "to be buffaloed" meaning to be unable to answer or proceed, as with the creature chased to the edge of the cliff or stampeded into the pound and there experiencing that instant of awareness, too late, of no where else to go. An inexcusably benign face is put on the word by the *Gage Canadian Dictionary* in the example "We were all buffaloed by the last question on the exam." More malignant were my own feelings of being buffaloed as I flailed about to find an outlet or any means to build a trestle to firmer ground. Although Dad's body was buried and his proximate grave settled with stone, the whole thing remained unsettled in its telling, all too terrible to look at directly, and the story now bearing the added weight of a mother's curse. With heaviness and regret, I set that poem aside, buffaloed and feeling dirty, soiled by all the drafts that went nowhere with their themes of nowhere to go, along with my secret documentation of events in the corral, humiliated to be allotted a story so powerful that it deshapes the whole world but that I couldn't get a grip on while dodging the blows of the living of it and resisting my own settler history that puts me here and sets me up in an intractable tale, written and unwritten. Granted, "Corral" stands on its own as a family story, however suppressed, or as the rodeo or ranching news in print or told around the campfire or by Anonymous in a church basement AA meeting.

I thought to extricate myself from the place I was in through a revision, modest or drastic, of the whole country and western story. At that time, I could not imagine who would listen to or read such a story of cowboys, Indians, with my father dead, my mother writing her own version and forbidding mine, and who else would care, in the world's deafening uproar of protest and pain, settler and Indigenous, about what could not be said? So, in the off-hours, I conjured up a list of imagined readers, a list that will grow and grow, I hope, initially arranged as a top-to-bottom ordering from most to least important. Maybe it's better contemplated on a horizontal plane, like the laid-down telephone poles around Johnny Bradley's pasture where his buffalo grazed. Only all readers are at the top of my list, there being so much work to do and ground to cover.

The readers of *Unsettled*:
- Descendants of settlers to the Americas
- Descendants of Indigenous peoples displaced by European settlement of the Americas
- All those who demand redress for Indigenous peoples cleared from the land for settlement
- All those whose loyalty is yet with the pioneer settlers over the claims of Indigenous peoples
- All those who grieve for their parents
- All those obliged to depart from the pathways taken by their parents
- All those who walk the line between laughter and tears
- Students of geometry, orthodox and absurd
- Teachers of settler and Indigenous literature, Great Plains history, cultural geography
- Film directors and cinematographers who can't take their eyes off the Great Plains
- All those with an uneasy affinity for cowboys, their boots, pearl snap-button shirts, string ties, horses, country music, western movies, and pulp fiction
- Followers of Americana roots music at Farm Aid and in the journal *No Depression*

- Readers of *Don Quixote*, *Facundo*, and other works of Spanish and Spanish American literature in any language
- The Roma, formerly called Gypsies, wherever they find themselves
- Eastern European writers seeking readers in North America
- German and British readers fascinated by the cowboy and writing that confronts colonial history
- Left-handed, pipe-smoking, guitar-swinging poets with knives in their boots and pens in their pockets
- Cowboys of Latin America: *gauchos, charros, llaneros, vaqueiros, pantaneiros, chagras, huasos*
- All those thrilled, secretly or openly, by writing that blends fact and fiction as a matter of historical necessity and because it is lifelike yet who remain concerned about the consequences for truth and consensus about what is real
- All those who imagine forms of communal land tenure beyond the tyrannical extremes of private property and centralized (state) ownership
- All those made to shut up about what they see with their own eyes
- Victims of compulsory cheerfulness no matter what
- Victims of discouraging words
- Desperados, out tending fences
- Lonesome travellers
- All those cut in half by the rural/urban divide
- All those who have never fired a gun and prefer to live in a world that does not call for it yet would never shoot themselves or anyone else over it
- All those overwhelmed by sadness at the depraved extremes of plenty and want
- All those taking cover in the library, unwilling to leave a single word unread

So many of the readers listed well know what is permissible to say and what is not, that boundary put to the test from time to time, as it was in a Regina high school not so long ago. "Got land?" said the front of a young girl's t-shirt one day. "Thank an Indian," it said across her back. The story made the national news before disappearing without a trace, and the girl was sent home to change. She was forced to apologize, and I have pondered long and hard those to whom she was to say she was sorry, the unnamed offended (who are they?), so eager to take offence and shut her up, since they seem to have a hand over my mouth too, like my mother's hand, to keep all the words from pouring out onto our t-shirts or any number of pages, words that might give shape to the choking contradictions moving up our throats to be spat out and said in whatever form or lack of it. I hail them as my readers too. We are going to have to talk to each other.

An even more insistent poem, "Circling," soon replaced "Buffaloed" when I set it aside. "Circling" took the intense focus and slow winding approach of the predator instead of the prey, a coyote stalking a buffalo calf, slowly, very gradually, nonchalantly separating it from the rest of the herd, enticing it toward the fatal moment, yet the poem never ceases to break off when I falter, not having the heart for jaws on jugular, squeals and groans, tearing of flesh, yelps, gunshot heard as though from under water, bottom of the river. The ceaseless motion and directionlessness of circling, interchanging the positions of predator and prey, occupy my mind to this day, like the circling of the wagons for protection from the danger my own presence on the Great Plains has provoked. Eventually, time loosens the tensions of grief and gives way to resignation, in my poem distorting the circle to a stretched oval that is then dispelled into faltering lines, and that poem too dwindles into faint traces of meandering ideas, dawdling stories, falling behind, as Laura Smith sings about recalling her own father in "What Goes Around"; it's all I can do to pack up and carry it all along to the next town, hands crabbed and numb from years of maintaining my grip across the miles of wandering unsettledness, clutching onto the bits of incompletion, resistance, frustration, melodrama, smears, write-overs, scratchings-out, messes, complete lack of formal integrity.

Sometime during those early years of compulsion and resistance to writing, I happened on a letter written by Leonard Cohen to a friend, dated March 1962, about a principle of composition I had not even been aware I might be searching for: "I've taken a scalpel to my novel," Cohen wrote. "I won't be able to save it, but it's the most interesting corpse I've ever seen." That was when I began to see my attempts at telling the story as indistinguishable from the corpses I carried, Johnny Bradley's and Dad's, the buffalo and the Assiniboine. A most interesting body of work I was amassing, corpses inviting their own anatomy, layer peeled from layer in the pursuit of knowledge of what is invisible while the organism is alive and kicking, corpses now rotten with my failure and resistance to putting them back together in the exact condition they were in at dissolution by whatever cause. Johnny and Dad I did not want to make whole or restore to their origins, bloodied and compromised. I wanted them altered somehow but could not see exactly how. The buffalo and the Assiniboine I did want to return to pristine original conditions by a kind of taxidermy. Neither was going to work, I knew, but I kept on trying for some time.

I tried my hand at drama, though inwardly I was appalled to think my problem and therefore the solution could be a matter of literary form, as if there were set forms that could give the story communicable shape, if only I could find them. But let's face it, I thought, the story has gotten out of hand, and too much time has slipped by. Johnny gored to death, King, the last buffalo, and then my dad shot in the head for the horror and grief of it all, and my mother prohibiting what I had timidly begun to write about it, and I experienced all that as a formal problem? Literary form seemed too paltry a thing to address the weight of history and psychology and colonialism, genocide and gender trouble, and all that tethered me to my grief. On top of that, literary form seemed to confuse orders of being and knowing that needed to be kept separate, any fool knows that, yet what I wanted reunited and reformed by writing in some as yet unimagined way, a form that could contain the weaving and unravelling of stories at the same time to include the already written country and western story and the as yet unwritten settler-Indigenous coexistence or resettlement story, a genre of some reckoning, whatever it turns out to be, both of which would have to be on the same page for historical accuracy and for positioning myself as an author with a future, even if only of my own story and its readership, if such is out there or amenable to coming into being, by a certain kind of book finding its way into so many hands. "The prudence that restrains us, normally, from venturing too far ahead in a sentence," writes Theodor Adorno in his work bearing the subtitle *Reflections from Damaged Life*, "is usually only an agent of social control and so of stupefaction." So I resolved to disrupt my silent stupefaction, to escape the unspoken social control, neo-colonial, parental, racialized, racializing, whatever it was that was jamming me up, I pulled the plug and let my lines go slack, giving free rein to my sentences as you find them here, to see where they might lead, as if letting go of the reins so my horse decides which path to take, the way Don Quixote's does, all the while appearing to respect the various restraints and prohibitions against telling the story by going my merry way in the stacks of the library, wending my way through the sentences and songs, the words and voices of others, and making a home for myself there where no one might notice.

In the opening scene of my play, which I could not keep from writing in the margins and at night in spite of all my misgivings and prohibitions, I looked into the backstory of the land the corral occupies, its original survey and mapping prior to settlement, to give events in the corral the full weight of the past, a greater anchor and claim on the attentions of my readers than mere rodeo news or the sad story of one unsettled country and western family. In the opening scene, a journalist is interviewing the scholar Dr. Irene Spry, just as I had interviewed her when freelancing as a journalist in Ottawa, and she was already elderly and, as it turned out, just a few years before she passed away of old age in 1998, grand and accomplished. Spry had been a student of Harold Innis, the historian of the fur trade and scholar of rivers, and she took on the editing of the Champlain Society–sponsored research of the Victorian Anglo-Irishman John Palliser, who, wishing to make his mark and repay the Crown for allowing him to hunt the plains buffalo to his heart's content, reported confidently to the dominion government that the triangle of territory, its base formed by the forty-ninth parallel of latitude, now the Canada-U.S. border, and its apex between Manitou Lake and the present town of Unity, just east of the Alberta-Saskatchewan border, from that point drawing a line descending southwest to the forty-ninth parallel, intersecting the U.S. border at the 114th degree of longitude, and another running southeastward to 100 degrees, or 101, just into what is now Manitoba, that triangle of territory, about 80,000 square miles, Palliser wrote, was not fit for cultivation or settlement.

Above the western and eastern angles and tip of the triangle was the fertile belt of western British North America, the whole, including the triangle, called Rupert's Land. The northern fertile belt Palliser highly recommended for settlement and agriculture. But what became known as Palliser's Triangle to the south was irredeemably arid or semi-arid, a desert wasteland that was the northernmost extension of the Great Plains of North America, the very heart of the northern continent dry and able to support only limited plant life, the short, wiry bunch grass, sagebrush, and cactus, where plagues of locusts visited regularly, and home to the enormous herds of grazing buffalo, which chewed the grasses to the very nub before moving on. Palliser found the climate severe, heat and frost, with insufficient wood or food sources to support settlers before the first crops would be ready, if any, if ever.

"A great deal of trouble, expense, and heartbreak would have been saved if the expedition's conclusions about the triangle had been taken more seriously," writes Dr. Spry, and surely it is true that all my central scenes and characters— troubled, broke, broken—dwell inside that dread triangle: Johnny Bradley's ranch at Cantuar, the Great Sand Hills, the lost Morgan homestead, now sunk into the ground, Johnny's office just off the kitchen, all are located about dead centre, with Wood Mountain, Assiniboia, and the Big Muddy badlands off to the southeast but well inside the damned geometry. Palliser's Triangle, the more I looked into it, was colonial geometry that began to bear the weight not only of its survey of the land but also of prophecy, the very presence of farmers and ranchers there a matter of chance and chicanery, historical happenstance, ultimately the outcome of bitter controversy in the 1850s, then mounting to a crisis, writes Spry, over the future of the plains west of the Great Lakes. The controversy turned on the possibility and desirability of settlement in the vast territory, until then under charter to the Hudson's Bay Company, and known only to company fur traders, mostly Métis, then called the Red River men, and the nomadic Aboriginal tribes whose hunting ground it was. The company's charter was set to expire in 1859, and the British government, distracted just then in the Crimea, and alarmed, so it said, at the prospect of incurring taxpayer expense in the development of barbarous and immeasurable districts of the continental interior of North America, realized it did not know with any certainty the location of the boundary separating its territory from that of the United States. The line presumed for the purposes of the Treaty of Versailles in 1783 had been shown to be nonsensical, physically impossible. At the leisure of the parties, a more "feasible line" was agreed to as set out in the London Convention of 1818, and only a full eight years later David Thompson was sent with the Boundary Commission to survey it. He got only as far as the Lake of the Woods at the present border between Ontario and Manitoba. So even in the 1850s the international boundary west of the last surveyed point remained a matter of guesswork. The Hudson's Bay Company had its own surveys and maps, of course, but they were jealously guarded private and proprietary intelligence, and Spry notes that the company saw no reason to incur the expense of publishing or publicizing what it knew. A cloak of mystery about its territories and borders served its interests very well. The Company considered Thompson's map, and the later Arrowsmith map of 1854, used by Palliser, to be polemical documents. There was speculation that Palliser himself might have crossed the international boundary line without knowing it while hunting buffalo in the Missouri River valley in 1848, but Spry, in her article "Did Palliser Visit Saskatchewan in 1848?" published in *Saskatchewan History* 16 (1963): 22–26 concludes that, because of the lack of a reliable survey to that date, there is no way of telling. Meanwhile, the railways were drumming up support for spending public money and creating public interest in a rail link between the as yet unconfederated Upper and Lower Canadas in the east with the settlements and ports on the West Coast. The American Corps of Topographical Engineers was busy with their own survey and would surely set the boundary where they would, and could they be trusted with the task, especially when American railway interests, at the very time, were scouring the uncharted borderlands in the Rockies for a rail route through to their own Pacific Northwest coast.

In the end, the British Colonial Office was resigned to annex the western plains, not as a positive expansion or an embrace of empire, Walt Whitman–style, but as the least undesirable alternative to absorption of its putative territory by the United States and thus my matrix, country and western, from a kind of begrudging imperial attitude of necessity and annoyance. The Palliser Expedition was reluctantly underfunded and dispatched to determine the physical features of the boundary line of the forty-ninth parallel of latitude and seek a route to the West Coast on British territory through the Rocky Mountains. Yet the ink was still drying on Palliser's report, published as government "blue books" in the early 1860s, when the campaign to discredit his findings and his person began. The railways agitated for government-sponsored agricultural settlement all through the undifferentiated west to justify the public expense of building their railways, inventing the verb *to railroad* as the exact opposite of what it was to be buffaloed. The railway men challenged the triangle theory and ensured that later surveys, including their own, conflated Palliser's distinctions between land types so the entire West was portrayed as yielding sweet water aplenty and smiling meadows all the way from the Red River to the Rockies. Palliser himself was portrayed in such a way as to shape the country and western cowboy and the imminent settlers as his opposite: he was dismissed as an opportunist, a recreational sportsman who concocted his expedition and its findings only to legitimize three buffalo-hunting seasons for himself and his aristocratic friends, from 1857 to 1859, on the public purse. Palliser was disparaged as unmanly, especially in his European attitude to horses, unable to tolerate their treatment as expendable, on numerous occasions shamelessly halting progress to allow them to rest and even going far out of the way to find adequate pastures and making elaborate guard and shelter arrangements to protect them from wolves and theft. Well known also, or at least so the word was spread, was his unforgivable lack of ruthless drive, his reluctance to carry his point no matter what, in the usual manner of heroes, and, worse, his tendency on at least two occasions to defer to local advice—that of his Indigenous guides.

That Palliser was a weak and ridiculous figure was taken for granted, however slanderously and erroneously, even by schoolgirls, for over 100 years, myself among them, taking it in with the air we breathed and the sour, malodorous water we drank in Assiniboia, as he predicted we would. For "it is incontestable," writes Dr. Spry, "that some of the land the expedition judged would be forever useless has since become some of the finest wheat land in the world." As a prophet, Palliser has indeed been proven fallible by bumper crops—in good years—and an entire period of Canadian economic development based upon the flow of grain from the western plains. Yet, Spry continues, "his warnings have had desolating justifications in periods of drought such as the Dirty Thirties and in parts of the triangle that have gone back—or been put back—to grass," not to mention those never put to seed, like the Great Sand Hills or the southwestern-most grasslands or the Big Muddy badlands, all the coordinates of the dead centre of my misfortune and being. And the success of dryland farming within the triangle has depended heavily, since the dustbowl of 1935, on sustained government assistance to develop the cultivation methods and new technologies, high-priced inputs, as we call them, such as chemicals and fertilizers needed to keep the short-grass prairie productive of grains and other food crops, the export of which could be depended on to tip the balance of trade to the benefit of the entire nation. Then, too, the insistence of the Palliser Expedition's report that there were exceptions to the conclusion of generally arid lands within the triangle is often overlooked in the general disparagement of Captain Palliser around Assiniboia. Isolated tablelands where vegetation became luxuriant were noted in limited areas deemed able to support agriculture. Surprisingly, and only after a thorough examination of the hundreds of pages of the *Palliser Papers*, I realized that neither Palliser nor his expedition ever traversed the entirety of land within the triangle; they only peeped into its southeastern corner at Roche Percée on a brief side trip from the Red River settlement on setting out in 1857, and later they intersected its western half almost to the international boundary, in the summer and fall of 1859. In one of the notable instances when Palliser accepted local advice, he did not penetrate or trace the entire triangle, largely because of its function as a buffer of territory separating and sheltering Indigenous peoples at peace or in competition with each other for buffalo and other sources of food, water, and wood. Inside the triangle itself was mostly the territory of the Plains Assiniboine, who periodically joined forces with the Qu'Appelle Cree farther north in fighting against their traditional enemy, the Blackfoot, who occupied the triangle west of the Cypress Hills in what is now southern Alberta.

In September 1857, in its first season of exploring and surveying, the Palliser Expedition made a northwesterly foray along the eastern line of the triangle to the Qu'Appelle Lakes and spent most of that year in the elbow of the South Saskatchewan River before it was dammed, just across the river, it turns out, from where Pop Morgan and my mother's McLeods would homestead, not so far from where Johnny Bradley built his corral. Palliser always took care to keep within a day's ride of the fertile belt to the north to ensure access to buffalo, water, and wood. None of the Cree or Red River guides much relished accompanying the expedition farther west or south in that first season, where they might step onto Blackfoot territory without any assurance of assistance from the Plains Assiniboine to the south, who more or less kept to themselves and would not go looking for trouble, even to support their Cree or any other allies, should they be so foolish as to get into it. The Assiniboine descended from a branch of Lakota Sioux who had broken away and moved north from the Black Hills of what became South Dakota to occupy the triangle as early as the sixteenth or seventeenth century. They dominated southern Saskatchewan, though hunting by other bands, Métis, and other fur traders was tolerated, and they often depended on the hospitality and firewood of the Cree in the Qu'Appelle Valley during the harshest winters.

When the Palliser Expedition headed south to survey the Cypress Hills and the surrounding topography of the forty-ninth parallel in its third and final season, in July 1859, only Blackfoot and their Blood allies would venture to guide the group, with some trepidation, keeping to the west of the trail followed by the surveyors. Palliser noted repeatedly in his journal how they contrived to keep a route west of the Great Sand Hills to avoid inadvertently entering Assiniboine land and provoking a defensive attack. For their part, the Assiniboine seem to have allowed the expedition to pass without incident. Palliser's instructions were to use local guides and assistants wherever possible, and to avoid hostilities of any kind, but the forts and outposts where the expedition provisioned and spent the winters, and where Palliser hired his guides, were necessarily outside the triangle, since even the Hudson's Bay Company had retreated from its sandy wastes by the 1830s, the harvest of furs not sufficient to justify the hardship or expense of palliating or fighting the Assiniboine. In choosing his guides, Palliser found himself allied now with the friends, now with the enemies, of the Assiniboine inside the triangle. Sometimes called the Stone Sioux because they cooked with hot stones, the Assiniboine were so named from what the English heard the French call them, from how the French heard the Ojibway call them Assinaan (Stone Sioux). The Ojibway, for their part, only followed the Plains Cree, who called them Assnipwan, from the words for rock or stone plus enemy, which, for the Cree, the Lakota Sioux had been when they first arrived from the south, from what is now North and South Dakota. The Assiniboine spoke a variant of the Sioux language, as did the Stoney Plains communities farther west in the foothills of the Rockies after arriving there at a later time and from a different direction.

Palliser's *Journal* assumes and even treats as self-evident the Sioux language affinity between the Stoney and Assiniboine peoples when his expedition assembled, in July 1859, at the confluence of the Red Deer and South Saskatchewan Rivers near present-day Leader, to the northwest of Cabri and Cantuar, and prepared to move south to survey the Cypress Hills and the forty-ninth parallel before heading west in its last season in search of land routes through the Rockies on British territory. First, a Métis Red River guide, Old Paul, backed out of the southern trip, saying something about a "mother-in-law," a term Palliser put in quotation marks maybe to indicate how Old Paul's excuse strained credulity. Old Paul claimed she-of-a-higher-authority was summoning him away, and to Palliser the seemingly lame excuse only betrayed Old Paul's terror at the prospect of travelling through the heart of Assiniboine country with the Blackfoot, accompanied by their Blood and Peigan allies, making the expedition possibly appear to the Assiniboine as a threatening invasion. Palliser reluctantly let Old Paul go, and he succeeded in keeping the rest of his men together thereafter only by ridicule and constant persuasion. The Blackfoot, keeping close to their portion of the triangle to the west, seemed intent on following the expedition, but at a distance, planning to ride and camp alongside the caravan as it moved south, perhaps ready for a fight if one should break out. When Palliser finally quelled a more widespread mutiny among his guides, among whom were Blackfoot, two Bloods, and a Stoney, and they got under way, his journal entries record the sustained restlessness of the men and portents of trouble to come. "A wretched soil everywhere," he wrote. "The horses miserably off for grass. In Lonesome Coulee south of Bindloss, a cart breaks down when a wheel sinks to its axle in the sand. We are now halted on a salt lake," Palliser lamented, "the only water we could find and are forced to drink after straining it through silk handkerchiefs." At the time of this journal entry, the expedition would have been about fifty miles west of Johnny Bradley's ranch. "We have had a severe spell with the carts in the sand-hills," Palliser wrote. "The travelling very severe for the horses. Soil worthless. Found a human skull on the plain. Where we camped, we killed several rattle-snakes."

As early as July 24, the Blood guide Amoxapeta and the Blackfoot Petope (Perched Eagle) began to talk of turning back for fear of inadvertently engaging the Assiniboine. Then Amoxapeta's wife, travelling with them, gave birth, and the couple argued. Amoxapeta wanted to turn back, but she insisted on staying close to Palliser's Dr. Hector, a medical doctor whose fame, Palliser records elsewhere, was a wonder and a byword among many a teepee that never saw the man, largely because of medical treatments administered when he came across anyone suffering illness or injury. "In the afternoon, a Blackfoot chief invites us to a feast," wrote Palliser, "and gives me advice not to go further into the country, for . . . we should certainly get into trouble; that only two white men had ever crossed the country between the Cypress Mountains and the forks of the Red Deer and Bow Rivers to the west in Blackfoot territory." The chief gave such an account of the Assiniboine, surely to be met with in the Cypress Hills or on the way there, that Palliser's men were much frightened and "went pale at his words." Undeterred by local advice in this instance, Palliser was again warned two days later, on July 26, when the Indians, as he wrote, "tried to persuade us to stop, assuring us that we could not possibly reach water before nightfall; nevertheless, we pushed on; they will now hardly travel further to the southward in this longitude, on account of the Assiniboines."

"We made a very long spell, and found middling water, although it was a little brackish. A young Indian and his wife rode up. They had been out two or three days on an unsuccessful hunt, and when they came on our track, followed us, arriving very late and half-starved." The next day, within sight of the Cypress Hills looming up out of the flat prairie, Palliser found the men most unwilling to approach any nearer. "Our latitude was now 49° 44′ and I see that we have imperceptibly been led several miles off our course by Felix, who goes in front of the carts and out of fear of the Assiniboines keeps too much to the westward." Correcting their course, Palliser later that day confirmed "the Cypress Hills indeed form a great contrast to the level country through which we have been travelling, a perfect oasis of wood and cool shade in the prairie desert. Still the guides are agitated and troubled, and Felix finally told me they were planning to murder the Stoney.

"Poor Nimrod seemed fully aware of their intentions even before we warned him," wrote the captain, "and was very much alarmed. We are all now armed, on the plea of guarding the horses; the Indians are also armed and one is now cocking and uncocking one of our rifles. I desired Daniel, in the tent along with the Stoney, to tell him quietly in Cree not to run, that we would protect him, and shoot the first man dead who pointed a gun at the tent. All the horses were saddled and fastened close at hand, which also signaled mischief. Then, at a little later than midnight, all rose, who had been wanting to do away with Nimrod, and with one accord jumped on their horses and galloped off."

"I may as well mention," Palliser wrote when the southward expedition set out from Edmonton as early as May that year, "that I strongly objected to this man being brought along with us, anticipating difficulties with the Peigan and Blood Indians as we advanced; but my poor friend Capt. Brisco was so impressed with Nimrod's great powers in hunting, and so anxious to obtain his assistance, that he requested me so strongly to allow him to come along with him, that I reluctantly consented." Brisco was Palliser's friend, late of the 11th Hussars, whose regiment, if not Brisco himself, rode in the Charge of the Light Brigade, even, according to Palliser in a letter to another friend in Toronto on March 21, 1858, distinguishing himself in the Balaclava charge, though Dr. Spry has been unable to verify this claim from the official war records. When the scientist Blakiston left the expedition the previous year, Palliser invited Brisco to join the southward penetration of the triangle along the border of Blackfoot and Assiniboine territory, probably the instance that attracted criticism of the expedition as a publicly funded cover for aristocrats to hunt buffalo.

Although Brisco was in the country with Palliser for the sole purpose of hunting buffalo, the expedition journal entries of Dr. Hector offer the most arresting accounts of buffalo hunting and what might be the Aboriginal form of the rodeo on the northern plains. The word translated as *pound*, from whatever language, likely Plains Cree, is the most nearly associated with what we know as the rodeo that I have come across. A pound or enclosure for entrapping animals is really the Indigenous counterpart to the corral and refers not just to the *round-up*, the English meaning of the Spanish word *rodeo*. When I look up the terms "buffalo pound" and "buffalo jump" in a Cree dictionary, I get *nâcipahâw*, as it transliterates into the modified Roman alphabet, and the sample sentence in which it might appear is given as "S/he rounds up the buffalo to lead to a pound, buffalo jump or enclosure." So the Cree word for *pound* seems to include both the *round-up* of the Spanish *rodeo* and the English *enclosure*, *pen*, or *corral* into which the buffalo are herded, which involves a stampede. The stampede of the buffalo into the pound, the practice of the Indigenous nomadic buffalo hunters described by Hector, could be why the rodeo is more likely to be called a *stampede* north of the forty-ninth parallel, whereas to the south the Spanish *rodeo* prevails, which vocabulary choices, as Wallace Stegner eccentrically noted, marked what he takes to be the sole substantive difference between Canada and the United States: they say *rodeo*, we say *stampede*. Stegner does not explore the significance of that distinction, though I notice from reading Hector's account how the word *stampede* takes the ground-level perspective of the animals and unmounted Indigenous hunters, whereas the word *rodeo*, the round-up, assumes the raised perspective and overview of the mounted rider.

"On the morning of December 26, 1857," Dr. Hector wrote,

> we were off by 4:30 a.m., and had gone a considerable distance, when we saw fresh traces of Indians, and soon heard the bawling and screaming of an immense camp, all in a high state of excitement. Diverging from our path to pay them a visit, we found that they had succeeded in driving a large band of buffalo into their "pound" during the night and were now engaged in slaughtering them. The scene was more repulsive than pleasant or exciting. The pound is a circular strong fencing, about

50 yards in diameter, made of stakes with boughs interlaced, and into this place were crammed more than 100 buffalos, bulls, cows, and calves. A great number were already killed, and the live ones were tumbling about furiously over the dead bodies of their companions, and I hardly think the space would have held them all alive without some being on top of the others, and, in addition, the bottom of the pound was strewn with fragments of carcases left from former slaughters in the same place. It was on a slope, and the upper part of the fencing was increased in height by skins stretched out on poles, for the purpose of frightening the buffalo from jumping out. This is not needed at the lower part of the enclosure, as the animals always endeavour to jump up-hill.

I thought of Johnny Bradley's pasture fenced only with horizontally laid-out telephone poles, or so Johnny claimed, in earnest or in jest, and I realized he might have had his own sources of the Indigenous knowledge that buffalo jump highest not from a flat surface but when running uphill.

"The entrance to the enclosure," continued Dr. Hector,

is by an inclined plane made of rough logs leading to a gap through which the buffalo have suddenly to jump about six feet into the ring, from which there is no return. To this entrance converge lines of little heaps of buffalo dung or brush from several miles into the prairies surrounding the clump of wood in which the pound is concealed. These lines serve to lead the buffalo in the required direction when they have been driven into the neighborhood. When first captured and driven into the pound, which difficult matter is effected by stratagem, the buffalo run round and round violently, and the Indians affirm always with the sun. Crouched on the fencing were the Indians, even mere boys and young girls, all busy plying bows and arrows, guns and spears, and even knives, to compass the destruction of the buffalo. After firing their arrows they generally succeeded in extracting them again by a noose on the end of a pole, and some had even the pluck to jump into the arena and pull them out with their hands; but if an old bull happened to observe them they had to be very active in getting out again. The scene was a busy but a bloody one and has to be carried on until every animal is killed to enable them to get the meat. I helped, by trying the penetrating power of rifle balls on the shaggy skulls of the animals, with invariable success; and it is the least cruel way of killing them, as they drop at once.

The doctor continued,

There are many superstitions connected with the whole business, and the Indians always consider their success in procuring buffalo in this manner to depend on the pleasure of the Manitoe, to whom they always make offerings, which they place under the entrance to the pound, where I saw a collection of Indian valuables, among which were bridles, powder horns, tobacco, beads, and the like. . . . In the centre of the pound, also, there is a tall pole on which they hang offerings. To which piece of idolatry I was in a manner accessory by giving them my pocket handkerchief to convert into a flag.

Despite his disparagement, quite uncalled for, of the Indigenous solemnities of the hunt, Dr. Hector here gives what may be the first recorded account in English of a rodeo or stampede in Rupert's Land, though it was an earlier impromptu bucking bronco event that impressed his name or rather his horse most permanently on the country and western landscape. The following August a party led by Nimrod, then serving as Hector's guide, left Rocky Mountain House and rode up into the mountains to about fifty-two degrees latitude in search of a land route through to the coast. At a sharp V-turn in the river, "just above the angle there is a fall about 40 feet in height," since named Wapta Falls. Hector writes how

> one of our pack horses, to escape [a] fallen timber, plunged into the stream, luckily where it formed an eddy, but the banks were so steep that we had great difficulty in getting him out. In attempting to re-catch my own horse, which had strayed off while we were engaged with the one in the water, he kicked me in the chest, but I had luckily got close to him before he struck out, so that I did not get the full force of the blow. However, it knocked me down and rendered me senseless for some time.

In another account of the same incident, published in his book *Buffalo Days and Nights*, the half-Danish, half-Cree guide Peter Erasmus records that the doctor lay unconscious for two hours and was watched anxiously, and the men had already sorrowfully begun to bury him when they noticed he had regained consciousness. Still unable to speak, Hector managed to wink, as I imagine my dad winked, catching the eye of his mourners and so saving himself in the nick of time from untimely interment. The Kicking Horse Pass through the Rockies, just west of Lake Louise, still bears that name commemorating Hector's carnival resurrection from the very kick, the very horse, the very pass through the mountains later taken by the Canadian Pacific Railway.

After the hour or more delay spent watching the stampede and hoisting his flag at the buffalo pound, Dr. Hector and his men continued on, soon coming to a large plain bounded by high hills on each side. "The plain . . . looked as level as a bowling green, being about 10 miles across, and is evidently the bottom of a drained lake," he wrote. "The whole of the extensive flat was covered with immense herds of buffalo, and as the afternoon was bright and fine, with just enough frost to keep the snow crisp, the scene was very enlivening, reminding one of a huge cattle fair at home," calculating later that the "first cost of the buffalo as a source of food, when killed in the plain, is merely nominal." But even then it was apparent the buffalo could not support a population much larger than the existing Aboriginal bands, there being about 150 additional souls then subsisting at Fort Edmonton, only 50 of whom worked for the Hudson's Bay Company. "These are all fed on buffalo meat," Hector wrote,

> and if there happens to be a good crop they get a certain small allowance of potatoes. The consumption of meat is enormous, amounting to two buffalos a day on average. It is no easy matter to supply this demand, especially of late years, and the loss of horses from dragging the meat during the severities of the winter, and the number of men employed for just this purpose, alone renders it a very expensive mode of feeding the establishment.

There was also the danger to the men, Hector having treated, just a month earlier, a man brought in from the buffalo hunt and dangerously injured when he was thrown from his horse and then charged by an old bull. The man had a burst blood vessel, one or more, and his chest was injured severely, though the doctor does not provide further medical details or a prognosis following that stampede.

Dr. Hector witnessed and treated numerous illnesses and injuries, "even from the bites of rabid wolves to be met with typically in the spring, when the grey wolves go mad and do not hesitate to attack any one they meet with. Hydrophobia results from their bite, and the Indians are very drunk today," he blurts out disjointedly, such outbursts appearing frequently throughout his entries on the deleterious effects of trading alcohol for furs and meat, and creating disastrous addiction and malnutrition widespread even by that time, not only among Aboriginals but also among lonely non-Indigenous men seeking or escaping their fortunes there. On November 21, 1857, after a hiatus of some several days from writing in his journal, Hector wrote that he was detained in the fort, "busy with maps, reports, &c., so that many days afford no remarks worth recording. The hunters returned to-day from the plains, and the fort is the scene of riot and drinking again." On returning to the fort at Rocky Mountain House some months later, Hector found

> a group of Blackfoot also just arrived to trade, so that the Company's people were now much relieved, as they were almost out of provisions. As the buffalo were far out in the plains, owing to the open winter, the Indians were themselves badly off for provisions. In coming to the fort they had nearly consumed their store, owing to the length of the journey. The desire for rum, however, soon induced them to part with some of their scanty supply, and now the environs of the fort presented a dreadful scene of riot and disorder. Even diluted to the extent of 11 of water to 1 of spirit, yet the trade in liquor is always one of great trouble and even danger to the Company's servants, never mind that they instigate the trouble by depending on liquor to lure the Indians into supplying their food.

Later that winter back in Edmonton, Hector wrote about a Norwegian trader who died in a fit of drunkenness at Christmas time, there being nothing the doctor could do for him.

On the branch expedition south into the Palliser Triangle, the threats to poor Nimrod, the same Nimrod who accompanied Dr. Hector to the Kicking Horse Pass, threats one after another were foiled until they made camp within the Cypress Hills, after all Blackfoot and Blood, to a person, had fled back north or west. Neither the *Journal* nor Palliser's *Report* ever fully explains the reasons for the plot to kill Nimrod, it seeming self-evident to the writer, so the reader can only surmise it was because of Nimrod's Stoney language, a dialect of Sioux, and the presumption of his likely collusion through that language with the Assiniboine no doubt lurking watchfully at the boundary of their territory as the expedition moved south. Nimrod must have been suspected of secretly signalling his kinsmen, and together perhaps plotting an ambush, so the Blackfoot aimed to prevent it by doing away with Nimrod first, which probably would have had the effect of setting off the armed conflict Palliser feared and wanted to prevent. But just as this sequence of terror and portents, so closely recorded by Palliser, is never fully explained, and comes to naught, neither is the fantastic name of Nimrod for a Stoney Indian who, as I recall from my reading through all *The Palliser Papers* until quite bleary-eyed, into the sleepless buffalo nights, was recruited by Hector at Rocky Mountain House the previous season for this southward penetration of the triangle. Nimrod's Stoney name Hector could not pronounce, but he heard it translated into English as "One with a Thumb Like a Blunt Arrow," in reference, perhaps, to his famed prowess as a hunter, having killed fifty-seven moose in the season when he and Hector first crossed paths in the foothills. In renaming him Nimrod, Hector saddled the Stoney guide with his own classical education from the University of Edinburgh and his schooling in the Christian Bible, in which Nimrod is introduced in the Book of Genesis and again in Chronicles as a renowned hunter and in connection with the Tower of Babel. Nimrod the son of Cush, Cush the son of Ham, Ham the son of Noah, he is a mighty hunter before the Lord and the beginning of his kingdom included Babel, where the whole Earth had one language and the same words. And as Nimrod and his people migrated from the east, they came upon a plain, and they said to one another, "Come, let us make bricks, and burn them thoroughly." And they had brick for stone, and bitumen for mortar, as Hector also noted at the site of La Butte Noire, the absurd rising up out of the plains to the east of Fort Edmonton, and named, I suspect, by a punning French-speaking voyageur, when inside the hill was found a round hole, from which oozed a black unctuous mud that would be treasure for the yet unimagined time to come, the dinosaurs' time bomb gushing from a gaping depression so deep that none had been able to fathom it, even with the longest pole that could be found.

"Come, let us build ourselves a city," said Nimrod to the people of his kingdom, "and a tower with its top in the heavens, and let us make a name for ourselves." Nimrod so ordered and oversaw the folly of the construction of the tower and is even portrayed inspecting the stone masons at work in the famous fifteenth-century painting of the biblical scene by Pieter Bruegel. And the Lord saw that this was "only the beginning of what they will do; nothing that they propose to do will now be impossible for them. Come, let us go down and confuse their language there," that story justifying the imprisoning in English of the pious and sober Scot, Dr. Hector, who struggled even with French, though he studiously collected and published vocabularies of four Native languages, while the Stoney with a Thumb Like a Blunt Arrow, from beyond and before God's deliberate linguistic confusion, spoke all the languages that made up the Babel of the northwest: his own Stoney dialect of Sioux, plus Assiniboine, Cree, Blackfoot, Blood, English, French, and these only at the least. His ability to speak to all and to understand the words of others made

him valuable but, at the same time, put him and the Palliser
Expedition in danger, according to Palliser's account, marking
but at the same time blurring the line between enemies and
friends, between the prairie desert and the mountains, on the
single foray bisecting the triangle from north to south, bearing
the name of Nimrod, and partaking of the very attributes of his
fabled namesake, the command of multiple languages, association with stones, the Stone Sioux, famed for hunting prowess,
and surviving, as the name of Nimrod has, to make the return
trip from the underworld, as did Hector in the Kicking Horse
Pass, on safely reaching and peaceably retreating from the rising fertility of the Cypress Hills, borderland between ancient
foes, deep inside the triangle, at once hallowed and accursed.

Almost as shadowy a member of the expedition as the
Stoney Plains man bearing the name of Nimrod was young
John Sullivan, about twenty-five years of age and actually
described by Dr. Spry as "a shadowy figure." She did manage
to find evidence—one scarcely imagines at what cost in time
and labour searching the brittle pages of registers in sailors'
reading rooms, ships' logs, and records kept in far-flung libraries—that Sullivan had some training in astronomy and had
worked as a sailor, serving on the HMS *Cyclops* as a caulker's
mate, and having just resigned for unknown reasons from a
position as acting assistant master in the nautical school of the
Royal Hospital at Greenwich, where he himself was educated,
when recommended to Palliser for the position of draughts-
man and assistant surveyor. Sullivan turned out to be very
good at mathematics, and was conversant in French, making
him the natural ally of Eugene Bourgeau, the Palliser Expedition's botanical collector, a son of the Alps, and, as Spry found,
named Prince of Collectors, with seven years of collecting
in Spain for the British Museum under his belt, and who, no
matter how harsh the conditions on the expedition, reportedly preserved and catalogued each growing plant as a matter
of supreme importance to the overall design of nature, many

specimens bearing his name and still to be seen at the Royal Botanical Gardens at Kew.

Facility with languages made Sullivan fast friends with Bourgeau, who spoke no English, but made him the natural enemy of Lieutenant Thomas Blakiston, late of the Royal Artillery, described as a branch of the British Army and considered a sort of penal corps in the eyes of the authorities, young men joining only after failing to get into the Royal Engineers. On account of his keen interest in ornithology, Blakiston had been trying to attach himself to a scientific expedition imminently departing for Chile and the Southern Cone when he joined the Palliser Expedition instead as a second-best option, fleeing what, if anything, the sources do not say. He was put in charge of the magnetic instruments and various other tools of measurement, and who knows but perhaps it was the jolting travel on horseback and cart and canoe over the rough country upsetting his chronometers, by which longitude and latitude were measured, that was responsible for the many small but not insignificant inaccuracies in the logs about the expedition's precise locations, which made him so cross at Sullivan, the poor sailor his scapegoat for most of the two seasons they were forced to work together. Blakiston depended on Sullivan to take regular shifts in the hourly astronomical and meteorological measurements, after two years of which Blakiston abruptly left, on October 12, 1858, as did Bourgeau, neither man making the trip south into the western part of the Palliser Triangle. Sullivan somehow early on had become Blakiston's *bête noire*, the representative of what Blakiston apparently thought the idiocy of the expedition, though the calumny that peppers his personal correspondence contradicts his formal reports sent to the government included by Dr. Spry among *The Palliser Papers*, as they were included in the published blue books. Spry does not discount Dr. Hector's belief that Blakiston was a spy set in their midst by the government, since the criticisms found in his personal correspondence were quoted on at least one damning occasion in the *Hansard* record of the

British Parliament of July 29, 1859. Blakiston called Sullivan a good-for-nothing fellow, careless in carrying out scientific tasks assigned to him, and when Sullivan left Fort Carlton, near present-day Prince Albert, for Jackfish Lake in February 1857 because of low food provisions in the fort, Blakiston called him a deserter, whose absence he was nevertheless glad of for the sake of the observations, and he wrote to his friends abroad that the only rational conversation he could have in the camps was with the Black cook, Dan Williams, listed by Palliser as an American, perhaps an escaped slave, whose evaluation of Blakiston's rationality or capacity for friendship I find nowhere recorded.

"It is not uncommon," writes Dr. Spry, "for men isolated in remote places to develop bitter animosities. Blakiston and Sullivan, with their contrasting personalities, were almost bound to clash when thrown together for week after monotonous week, tied by exacting work, with fifty-nine minutes for gloomy reverie between each hourly crisis of observation, and living under difficult conditions." Sullivan was ill once for eleven days, during which time the restless Blakiston's boredom was exacerbated by the news that his regiment had gone off to serve in the Indian Mutiny. "Only his sense of scientific duty kept Blakiston from rushing off to join them," says Spry. Tension was accentuated by an acute and increasing shortage of food. Thus, Spry mitigates time and again, as she reports, Sullivan's hapless eagerness to be of general use, the sweetness of Bourgeau, also a superb cook, returning always to reflect on Blakiston's uneasy temper, his moodiness, and his tendency to severely criticize anyone absent and to undermine the expedition at every opportunity. Spry thought Blakiston an insufferable purist, impatient and harshly judgmental, writing how even when honoured by the scientific community in the naming of a newly discovered beetle, the Beetle Blakistoni, actually *Carabus Blakistonii*, he ungraciously discounted the acknowledgement, writing that "putting men's names on the specimens of creatures is great nonsense; it would be far better to name a species from some particular feature of it." Despite his status as a well-respected ornithologist who had published on the birds of Nova Scotia in journals such as *Ibis* and the Smithsonian's *Report*, written a book on his travels in China, *Five Months on the Yang-Tsze* (London: John Murray, 1862), and later known as a leading authority on the birds of Japan, Spry takes the trouble to present evidence of Blakiston's mercurial temper and even his capacity for homicidal rage in an episode later in his career. In 1873, she records, in a footnote both pertinent and gratuitous to the historical import of the Palliser Expedition, while a merchant in Hakodate, Blakiston admitted a charge of battery and assault when he beat two local men who, he believed, had been stealing his property. One, confined by Blakiston in a wooden "godown," hanged himself. The other landed in hospital. Several European witnesses considered the actions justified since Blakiston could get no redress for the loss of his property from the Japanese authorities, which I think is a rich accusation coming from colonial experts and adventurers busy grabbing or having their way with other people's property all over the place. Blakiston's word was accepted as mitigation of the offences of assault and even murder, so a manslaughter charge was quashed, and Blakiston was fined a mere $500.

For the partial traverse of the westernmost third of the Palliser Triangle, all the way to the Cypress Hills in the third season, with Blakiston long gone to join his regiment and Bourgeau by then off collecting in the Caucasus, Sullivan was entrusted to survey the area south of the Cypress Hills, travelling south to the Milk River, which Palliser's map shows he reached but was just shy of the forty-ninth parallel. His failure to reach the boundary and to file a report on his survey of that parallel of latitude, the ostensible purpose of the whole enterprise in that third and final season, is noted by both Palliser and Dr. Spry but not explained or in any way compensated for that I could find. This gap in the record notwithstanding, the spectacle that unfolds before the mind's eye from Spry's diligent and extensive research in *The Palliser Papers* is of an increasingly strained and hungry, raggedy, scared, and bickering band of land surveyors employed by a distracted authority, along with their variously frightened and disgruntled assistants, the whole led by the potentially duplicitous or hapless or conniving Indigenous guides, also hungry and afraid, with interests and names and trajectories of their own, in the very midst of the Buffalo Wars that would rage for twenty years. In no way does the Palliser Expedition present what the novelist Joseph Conrad called "Geography Militant," the colonial enterprise combining science with conquest, in his article published in *National Geographic* 45 in 1924, but more what we should call the "Geometry Absurd" of the Palliser Triangle, especially its correspondence, in its characters as in its essence, with Franz Kafka's story in *The Castle*, which Kafka was writing in the early 1920s in Prague between bouts of laughter and discharges of consumptive blood. His fabled land surveyor, K., suffers the quarrels and antics of his clownish assistants, and finds the townspeople no less than the authorities of the local castle evasive and unresponsive to his claim of being a land surveyor, alternately revealing the clash of interests for and against redrawing the lines that demarcate boundaries between what is yours and what is mine, those lines ultimately excluding the land surveyor himself as he descends, peg by peg, to lower and lower stations in life, until by the end of the story, from a professional and educated man with court-appointed assistants, K. is reduced to taking orders from the chambermaids, and hoping for a bit of space on the floor to sleep between their beds, if Pepi will have him. Such is the thanks he gets for presuming to be qualified to redraw the lines defining properties and assuming the identity of a land surveyor, for only the supremely ridiculous Count West-West of the castle has the authority to determine his subjects' identities, and, likewise, it transpires, by implication, that the count's authority exists only to the extent that his subjects believe it does.

Had Kafka any command of English, which I do not believe he did, I easily imagine him rummaging through old English blue books of an afternoon, documents perhaps left in a cupboard by a departed diplomat or languishing on a shelf in the converted offices of the insurance company in Prague, where he might flip through them idly while awaiting adjudication of a claim. How amusing he would find it, and how we might laugh darkly together at Palliser's troupe, which Kafka would easily recognize, characters such as Nimrod resembling his hero, K., both with targets on their backs, and everyone else quarrelling and on edge for fear of their lives, hunger gnawing their insides as they traverse the arid triangle that would soon be argued and scorned out of existence, so that my ancestors, wombs within wombs, would soon arrive at their promised land none the wiser, the diminished buffalo herds nowhere visible on any horizon, stealthy Assiniboine hunters tracking the processions of men and instruments in the dark, and the captain preoccupied, while he rides, with the unresponsiveness of the Colonial Office about the permissions and funds needed for the trip back to England, which he hoped would be, and did in the end turn out to be, by Pacific and then West Indies steamer, passing through the hemisphere by the shortest portage over the isthmus at Panama.

In the opening scene of my play about the Palliser Triangle, with the juvenile and now-embarrassingly hyperbolic title "The Never-Ending Death of Burn Maxwell," which then changed to "Triangle of Death," both discarded along with the play itself in my belated disgust with their melodrama and inaccuracy, a journalist is interviewing Dr. Irene Spry about the Palliser Expedition, and she talks about how, in all his journals and reports, it transpires that Palliser never fully explored the territory encompassed by his triangle. His fear of entering that territory seemed well justified by his practical assessment of the chances of survival without sure sources of water or wood, and given the hostilities in the competition for buffalo, but maybe if he had been able to complete a more detailed survey it might not have been so easy for the railways to pro-pagandize it out of mind, and the settlers would have known to avoid places like Cabri or Cantuar on the edge of the Great Sand Hills, the bloodied, doomed centre of the universe, and wrecked prospects of its settlement by my forebears. The eco-logical delicacy of the Palliser Triangle did impress the author-ities enough that the areas closest to the fertile belt, between and above the branches of the Saskatchewan River, north and south, were settled first, though my grandparents from the Scottish Highlands via Prince Edward Island and Mich-igan, and the others directly from the coal mines of Wales, received their grants of land south of the river at Cabri, the town named by the French word for the antelope that range there to this day, though the French-speaking peoples who left that perspective and word on the ground are long gone, fled, Englished, or died out, from west of the elbow of the South Saskatchewan River. By 1912, both sets of settler grandparents were married and had begun their begetting of large families to help with the work of settlement and proving up that trans-formed the communal lands of the Assiniboine into their own private property. By the time the southern Slavs arrived in the prairie west, among them Suknaski's parents, only the most arid and marginal lands around Killdeer and Wood Mountain and on over to Climax and Eastend and beyond were left, and much of that was designated as rangeland, unfit for the plow, and already leased, some of it for ninety-nine years or more, to a previous generation of ranchers.

Meanwhile, in my drama, in which the interview about Palliser's avoidance of his own triangle is taking place, amid microphones and patch cords, tables and chairs, it is made visually apparent that yet another drought is burning up the southern grasslands. The dunes of the Great Sand Hills are advancing perceptibly southeastward at the rate of a few inches per year, lightning speed in geological time. Long, slow pan shots of the grasslands are projected onto the back wall of the stage, and maybe the interview breaks for the grim drought and global warming news broadcasts on a TV monitor upstage right.

Sundays we spent at the Sceptre Sand Hills, there being a road through the town of Sceptre into the northern range of the dunes. Dad took us there to roll down the soft slopes and bury ourselves to our chins in the fine white sand, so fine we could see the tracks of the tiniest bugs crawling about, though the bugs themselves were too small to see. We squealed and lolled away the scorched summer afternoons. How many arrowheads did my brothers find, gathered up by the jarfuls, and they traded them like marbles at school, making toys of the weapons of hunting and war of vanished peoples whose presence and fate were eerily felt all the same in the sublime silence that always reasserted itself, dry unsettling winds dispersing any yells that didn't fall dead into the folds and banks of sand. The Great Sand Hills were haunted in the same way that, driving to picnics down around Wood Mountain, the sudden steep hills that made the roads swerve and threw us around the back seat, tumbling over each other and making us laugh from the butterflies in our stomachs, were explained as burial mounds for the heaping piles of dead Assiniboine, even kids just like us we imagined, when their numbers crashed from more than 10,000 in the eighteenth century to 2,600 by 1810, by legend because of smallpox lurking in the blankets traded for furs. Old Trottier wore a blanket draped over his shoulders against the cold of early morning, his rifle cradled in his arms, and he was tall in the saddle, facing west, both harmless and menacing, the reins of his horse fallen slack, and all was still. My mother told and retold the story told by her father, my grandpa, of Old Trottier's silent visitation from sun-up to sundown at the road-building site west of Swift Current during the 1930s, the road that is now Trans-Canada Highway 1, the southern boundary of the Great Sand Hills. That east-west road my grandpa built intersects the north-south trail taken by Palliser's troupe with Felix leading the way and the Stoney, the Man with a Thumb Like a Blunt Arrow, and Dr. Hector and the others straggling down to the Cypress Hills seventy years before the road was built in fear or under the protection of the Assiniboine, even now, or still, missing from the scene.

Old Trottier would have been the grandfather or great-uncle of Brian, the NHL hockey player from Val Marie, deep inside the triangle, and we all knew they were Métis or Stone Sioux. Old Trottier might have known Sitting Bull, it was said, since he would have been a kid in the 1870s. Grandpa, fore-man of the construction crew, told Mom, and she told us, over and over, how Old Trottier arrived at the road-building site each morning and watched from a distance, never crossing an invisible line. The significance of his visitation was never stated, or known, Grandpa and Mom only remarking repeat-edly that it happened, and Grandpa especially seeming to assume Old Trottier stood in admiring awe, as Grandpa was, of the skill and labour and technology involved in making the road, whereas Mom was discomfited by the story. I could see she knew it wasn't right and was agitated and unsettled, as if she recognized Old Trottier was pointedly bearing witness to an ongoing atrocity, our presence crowding out the peo-ple already there, never mind the tearing up of the land and building of a road to bring in more and more, and Mom's torn loyalties, and Old Trottier's vigil was a silent reproach for the loss of territory and displacement of the Assiniboine and the Métis, whose disappearance made the road possible and nec-essary, if it was.

Interspersed with the interview with Dr. Spry in my play, an exchange that would be dramatically riveting, the audience on the edges of their seats despite my script being heavy with geological facts and historical research, among all that there would be periodic glimpses of the actor playing my dad. He would be slouched at Johnny's desk in his dark green khaki work clothes with a revolver cocked. When I wrote that play, I didn't know it was a rifle he used. In the lulls of the inter-view, back and forth, specially calibrated to build toward the impending catastrophe, Dad's profile, set off centre stage, comes into and out of view by lighting effects. Dad raises the gun, pointing it straight at himself, his finger on the trigger, and then the tableau freezes, the audience holding its breath, until, at a murmur, the gun quivering, he slowly lowers hand and gun, resolve wavers, the light dims, and life reasserts its dominion as the interview, closer to centre stage, brightens and resumes.

The drama never went beyond that point. I always hit a blank. The problem was maybe the predictability of the interview's revelations about Palliser's triangle, Dr. Spry's account of his warning against settlement and the gunshot coming together at the end, the trigger pulled, there is no other end, and the theatre would go dark in the apocalypse beyond time and space, heightening the uncanny accuracy of Palliser's judgment about the non-viability of farming within the triangle, the Morgan farm in particular, which, however, my dad did not lose to drought or dust storms or soil salination or bankruptcy, though there might have been, as on any prairie farm, the haunted thought that always has to be pushed back and suppressed of the ghosts of the Assiniboine, come to reclaim the land and wreak vengeance, maybe playing a role in the fascination of the buffalo bull King, then Johnny, then Dad, and, really, no leg to stand on for resisting the retributions of fate. But that was all in the wind, while in the everyday world of Cabri, Assiniboia, Main Street, and the banks, Dad only had no access to credit for expanding beyond the home quarter, fully paid for by the mid-1950s. The dramatic logic of my tragic drama falters without recourse to haunting by a supernatural agency, and the Assiniboine are reduced to malignant yet righteous ghosts, a metaphysical absurdity that fails to do justice for them or my dad, or in any other way compensate the audience for the bureaucratic lumber and dramatic turgidity of my script, however well intentioned and passionately felt. Neither Dad's giving up the farm nor his death can be linked to Palliser's prediction about the non-viability of farming in the triangle in any direct way; Dad and Palliser, the surveying expedition, brought together not by cause and effect but by the lack of it and by something else I was trying to figure out. Johnny's last ride on the horns of an angry bull, the last bull fight, what might be considered his and my dad's reparations for the extinction of the buffalo, made with their lives, their own extinctions, the territory where the events took place at the centre of the Palliser Triangle, superimposition of one over the other, joins them in space, where they are not portents or consequences, one of the other, maybe, but events merely, yet consequentially, coinciding right at the place where my compulsion to tell the story meets my resistance to saving Johnny and Dad through reconstitution of that cowboy-settler world to make them whole again because that can only be done at the expense of the Assiniboine and the buffalo and the land itself and so many stories yet to be unearthed and unspun and unravelled all across the Great Plains.

Not only that but also the story could only begin, as it does, too late, after the horns have already pierced flesh and shots fired. I never got beyond a page and a half of "The Never-Ending Death," and another reason for my inability to compose a tragedy might be that a suicide can never be represented in itself but only as the symptom or sign of something else, failure in life and its imputed cause, always a story that has to be made up, in this case conjoined biological and ecological suicide caused by industrial-scale drinking and farming on land, the possession of which depended on the railroading of Palliser's report, wiping out of the buffalo and the Assiniboine and whoever preceded them, the makers of the arrowheads, displacements back through time, and all depriving the actual suicide of any significance of its own, what I was reaching for, however misguidedly, since there is no such cut-off of implications in truth, only in fiction. What could my play promise but a parable of revenge of the land, and in the end my story, my dad's, Johnny Bradley's, would forgo any claim to resolution, instead dwelling in the profound unsettlings of lives and land and land titles, for which there is no remedy in this late aftermath, except for turning the page on the country and western story and confronting, full on, the blank page of a shared future, if any, if ever.

What is true about the Palliser Triangle, whatever else it means, is that it fixes in place and on maps all my anchoring absences—Johnny; his buffalo, King; the Assiniboine; my dad—the points of grief that loom large, a little larger than the Western Hemisphere itself, that persist in the ongoing deshaping, geometric absurdity that binds us to that ground, country and western, and whatever will dislodge it. The Palliser Triangle with Bradley's corral at its centre corresponds with the symbol of the trinity enclosing the all-seeing eye engraved by the German shoemaker Jacob Böhme when he was visited by a vision 300 years earlier, in 1612, what he could not avert his eyes from and quickly transcribed in a work that borrows from alchemy to express the secrets of God as they unfold, the trinity he finds everywhere in nature, described in the work he called *Aurora, oder die Morgenröte im Aufgang*. The *Aurora* study, like mine, was a story no one—not his family, the townspeople, the powers that be—wanted to hear or read and was swiftly denounced by the local pastor as heretical in the still controversial conditions of the Reformation and threatened to attract the attention of the Inquisition. The book was seized by the town council, which ordered Böhme to refrain from such writings. Loyal to, and at the same time perhaps wracked, even to the point of recklessness, by his vision, he continued to explore what he saw, but in secret, publishing further mystical works in Amsterdam, which gained an underground currency through the seventeenth century, where Prince Rupert of the Rhine grew up with his family in exile from the courts at Heidelberg and Prague after the outbreak of the Thirty Years War. The triangulated eye depicts the essence of the light of eternity, the all-watchfulness of the presiding deity, the opposite of the absurd in asserting that someone watches over all this, some being who has designed and oversees events that cascade in happening, one after another, as seen from that supreme point of view. Yet the frontispiece of Böhme's *Aurora* features not his engraving of the all-watchful eye in the triangle but a proliferation of perspectives in a globe wrapped with eyes on surrounding bands. The entity bound by multiple eyes is not Earth but a planet hovering near by, with Earth in its shadow, and it seems shockingly modern, decentring both sun and Earth, almost surreal, beyond and above the real, and prophetic of the perpetual contest and circulation of perspectives that was only then, in that century of European wars of religious and political strife, becoming the world of little Rupert, whose name displaced all Indigenous names that had been attached to Rupert's Land.

I always thought of Rupert as a small boy in short pants, tumbling and laughing like us in the dunes, in the back seat of the car, even his name was unusual and colourful, like Rudolph the Red-Nosed Reindeer, and he was, it turns out, the child of a volatile wedding between Princess Elizabeth Stuart, daughter of James I of England, and Frederick, the Elector Palatine, the Protestant German prince with a vote in determining who would be emperor of the Holy Roman Empire, both attending the court of Rudolph II when he moved his capital from Vienna to Prague and proceeded to bury himself in abstruse studies, his court becoming a centre of alchemical, astrological, magico-scientific studies of all kinds. Hiding himself in his great palace at Prague, maybe like Count West-West, and as Prospero does in Shakespeare's *Tempest*, thus leaving his kingdom vulnerable to invasion or usurpation, Rudolph's castle with its libraries, wonder rooms of magico-mechanical marvels, water organs, speaking fountains, and statues that give out sounds and noises when struck by the sun's rays, signalled his withdrawal from the problems caused by the fanatical intolerance of his religiously sectarian and belligerent nephew, Philip II of Spain. Rudolph died in the year of Böhme's visions, variously depicted in woodcuts or engravings published in *Aurora*, and the following year Rupert's parents were married with great pomp, their wedding the occasion of Shakespeare's writing of

The Tempest and its first performance, the comedy resolving in the joining together, in the end, of Frederick and Miranda, daughter of the magician Prospero, and the couple's escape from the enchanted island, at once in the Mediterranean and the colonial Caribbean, while its original inhabitants, the Indigenous Ariel, the angelic sprite, and Caliban, earthly clod, prefigure the New World actors and storytellers to come.

There were high hopes for a Protestant Europe in the union of Rupert's parents, named the Winter King and Queen of Bohemia, ensuring, so it was thought, the support of England in the coming conflagration. When the lines were drawn and the swords came out, however, King James did not rush to send armies to his daughter's aid, and her son, Prince Rupert, born in Prague, was almost left behind and then remembered at the last minute, and carried out in the arms of his parents as they fled to Berlin and then on to Amsterdam, the child with just the clothes on his back, and there in exile growing into a man of science and war himself, a cavalier in the English civil wars, founder of the Royal Society in 1660, first governor of the Hudson's Bay Company, and lending his name to several ingenious inventions that he allowed people to believe were his own but were probably only introduced by him from Germany, including a naval gun known as the Rupertinoe, another that fired multiple rounds at high speed, and a handgun with rotating barrels. What stands out for me are not the guns but his new method of casting objects into an appearance of perspective, what Rupert might have conceived of after reading *Aurora*, which I am looking into, and, most of all, his glass teardrops that explode when the tail is cracked, a revelation in the distribution of surface tension for tempered glass, known to this day as Prince Rupert's Drops.

At some point, I finally ditched my tragic drama that absurdly relied on mixing documentary realism with supernatural forces, malignant or benign, and tried outright fiction, churning out hundreds of pages of "A Legend of Ruined Children," the title taken from a psychologist's account I read of a story that recurs in case studies of the troubled and tormented. I was shocked at how common it is to concoct and nurse stories of our ruin to explain unspeakable night terrors, even those deriving from historical culpabilities accruing long before our births and lasting long after our deaths. The problem that came up right away in my "Legend" was that there was no professional listener, no one qualified, no one standing outside of things and sufficiently undamaged to make sense of the ruin or what caused or sustained it, like there was in the psychologist's accounts, the psychologist herself coming to the rescue as an author and authenticator, a verifier of the pain and distortion and their causes, and lacking my inability to verify the truth and full meaning of the story, verification being the whole problem, fact and fiction, the story lacking direction and propulsion, no steady and all-seeing eye in the triangle to guarantee the truth from which all other versions depart and, with the recovery of health, the truth to which they return. For what could be said by creatures whose ruination rendered them speechless and mute? By those who couldn't recognize their ruin until after the work had composed it, the very work in the continual process of its decomposition because of the ongoing distortions of perspective on their ruination? I received a small Saskatchewan Arts Board grant for the plan and some pages of this self-extinguishing attempt and dragged it around for years, another layer of dead skin, before adding it to the stacks and files, now reaching almost to the ceiling of my archives of industry and failure.

Why do they fail, I wondered in my kinder moments, when they seem to take on a life of their own? Now and then it occurred to me that maybe it wasn't failure but resistance. Maybe I had hit against something that would not give, either in language or on earth, like the gravedigger's shovel hitting the coffin already in the place where they were digging somebody else's grave. And that led me to think the resistance was not mine, or not mine alone, not an individual failing or a repression of something but an external and a formal prohibition of some kind, a curse or taboo that cannot be overcome but is lodged in the ground itself, and disturbance or violation would be deadly not only for me but also for others, my sisters and brothers, mother, her sisters and brothers, her parents, my dad's sisters and brothers, his parents, and so on, plus all the towns and territories where they live and where they die. I could not refuse the gift of the tea towels, that was never an option and never even occurred to me, but they were the sign that alerted me to such a curse, what threatened exile and worse for the treason of questioning the primacy and righteousness of the settlement of my ancestors in the Palliser Triangle. The tea towels were so mired and stained in all that, even before I ever used them, as I dawdled over the pages and wrestled with the story, and soon enough I would be interrupted to finish the dishes and get on with things, so I would put them away again, always failing to forgo the writing entirely, or give it up, like an addict who never stops quitting. I could not keep from trying to write the story, whatever it was about, my parents or me, the triangle of absent buffalo, missing Assiniboine.

In one of the aborted versions of my "Legend," the damage or ruin registers not only in mental or perceptual derangement but also in the language disorder of the narrator, which forces her to speak in the second person, as in "you are happy," you-this, you-that, when you think of it that way, and so on, which you might do to gain some distance from the trouble you're in, to imagine yourself here or there, barrelling down the road without making any progress, yet unable to stop, and I tried to maintain it, the second-person you, in the present tense, to harness the imperative mood and imagine a future against a nearly overwhelming sense of impending destruction, unable for some time to distinguish my own prospects from those of the buffalo, Johnny Bradley, Dad. The result was that my "Legend" was all feverish and breathy, events seeming to happen even as I wrote. "Take a deep breath, sister, and confess," it begins. "You got no place to go." I needed, without knowing it in so many words, to locate the corral in history, geometry, topography, from perspectives I could countenance and communicate and bear. For that, I needed distance, but I kept running out of gas. I found the second-person you could not be sustained without extreme fatigue by about page 15. Then I truly had no place to go, as all the pages say about my ride back from Toronto in the transport truck on receiving the news of my dad's demise.

We broke down east of Thunder Bay. "All that thunders round the bay is this truck and the convoy we're in with dozens like it and all the trains rolling west," I wrote.

> Down two-way roads of cracked asphalt, mud shoulders, deep ditches, and piles of smoking tires, the smouldering sores of hell. You and the Driver set to race right through town when something gives out, something falls off the chassis, or a bearing flies out of the power train, something like that. They don't have the parts and won't have the time until morning to pull the whole thing apart and put it back together for the driving road. Three in the afternoon so what are you supposed to do. Your Driver idles outside the truck stop, grunting and climbing down and scuffing a boot in the dirt, kicking tires in code with all the greasy gone guys, so you say, okay, you disappear down the broken sidewalk towards Town past the Burger Baron and the Dairy Queen like you're in some junk food kingdom trying to make you feel you come up in the world, but really you trade time for money, dreams for work, food for sawdust wrapped in pickle-flavoured tinfoil and thrown at you with the vacant cheer of ruined part-time kids working day and night in their younger and younger youths, the road a gone place for them, and you see no sympathy or curiosity about anything there where you line your stomach with rancid fat whose stench coats your skin and teeth until you

got to wash it off or die. A motel neon struggles out of the clutter blinking Vacancy, Welcome, Free Movies, okay, so one night you could get a sleep worth paying for, how much is the hopeless question. You ask it, and twenty-three bucks gets you a saggy bed, bedspread with blue ridges, the knobby old covers in the farthest gone places of memory. So you pay the fee and stretch out, the bill leaving three-fifty for the rest of the way home, likely just a day and a half and the food on this road isn't worth paying for anyway.

You can see how drunk I was on Jack Kerouac and tried to catch his driving rhythm of the road to give myself and my reader that same ride, everything "gone," your dad, the driver you are half afraid of, and so on. Kerouac's "gone" worked like the song "Lost Highway" by Hank Williams, where the condition of the traveller as lost is transferred onto the road he's travelling, as if the road is at a loss about where to go or take you and making the whole thing even more unbearably forlorn and without any sense of a destination. But then,

that Driver offers you a hot Denver sandwich, interrupting your gone Dad's handling of the gun replaying in your ruined mind: "He raises it, then sets it down, stares at it without words, knowing only a dull thudding pain behind his eyes. He picks it up again, checks the chamber, cocks the barrel, sets it down. Maybe he hopes it will go off accidentally, shoot him of its own accord," I'm caught thinking. "All he has to do is sit there, and he does, he sits there for hours and days. The calendar on the nail reads March, but you know in the end it will be April, the beginning of April, April 1st, that's why the page hasn't been turned yet, it's April Fool's, and no one thought to turn the page over after Johnny died."

Of course, it's May or June by the time you piece all this together, most of it you never hear out loud, you glean it and make some up yourself. You need to tell yourself something, everybody else skimping on details just when they matter most. What was he wearing, what time of day, what was the weather outside, and how long before they found him? Could they open the casket, or was his face too gone? This you are denied, sister, and whether you know it or not you are haunted and careening west forever in a truck that roars but that will never get you there in time. . . .

Now the Driver is suspicious, so you say less and less. The Denver he went to so much trouble for, gift of the road, turns to dirt in your mouth. The trees are shrinking out the window, and the rocks are crowding into pile-ups at the corners of fields opening to prairie. You know what's at the end of this road, and it fills you with dread. The Assiniboine could feel the ground move for days before they caught a glimpse of the thundering buffalo herds forever moving over the sloping land, like you now, sister. You are looking squarely at the massacre coming to meet them on arrival. They are stampeded into a frenzy, thinking they are escaping or going home, when in truth they are rounded up into the pound from where there is no exit or they are driven over a cliff, heads-smashed-in. Now your dad is extinct, and you can feel it happening to you too, driving to save that dad, those beasts, from hopeless forgotten silence and death. But all this you will never have the strength to face up to if you don't eat more than sawdust along the way.

Even then food was pretty much my only other preoccupation, food and space, or distance, and I'm sure it's what saved me in the end, the food part learned from my mother, who only threatened to kill me in other ways, and, as also learned from her, why the preparation of food is the antidote to death, buns and pies and casseroles to take over and bring the mourners back to the life of the appetites. I won't belabour it any more than I already have but only say how I could find no way for that truck to reach a destination, just like I could not imagine any dramatic progress or action in my Palliser play starring Dr. Spry. I was stuck wanting to live my whole life in the moment beforehand, lest the second-person title "You Are Happy" silently revise itself in my hands to "You Are Ruined," and who would look twice at a book called *You Are Ruined* or *You Are Miserable* or, for that matter, *A Legend of Ruined Children*, ruin and misery being what drive you to the library or bookshelf in the first place?

As for the word *legend* in "A Legend of Ruined Children," I was only after a kind of solidity and weightiness to anchor the idea of the ruins I found myself in, like a stone that cannot be dislodged or discounted so easily, no matter if this or that passage does not quite add up or move things forward or cannot be corroborated or if, in my headlong quest, I got a fact wrong, and my findings somehow came untethered from where I began. I considered replacing "legend" in my title with "ballad," with its more modest, working-class, musical connotation. And then I thought, not only that, it's a country and western ballad. So then I wrote down the titles that instantly came to mind: "The Ballad of Johnny Bradley," "Pity the Rodeo Clown," "Transport Heading West," "Death in the Badlands," "Stolen Ponies," "The Tailgate News," "Outlaw Trail," to name a few that remain unwritten and unsung. Not yet legends or ballads, they are hollowed-out places made ready for the farmers and ranchers and their progeny, settler or Indigenous, the cooks in their kitchens and the children out weeding the gardens or cleaning the corrals, all borne on events too terrible to look at, where they work up the courage and open their hearts for the reckoning they know is coming and will have to face up to.

Legend. Ballad. You see how every last word has become unsettled and put up its fight against me. How to proceed, then, when all the deaths and enraged bull's horns have punctured and bloodied my words and lens, as Hemingway would say? In "Literature Considered as a Bull Fight," the preface to his autobiography, the French surrealist and anthropologist Michel Leiris compares the writer to the matador or bullfighter in a way that speaks directly to my story and condition. "If there is nothing in the fact of writing a work that is the equivalent to the bull's keen horn," he writes, and he means something of the encounter with reality, the real, or even the mere shadow of the bull's horn, what the British writer Tom McCarthy describes as "some roving black hole . . . the point at which the writing's entire project crumples and implodes," like the impossibility of telling my story that I've been describing, that must be written and unwritten simultaneously, the cowboys and Indians story, if there is nothing like that at stake, "then we are left with empty style," with a work that Leiris fears, in his own case, will be merely aesthetically pleasing but insignificant, insipid, though it might be beautiful and even satisfying in going only to the brink of disturbance in the geometry of things.

Leiris confronts the potential insignificance of the confessions he makes in his autobiography, his exposure of "personal peccadilloes," especially what had been his covert homosexuality, which, granted, can be life-threatening in some contexts. "What is the use," he writes, "in the world's excruciating uproar, of this faint moan over such narrowly limited and individual problems? . . . [Yet] I found it hard to resign myself to being nothing more than a *littérateur*," he goes on. "The matador who transforms danger into an occasion to be more brilliant than ever and reveals the whole quality of his style just when he is most threatened—that is what enthralled me," he writes.

With this, Leiris resolves to "reject all fable" in his life story, to admit only facts, and write "a negation of a novel." Yet, in the very next paragraph, he defends the poetic value he attaches to dreams and to Freudian psychology, vestiges of the surrealism he had already broken with. At the same time, he insists on speaking frankly, especially about love, and wishes his work might amount to a kind of surreal collage or photo-montage of elements of strict documentary value. The elements are factual but pieced together in a fanciful or fictional montage of relationships, the normal logic of connecting elements like chronological sequencing or cause and effect dispensed with beforehand. "Each of my sentences would possess a special density," he claims, "an affecting plenitude. To use materials of which I was not the master, and which I had to take as I found them (since my life was what it was and I could not alter, by so much as a comma, my past, a fate as unchallengeable for me as for the *torero* the beast that runs into the ring)—such was the risk I accepted and the law I fixed for myself." Similarly, "the *corrida*, the bullfight, is a rigid framework imposed on an action in which chance must appear to be dominated." This Leiris takes as his principle of composition, what he calls his "tauromachic" code, his "guide for action and guarantee against complacency" in his writing, which I take to mean his taking hold of and seeing through the prism of what is true, the truth of the story, rather than excluding what does not fit a heroic or preconceived notion of how the story should go according to the conventions of genre, in my case, genres of country and western, the good cowboys always winning in the end, when victory for all is never the case in the colonial settler story. Those works in which the horn is present in one form or another are what Leiris is after, works in which the situation is confronted directly, "taken by the horns," as he says, allowing us to see, and more or less directly experience, "life engaging its partisan—its victim."

"Literature considered as a bullfight has an attitude of something like humour or madness towards things," Leiris

writes. The "mouthpiece of the great themes of human tragedy," it deposes as in a courtroom, contributing "evidence to
the trial of our present system of values and tips the scales .
. . toward the liberation of all." Olé! I say, but, if the threat of
the goring and tearing overcome is the principle of composition, then not only occasional brilliance in managing that
danger but also occasional failure and near failure to manage it
entirely feature in the very content of the work, deshaping and
deformation giving shape to its telling. Oh, that's it, I thought.
I'm in a bullfight with a story of a bullfight, the setting and
scene of which I disavow and distance myself from, the land's
colonization my precondition, yet the same land my only destination, a most contradictory, even annihilating, principle of
self-composition, and why the story so struggles to be told.

Another renegade French surrealist, Georges Bataille, tries
another method of negation to get at the truth of his story that,
like me, he resisted yet could not leave alone. Our existence
is a relentless and ongoing process of deformation, he insists,
a straining and bucking against the harnesses and bridles of
form. The risk is not so much in the selection of form as in the
surrender to writing as deshaping, which releases the writer,
the bull, the fight, and the world, all that overflows boundaries
of definition, identity, bull, fence, ring, corral. Bataille draws
to himself the bloodied tips of the horns in two characters
attending a bullfight in his *Story of the Eye*. They keep "disappearing together all through Andalusa," he writes, when they
have to change disguises again and again after committing out-
rages—violent, sexual, blasphemous—against propriety. Then
on May 7, 1922, he records, in the person of his extremely horny
narrator, a young man revelling in truancy from school and
unbridled debauchery with his equally wild friend Simone, and
how they go to the bullfights together where the well-known
matadors "La Rose, Lalanda, and Granero were to fight in the
arena of Madrid." Manuel Granero was a real historical bullfighter. The narrator attests to having still in his possession "the
round paper fan, half yellow, half blue, that Simone carried that

day, and an illustrated brochure with a description of all the circumstances" of the bullfights "and a few photographs," all that attests to the non-fictional status of an otherwise outlandish story. Later on, Bataille writes, long after the events about to be depicted, while boarding a ship, "the small valise containing those two souvenirs tumbled into the sea, and was fished out by an Arab with a long pole, which is why the objects are in such a bad state" at the time of writing, but still essential to the telling, functioning like the coordinates of my Declarations of the Coroners, the map of the Palliser Triangle, and other specimens of proof like my thirteen porcupine quills from the stone ruins of Pârinti's house. "I need them," he writes, "to fix that event to the earthly soil, to a geographic point and precise date, an event that my imagination compulsively pictures as a simple vision of solar deliquescence," the act or natural process of passing away gradually, not death but a dying out.

Bataille writes as himself in Part 2 of his repulsively exuberant *Story of the Eye*, a part titled "Coincidences," to explain how he wrote the story as a way of trying to forget "the things I can be or do personally." He was trying to avoid autobiography but ended up showing the impossibility of that avoidance. In the years following its publication, he discovered by a series of coincidences startling correspondences between images in his story, beginning with the bullfighter Granero's eye that famously took the tip of the bull's horn as it bore through the matador's skull, between that bullfight as graphically depicted in his story and traumatic events in Bataille's own life, mainly the lonely death of his father, blind and partially paralyzed. Bataille, at age seventeen, along with his mother had abandoned him, an invalid, to the housekeeper and fled ahead of German forces advancing on their town in rural France in August 1914. When the housekeeper sent word that his father was dying, Bataille and his mother decided to return to the town despite the advancing bombardments just miles from the front line of the war. They arrived in November of 1915, at some risk, a few days too late, and found him sealed inside a coffin in the bedroom. Bataille's mother, "unable to bear the thought of his lonely death, loses her mind. I wanted to escape my destiny at any price," wrote Bataille in 1943. "Today, I know I am blind, immeasurable, I am man abandoned on the globe like my father. No one on earth or in heaven cared about my father's dying terror. Still, I believe he faced up to it, as always. What a horrible pride, at moments, in Dad's blind smile!"

For Bataille, nothing more terrible can be imagined, no matter how violent or debased, and his filthy *Story of the Eye* is a parable, in spite of himself, that seduces writer and reader into looking at the very thing we would rather not see: abandonment of a father by his child and that father's lonely death. The story is Bataille's way of avoiding and at the same time confronting what is too terrible to look at. In retrospect, he sees how its images and events tell that story all too clearly in seeking the eye made blind and dead, the eye that sees and is gouged out, whereas in my story of a bullfight I also try to face up to and at the same time evade what is too terrible to look at, only hesitantly piecing it together and putting parts of it into words after years of working up the courage and lying in wait, gathering documents, evidence, oral testimony, circling the corral, now looking squarely, now averting my eyes, even as I quail at the thought of exposing what I'm up to, showing how it was and what was lost, looking further into that story, for shame, what needs to be written and read for our reckoning of mourning and answering in time.

So Bataille's avoidance and my pursuit of autobiography get us to roughly the same place, what I guess to be the point of his bullfight imprinted in a pornographic tale that so indirectly faces up, in the image of Granero's disgorged eye and the horny prankster's obsession with the eyes of their victims, life's victims, their perspectives and stories enabling their author to see his own abandonment of his blind father and his anguished death. My bullfight, imprinted in my reconstruction of Johnny Bradley's wrestling with the bull's horns, fixes my coordinates in territory occupied by settlers and mapped onto my being, the corral our destination and primal scene, where we landed in history at such cost. Like Bataille in his story, Leiris in his preface, Borges at "dawn," Suknaski in Wood Mountain and at the gravesides, we chafe against the bridles of form even as we surrender to the bull, the horns, and the fight that deshapes and reforms. For no one are the received forms adequate. The truth of the matter, of what transpires in any corral, exceeds all boundaries, punctures eyes, disgorges, disarticulates perception. In my case, it only ever takes shape in the fences and corrals repeatedly circled and then smashed, trucks idling and bearing down, cowboys gored and shot, the horns on stuffed heads gracing the living rooms and community halls, Indigenous riders and the beasts they hunted mimicked at the rodeo, stampede, by hired hands, young lads, surveyors, guides, boundary commissions setting out in disputed or uncharted territories and generating stories by following the polemical maps that cross the boundaries of known genres, scientific and literary, alert to signs of where, at any given moment, we sense the unrelenting swishing of the bull's horns, just beyond perception, about to disrupt and tear up every page and scene, from cradle to corral to grave.

The poet Lorna Crozier, whose father sold or lost the farm near the town called Success on the road between Cantuar and Cabri, well within the Palliser Triangle, and whose father also drank at the Healy Hotel in the 1970s, wrote in support of my application, either in a letter of reference or as an adjudicator, I do not recall which, for the grant to bring "A Legend of Ruined Children" to completion, and I've always been sorry about not being able to make good on it, especially since Crozier has gone on to considerable success as a writer, even writing, bravely, "Facts about My Father" that reveal how life imprinted and impinged on his body, bit by bit, nails chewed to the quick, three fingers severed at the first joint by a lawn mower, throat cancer, a smashed left hand, gall bladder removed, and in the poem his life is a sustained deshaping, cataracts growing over his eyes, clouding his sight, yet never threatening victory at the pool tables he owned, later collecting the coins, profits, on top of the glory of defeating the sharpshooter braggarts who paid for every game. Crozier, the poet not the father, writes of a vision of "Hemingway in Spain," according to the poem of that title, looking gentle and at peace even after "the life he'd led, after his violent death." Papa is painting by the seaside, intelligence animating his hands, in common with the same feature noted in the hands of her father. Hemingway following

> the language of the light,
> his hands remembering
> what they had known before
> he was a man, the joyful colours spilling
> beyond the lines, beyond the form
> of things . . .
> as if they'd known
> only brush and paint
> and never held a gun.

When I read those lines, I thought it was not so far out of line in my Spry and Palliser play to dwell on the instant before the trigger is pulled, that instant of possibilities and choices and alternative trajectories when Dad "never held a gun." I could have stayed there forever, since I didn't know where to go with it, yet I was terrified by the formlessness, what writers face up to, Hemingway, Crozier, and I lacked the courage to see let alone wrestle the horn tips of the bull, and instead staged, over and over again, their gouging and goring of Johnny Bradley, the gun firing at my dad, his own hand pulling the trigger. But I was wrestling, after all, as I see it now. Crozier, Hemingway, Suknaski, Borges, all hover over that choice between pen and gun, my own choice in the matter long since decisively made, in secret and now here in the open, on taking up my inheritance of Dad's AA pen, which my sister gave me along with the funeral card, the pen I lost for a time and forgot to mention earlier, gold and ivory, with praying hands on the clip now tarnished with age. It might have been in his breast pocket when his heart stopped, his pulse transferring to the pen with ink that, miraculously, still flows and that I doubt will ever run dry.

I knew the poet John Newlove through Suknaski even before I knew Lorna Crozier, and he encouraged me, when I went begging to his office in the Regina Public Library one time, to pursue the figure of Johnny Bradley, the romantic irony of this cowboy at the vanguard of reintroducing the buffalo to the prairie, giving his own land for them to roam once more, and the tragedy that he was thanked by being torn to pieces by the very beast that his farming fortune had displaced and that made restoration and reintroduction of the buffalo necessary. I was advised by Newlove, I thought, to abandon Dad again in favour of Johnny Bradley, for where is Dad in Newlove's story, an after-the-fact minor character, too late even to play the picador to the matador, and where could I possibly go with that? I dismissed Newlove as a drunk, which he also was, even as I secretly thought he was trying to tell me something I should heed. I just hadn't calculated that there might be so many different ways to pursue Johnny's story, or that the resistance of the story to its telling, except in the most roundabout and deformative way, might be one of them, having instead the hazy idea in my mind of Johnny as a character in western pulp fiction by Louis L'Amour or Zane Grey, the story of a lone gunman eeking out a life on a dirt farm, ramshackle house, no women or children in sight, alone like Johnny was, maybe running from something, heartbreak or bootlegging, robbery or cattle rustling. A cussin', ill-natured shootist, as gunslingers used to be called, going it alone out on the bald prairie, preferring the company of animals to other people, yet turning out to represent the natural law that overcomes all contradictions, even gets the girl, maybe reforming or being reformed by a whore, Miss Kitty, in the end.

In Newlove's memoir about drinking, "Not Swimming, but Drowning," published in *Addiction*, the collection edited by Lorna Crozier and Patrick Lane, a sequence of vignettes of Newlove's own alcoholic stupors and puking borrows the form of the twelve steps to sobriety of Alcoholics Anonymous. Step nine is the riddle "How do you know when a drunk is lying? Answer: His lips move." The fact there are only eleven numbered steps in his essay dramatizes that, though Newlove did have stretches of abstention, including some when I knew him to be a clear-sighted and generous writer, the drink never let go of him, though I believe he died of some other ailment and wrote a lot of poetry through it all. I am awash in a sea of drunks, I thought, all dreaming outside the lines, randomly renumbering the graves, a hand hovering over the brush, the pen, the gun, the facts not quite adding up, and it has taken me the longest time to quell my terror of following them, not shooting or drinking but writing.

DAYS OF HEAVEN

In the season before I put myself out of reach by moving to Toronto to write polemical poetry, and before I took possession of the gagging tea towels, before the buffalo charged in the corral and I went rushing back west in a transport truck and met Suknaski and we buried my dad or someone else just as good in the graveyard, before all that, during my blissful ignorance of that stampede and all that would soon befall me, that would provoke and at the same time obstruct the writing of any other stories to help me change course from the path I was on, I experienced what only now I see as portents and foreshadows, for good and ill, if only I had been able to recognize them, instead feeling myself all the while in heaven with a job and a crew and nothing to do but travel in a dusty colourful caravan following the wheat and maize harvests all through the Great Plains. In short, I was happy, with just the faintest intimations now and then of anxious dread emanating from nowhere in particular. I had been casting about for work when I heard about the custom harvest outfits gathering at my sister's farm and their need for a cook to go along with the crew cutting winter wheat down in Texas, then working their way back north through the cradle of the Great Plains in time for the Saskatchewan harvest in the fall. I landed that job, and in the night before setting out in early

May there was a heavy rain with high winds that disturbed all sleep and tore time apart until morning, when, ragged at the edges, we headed south in a convoy of grain trucks, each with a header loaded in the back to be mounted on the combine pulled on a flatbed trailer behind. The trucks and combines were followed by the crew boss in the service truck loaded with tools and spare parts. He was followed by the only car, which I rode in with his wife, my sister's sister-in-law, and their little girl. The crew took me on at the last minute because the crew boss's wife, normally the cook, was well along in her second pregnancy and not sure she could manage her own health, the toddler, and the work of keeping the men fed well enough to operate the machinery fifteen–sixteen hours a day for weeks at a stretch. Our car pulled the camping trailer, while his service truck pulled the trailer that would be bunkhouse and cook-house as well as laundry and gathering place for the crew, with built-in red vinyl banquette seating around a thin fold-out dining table. I took along my tent and bedding for sleeping under the stars just out of earshot of the snoring, exhausted, and crusty men in the mess of their bunks at the back of the trailer behind the kitchen.

We drove for two days on first heading out, the vehicles connected by two-way radios, with the boss at master control in the crew cab. The wife and little girl and I paid no attention to the jabbering on the radios, all about which routes to take and the hazards to expect, where to fuel up, and we moved along slowly. In the car, we played country and western music, especially Crystal Gayle, Loretta Lynn's little sister, at full volume on the eight-track, "Don't It Make My Brown Eyes Blue," and "River Road," that Sylvia Tyson song full of excitement about setting out, maybe never going home, whatever might happen, and in my case welcoming the daily distractions of our onward motion from what might otherwise have seeped into my days, fitful nights, the wretched noises and dreams of so many fore- and afterlives, my own and my family's. Besides the crew boss, his wife, their three-year-old daughter, and me, our crew and outfits were three, though we sometimes hired help along the way, extra drivers to keep the grain trucks in circulation back and forth between fields and granaries or railyards, and along with the crew boss that made four men to keep fed three times a day, day in, day out, nothing women don't do all the time, but a challenge for me, since I had taken my turn cooking one family meal a week and otherwise looked after only myself up to that time. Stan the Man was a clever skinny cowboy from a ranch down near Climax, deep inside the Palliser Triangle, whose joke we never tired of. On saying where he was from, and meeting blank incomprehension of where that was, his punchline was always "Aw, c'mon, everyone comes to Climax."

"Are you coming, Stan?" we would ask in any lull in conversation, always looking for ways to rephrase the joke in different settings, especially in front of girls he might be trying to impress.

"I'm coming, I'm coming," he would say, laughing.

Black Bart, the Italian Stallion, was from Wood Mountain, east of Climax. In stature, wiry energy, and talkativeness, he was the twin of Suknaski, in fact his contemporary, and I believe they knew each other, since a character named Labocetta, probably Black Bart's father or uncle, appears in one of Suknaski's poems. Bart wore a pitch-black ten-gallon hat, but only after work, so as not to get it covered with the dust of the fields we were harvesting.

Colorado Dave was a doe-eyed sweetheart of a guy, younger than the other two but way bigger, with a slow drawl and an unhurried manner that made it difficult to know if he was careless and sloppy or carefully belying the precise seriousness with which he completed every task.

We drove south through the Big Muddy Badlands down toward the lower eastern point of the triangle, a slow procession moving not much faster than a wagon train or stagecoach, and wound along the looming buttes and abandoned wolves' caves legendary for sheltering the Wild Bunch, Butch Cassidy and the Sundance Kid, before they escaped along the Outlaw Trail, if they survived, to Uruguay or Argentina, where they were glimpsed by the uncle, then a rancher in Patagonia, of the husband of a later friend of mine in the Maritimes. The horse thief Dutch Henry hid out in the Big Muddy, too, and so did the cold-blooded Sam Kelly and his band, but unlike those outlaws we crossed the border, papers and documents in order, at Regway, and the only other stop I recall all the way down to Texas was nearly straight south at Cheyenne, Wyoming, where we took advances on our first two weeks of wages and blew them on cowboy kit and country and western music cassettes, some eight-tracks, since that's what we had in the car. Black Bart bought an even bigger and blacker Stetson. I bought a braided leather belt with a brass buckle and a pair of tooled leather sandals, and we all got outfitted with jeans quite a bit cheaper than at home. Not so long after leaving Cheyenne, we pulled up just as the ripening harvest was about to get going full bore at Farnsworth in the Texas Panhandle, the exact place, or identical to it, where the actor Sam Shepard, playing the farmer, unknowingly hired among his harvest crew in 1912 his future wife, his murderer, and his murderer's little sister, the young girl who narrates the Terrence Malick film *Days of Heaven*, which won the Best Director award at Cannes in 1979 and was mostly shot near Whiskey Gap, a ghost town straight south of Lethbridge, near the southwestern point of the Palliser Triangle.

The farmer's fateful crew arrive by train at his tall lonely house surrounded by ripening grain fields and rolling rangeland where buffalo still roam, fantastically, since they were all but wiped out by the 1890s. Buffalo appear in the backgrounds of a few scenes, unfenced, tearing at the prairie grasses alongside the wheat fields, and they appear bemused or menacing, it's hard to tell which, and I later learned those shots were filmed in Montana, and the buffalo probably belonged to a rancher just like Johnny Bradley, who also was reintroducing the herds out of romantic glory and unfailing country and western optimism. The Montana buffalo scenes, according to the source I consulted, were inserted into the film afterward because it snowed in Alberta before the filming was complete at Whiskey Gap. As for Shepard, up to then, he was mostly a writer of poems and plays, and about to win a Pulitzer Prize in 1979 for *Buried Child*, his play about a family riven by a secret unmarked burial that, many years later, still could not be looked at directly, so we can assume Shepard well knew how many versions and variations of that story circulated at any given time on the Great Plains.

The *Days of Heaven* grifters among the farmer's crew were described by a reviewer as people "touched and then passed over by the divine," a phrase of journalistic poetry that gets at the mysterious grace of the three impoverished yet hopeful human figures on the horizontal plains of the movie, all vaulting sky, their tiny shapes inky along the horizon darkening just before the outburst of morning light spreads over all going awry. The murderer, played by Richard Gere, the wife-to-be, and the little sister are on the run after his enraged accidental killing of the shop foreman at a Chicago steel factory where he was working. They are thrilled to be taken on by the harvest crew because they are penniless and hungry and running from the law. The farmer is rich and dying, and he falls in love with the wife-to-be after watching her work in the fields from afar. Observing the farmer's growing infatuation, his murderer invents the story that he and the wife-to-be are only brother and sister and cynically encourages a romance between his "sister" and the farmer. His plan is to get her into position to inherit the farm when the farmer dies, which he thinks is imminent, but then he doesn't take into account how falling in love might arrest the farmer's illness and delay his death. After the marriage, the wife begins to love the farmer as much as she loves his murderer.

"She loved the farmer," the little sister says, and she narrates the story with sympathy for all three players in the tragic love triangle from some distance in time. The wife's love for the farmer was risked all along, yet was unforeseen, maybe because there is no more plot or hereafter once you are in heaven. The "days of heaven" referred to by the film's title are those few days of pleasure and freedom from want the grifters experience between the partly duplicitous marriage and the rash murder of the eventually jealous farmer. Under his gaze, the three intruders frolic in the brief suspension of their fears and cares. Nobody knows for sure if the marriage is sincere or insincere, not even the wife herself. No one knows who, or which man, will make the next move or if heaven will last for eternity. During what turns out to be only a brief hiatus in their hardscrabble wandering lives, the wife, the murderer, and the little sister don't have to work from morning to night or please any boss for a living. They spend their days cracking jokes, gorging on food, all they can eat, doing cartwheels in the yard around the tall house before the audience of buffalo, even hiring circus performers who arrive by airplane, and it's as if the buffalo aren't planning their next move either, only existing on Earth outside of time as they do in heaven. Still, they seem about to stampede into the story, as they soon would into mine. And like the little sister in that story, I've waited my turn. I'm the narrator now.

When we arrived in the Panhandle, dozens of crews were already gathered, and more rolled in by the minute. It was lucky our crew boss knew Bones and Lil from the previous year, so they let us park our trailers and trucks in their farmyard, a rented acreage really, since they didn't own any land and worked for the company we hoped would hire us, too, to take off some small portion of its crop. Farnsworth's park and all available parking lots around the town were already filled with combine outfits and trailers. Bones and Lil seemed to be having marriage problems, maybe because of his drinking, and then Lil disappeared soon after we arrived and long before we finished our first contract ten days or so later. I was sorry to see her go since she seemed to know how to navigate the swarms of men and equipment so well, the noise and dirt, get the groceries in and serve up the meals with lots of salt and Mexican hot chilis and even saltier jokes. That first night the crew boss gave us a talking to before taking us to the hotel bar for supper. He was sniffing around for contracts, but on the q.t., and he warned us not to blab details about which farmers we might be working for or where or for how long, information the other crews would be trying to get out of us in tricky ways while seeming not to care. "It gets pretty competitive in there," he said, and sure enough there was more than one loud argument and plenty of bullyish teasing and heckling of each other, and even a fight broke out between Texas and Dakota crews that busted into the street just like a barroom brawl in a country and western movie, all Willie and Waylon and the boys, broken tables, the men sauced up and yelling they thought they had a deal, a handshake, an understanding, and deserved to cut for the same farmers they had cut for last year. But the wheeling and dealing, deceptions, and undercutting of the crew bosses made that far from a sure thing, as our crew boss said. "Nobody is entitled to anything. You start at zero and earn your living each and every day."

What a cowboy world I'd landed in, and I don't recall going to the bars much after that first night of the brawls. I'd brought a few books to read and a journal to write in, and I liked playing with the boss's little girl, who was full of questions and busy learning things such as how to tie her shoes, which thankfully took up a lot of the time and attention of both her mother and me. We watched as she looked at her sprawling undone laces, and her thought to tie them up led to a shift in her shoulders and then moved down her arms into clumsy hands and fingers that sometimes tied the laces, or almost did, before the thought got distracted and the hands fell away and lost interest, and we'd have to do up the laces on the run as she made off after a toy or doll or up to the window to wave to her dad as he pulled out of the yard.

We left the bar that first night without our crew boss who had disappeared into the backrooms as soon as he wolfed down his supper. We assumed he was chasing work, and sure enough he drove up sometime later waving our first contract with a grin ear to ear, and he and the crew were soon poring over maps spread over the kitchen table in the crew trailer and making plans for the morning. We had a week or two lined up in Farnsworth and another two or three across the line around Hobart, Oklahoma, and jobs would come up suddenly in between when we'd be hailed by a farmer whose crew had failed to show up or whose combines had broken down. For me, the crew boss said, he'd draw a map the next morning once he calculated where the outfits would be at lunchtime, and he told me to lay in groceries or at least plan the meals for the next few weeks in Farnsworth. I did a quick inventory, shocked at the sudden realization of the relentless necessity of getting the meals together and delivering them to the fields, so much now depending on it, not just a pretty face anymore.

My largest pot was an old roaster that barely fit into the small propane-powered oven without the lid, so I planned to get lots of tinfoil. I dug out the cookbook I'd only absent-mindedly put in my bag at the last minute before leaving. The *Silver Chest of Recipes, 1949–1974* had just been published by the Assiniboia Kinettes on the occasion of their twenty-fifth anniversary. I had paid Caron Fafard, the crew boss's cousin (who had married and took the name of her husband and his cousin, however distant, the famous artist Joe Fafard from up around Pense), ten dollars for it, rather casually, a few days before, little suspecting it would be the most precious book in my travelling library. The signed recipes for fundamentally vague but hearty one-pot meals, such as Oven Dinner (Ann Vaessan), Seven-Layer Dinner (Carol Leach), Casserole for a Crowd (Mary Chipak), Meal in One Dish (Sophie McConnell), Variable Casserole (unsigned), and Caron's own Heavenly Hash, mostly called for some combination of rice or mashed potatoes, ground beef or chicken or stewing beef, celery, and a tin of mushroom soup or packaged onion soup mix, some with cheese or beans, some without, and the meal could be made in one pot and would keep well, even improve in flavour while I drove it out to whatever field the guys were working in by suppertime. I made a meal plan and grocery list, things I saw my mother do but had never been in charge of before. The first item on my list was a 100-foot roll of tinfoil, which I associate to this day with cooking in the 1970s.

The crew boss unhitched the car to level his trailer, while the crew detached and levelled the cookhouse trailer and connected the gas. The boss said first thing I should drive over to the store to get the groceries and be ready to head out with lunch before noon the next day. For breakfast, the crew said they preferred dry cereal, coffee, milk, toast, if anything, so that got me down to two meals a day, and I only had to make sure the breakfast things were in the trailer for whoever wanted to make his own. The crew boss was always up first, and he came over to make the coffee and rouse the guys out of bed around 6 or 7 a.m. When it rained or there was heavy dew and they couldn't cut until the sun dried the stalks at mid-morning, either he or I would make a hot breakfast of pancakes and eggs with bacon or sausage. Lunch would be sandwiches and fruit, rain or shine, sometimes a cake. I'd be pretty tired driving home after suppers in the field with a trunk full of dirty dishes, back to the little trailer kitchen where I'd been cooking and cutting up vegetables and washing dishes and folding laundry pretty much all day.

Lunches were loaves upon loaves of sandwiches packed in the original bread bags since there was never anything left of a single loaf once it was opened: tuna, chicken, turkey slices, ham, egg salad, cheese, tomato, cucumber. Colorado Dave asked for peanut butter and jelly sandwiches once, which made me think I was trying too hard, while all the time I chafed against the limits of my food and menu imagination. I took along watermelon slices, fruit salads, sometimes made a Lasagne (Bette Malesh), Chili con Carne (Ione Mireau), Tunaroni Casserole (Anne Pilkey), and one time I made a secret lunch—or did I only plan to?—for the crew boss's wife, her little girl, and me: Wieners Waikiki (Mary Chipak, who had lots of kids, so she would know), a dish involving canned pineapple chunks poured over hotdogs and baked at high heat.

I stopped making salads to go with sandwiches for lunch when I found the wilted greens left on the men's plates, whether out of distaste, fatigue, or awkwardness in eating with the plate on their knee in a cramped cab or on the tailgates where we sat or crouched at mealtimes. I had tried Party Potato Salad (Carol Leach), 30 Day Coleslaw (Marj Delyea), and plain old green garden salad, although I later overheard the boss complain that all the good stuff in my garden salads, the tomatoes or cucumbers, fell to the bottom, a comment I thought unfair since I hardly had a kitchen big enough for a salad bowl, let alone the implements or space for tossing and serving a salad properly, let alone having to drive for at least an hour to the fields in suffocating heat before dishing it up, all the anti-salad factors brought to bear by our working conditions that probably better cooks than me couldn't overcome.

I had two boxes for the field, one for dishes and utensils, bread and butter or sandwich loaves, salads, and the other for the hot roaster wrapped in tea towels to keep it warm. Desserts rode on the passenger seat beside me, levelled with a book or stone. The crew boss would drop by mid-morning and sit at the kitchen table to draw a map showing how to get to that day's fields and the estimated travel time to reach them. He was quite an artist and in fact had travelled to all the great galleries of Europe, and people in Assiniboia said it was a shame he couldn't make something more of this talent, returning home to take over the family farm instead. His skill at drawing was not wasted on me, though, or the crew I was feeding. Sometimes I had quite an intricate route to follow through seemingly trackless fields, a single company or farm enterprise by then owning entire townships, or many more than one, with only dirt trails to get to individual fields lacking boundaries that could be readily discerned. "Turn right at the third dip," the map's instructions would say, in a landscape where absolute geometric flatness was the norm and dips or undulations remarkable, but still I had to fight the tendency to second-guess myself. Was that a dip? Or was it just my hesitation and hovering over the brake pedal? "Turn left at the crossroads marked by a rusted can nailed to the corner post on your right," the map would say. If markers like a rusted can weren't handy, he would pound a stake into the ground and pile three stones in a triangle on top or nail a greasy rag or bandana or old cap to it. These treasure hunt trips filled me with anxiety but also a sense of adventure and fun, and, as my confidence grew in the accuracy of his maps and the crew's willingness to eat the food I was bringing, I was no longer surprised at going over a rise to see our three combines all idling together like tired beasts, or with a straggler just then approaching as I pulled up, or to see them as tiny specks on the horizon, my excitement at having found the rendezvous point and their ravenous hunger increasing as I drove up in a cloud of dust.

Sometimes other crews working for the same farmer would be visible in the next field, so I had to learn to distinguish our red Masseys and truck cabs from a distance to avoid landing in enemy territory. That would be a funny story, I thought. Or a scary one. I could write a harvest crew thriller, I thought, and I started writing it in my mind. The crew cook goes missing after failing to show up with supper in the field one night, and even when they find her it's not clear she didn't have something to do with her own disappearance. She seems to have a special regard for one of the drivers many fields over, where they find her and take her back to the crew trailer. *What the hell?* everyone wonders. The beginning of that story, as far as it went, is in a file here somewhere. In fact, I never ended up in the wrong field with a crew any better or worse than the one I set out with.

Besides my two packed boxes in the trunk, I hauled around a big cooler of beer, ice, and water, and the crew trained me to pop open the trunk so they could grab a cold drink to quench their thirst right away before I even got out of the car and started laying out the food. The urgency of it all, the timing and skill required, must have been how the chuckwagon races originated, a way to include the cook in the rodeo. The wagons would be parked inside the corral with the horses turned loose and the cowboys eating lunch, according to an account of the event in 1935 at the Wood Mountain Stampede by local rancher Pat Fitzpatrick. When the starting gun fired, they caught the horses, hitched their wagons, loaded the stoves and other equipment, and broke camp to speed around the track encircling the corral and finally turning back into its centre. The first wagon to show smoke coming from its stove, meaning the grub is on, was declared the victor.

At the spring round-up on the Turkey Track Ranch along the lower Frenchman River, where Palliser's Sullivan travelled and might have surveyed, but failed to file a report, inexplicably, and where rancher Tony Day some forty years later trailed 32,000 cattle and 700 horses from the Lazy F Ranch in the Texas Panhandle, the Cherokee Strip in Oklahoma, and the CA Bar in New Mexico, cowboy meals were prepared on a mess box bolted to the back end of the chuckwagon. So the mess box was more or less the pantry, storing all of the food and some of the cooking supplies, but it was also the countertop for preparing the food. I haven't seen a mess box except in the movies, but I've read about how the front panel of the box was on hinges so it could drop down just like a tailgate to provide that countertop, probably the original of all the tailgates to come. I always thought of that when I spread the lunch or supper out on the tailgate of the crew cab like a buffet, and, depending on how tired they were, the men ate sitting on the ground like cowboys, or leaned against truck fenders, or sprawled on dented and tottering old lawn chairs from my trunk, or sat in the solitude of their cabs, plates on their knees. The easy camaraderie of these meals was the highlight of days otherwise filled with uneasy awareness that my dad had left our house or been kicked out, and my mother was preoccupied with having things her way, maybe concerned to shut me up about something even then. What would my thriller or novel be about, I wondered, beyond the interesting local detail, and how would I ever get it written on the road and in between meals? I basked in what I thought would be Mom's approval of my finding serious work as the crew cook for a reputable harvest operation well known around Assiniboia. Sometimes the farmer we were cutting for joined us in the fields for meals, so I had to make sure there were extra portions. Sometimes he would bring the beer, or more often he was a teetotaller, so nobody got a beer that day.

The crew boss would calculate the acres done and those still to go, the payments due and what kind of time we were making, what the weather was likely to do. If the farmer wasn't around, the crew boss would tell us where our next work prospects were and the general plan for loading up and driving on in however many days. As we came close to finishing in one place, the boss would take off ahead to drum up work, usually no more than a day's drive away, so he'd get back each night. Over our supper plates, the crew would tell stories of nearly crumpling a header on rocks or in treacherous gullies not visible from high up in the cab, the damage heroically averted by last-minute attention and skill at the wheel and precision working of the hydraulics. Or they would tell of tough spots where the blades weren't cutting clean and how they solved that problem with amazing ingenuity, and everybody would get up and go over to check the blades and see, sure enough. Sometimes the talk went around to run-ins with other crews at the gas tanks in the mornings or at the bar the night before. I listened to it all, loving the sound of talk about our work without really caring what anyone said, feeling like I belonged there, I had a crew and work sufficiently tiring to put me to sleep every night. Always in those fields, there was the fading light, the perfect setting for the loneliness of evening, the body tired from work and the radio playing country music down low.

The crew was always polite about my cooking, though I don't kid myself that it was anything but just good enough. My one spectacular failure was when I added half a cup of ground coffee to the chili for some reason, something I'd read but didn't have time to fully understand, maybe thinking in a hurry how it made sense because coffee came from the same Spanish world as chili con carne, and I thought I would impress the crew with an ingredient that would not be identifiable as coffee but make the chili irresistibly flavourful. I could well imagine the flavour, I just couldn't make it. All the unbrewed coffee grounds did was get stuck in our teeth and make the whole mess taste like black bile, and the crew never stopped teasing me about that every chance they got, that supper a complete bust, and we all filled up on bread and butter or went hungry that night. I read that the chuckwagon cooks were rated in the Old West by the quality of their baking powder biscuits, the source of the jokes about the biscuits on *Gunsmoke*, when the seemingly dopey but good-hearted Festus, the cowboy clown who lacks tact and all the other social graces, complains about breaking a tooth on them. I don't think I attempted biscuits for the harvesters, but I have since, and they were not as good as Elly May Clampett's on *The Beverly Hillbillies*, who made them as hard as rocks and drew the scorn of her cousin Jethro, and I'm glad I never tried making them for my crew. I learned early on that it was quite enough to have something hot, edible, filling, and on the spot when they needed it. Lots of crews didn't have cooks, so they had to eat in diners and pay their own food bills, meal by meal, which would become pretty expensive over a harvest season, until they'd owe their souls to the company store if the amounts came off their wages, and often crews weren't allowed the time it took to get into town and back, so they had to take junk food snacks in their cabs to get through the day and eat just one big meal, usually deep fried, at the roadside bar when they finished for the night. On our crew, the food was paid for, our wages calculated accordingly, and it came to about five dollars a day for each person, which thriftiness was as important as the taste of the meals, and I was highly praised for my good planning, if not for my actual cooking.

I'd often linger in the field after supper when the machines had gone back to work, watching their lights hover off into the distance. I'd plan the next meal in my head and how I'd get a start on it as soon as I got the dishes done. Every night I repacked my mess boxes with the cleaned dishes and checked all my ingredients for the next day's meals, thankful all the while I didn't have to tend horses, too, or cook out in the field, or gather cow or buffalo chips to fuel my stove. In the end, I didn't spend much time reading that whole season except for the Kinette cookbook. I dawdled over the familiar names of all the women who had contributed their best recipes that were saving my bacon now. I imagined their families, most of whom I knew because I had taught their kids how to swim at the Assiniboia pool, and I thought about how a particular meal was their favourite as I prepared it, and how food was passed around like love at meal tables all over town, levelling the pecking order from the youngest female to the most senior male in the shared need for food. I was usually too tired to open a book I'd brought or a paperback picked up at a gas station, and anyway I usually ran out of light by the time I crawled into my tent with the flashlight, and I would be too tired to hold both the flashlight and a book, so I would fall into a deep untroubled sleep the minute my head hit the pillow. That was heaven to me, the physical tiredness at the end of the day, the sense of the day's work done, and down into sleep under the cold light of the stars, and I'm pretty sure that pleasure, however modest and ancient, must be how women get through the twenty or so years of raising children, cooking and cleaning for them and a husband, and I wrote in my journal, once we moved on to Oklahoma, that I didn't think I could do it for that long, or without wages, the little bundle of cash I'd have when I got home for setting out on whatever might come next, which might be anything, living as I then did in the ongoingness of my eternal youth.

My later journal entries, once we finished at Hobart and moved north along Highway 183 and then 83 to Selden, Kansas, were written with a memorable pen I bought at Karl's store. Over the counter, as Karl wrapped my things in brown paper that he tied with string, he told me his only child, his son, had moved to Alaska and thereafter flew over Canada many times, probably right over southwestern Saskatchewan, even Assiniboia, when he came home to Selden to visit, though Karl himself had not yet flown, having no desire to leave the ground, he added with a wry smile. The dreamy image of his son's flights, the contrails the plane would write across the heavens, connecting far-flung points, I knew well, having watched them form and then disappear from jet exhausts, the planes overhead so high as to be invisible, but drawing the only lines you could see across the prairie sky, and thinking, as I often had, of who might be up there looking down at that very moment and what they would see. Karl's attempt to draw a connection between his world and mine in the contrails of the jets his son was flying in, imagining our time and space intersecting, or almost, and connecting us, his reaching for something to talk about with me, a drifter passing through Kansas, to expand the ground of commonality in the most gracious country and western way, gave me pause to think of the daily and common criss-crossing of perspectives, how he saw me and I saw him, how we were positioned on either side of the wainscoted store counter, and, taking up my parcel, I didn't notice that he neglected to put the pen inside it.

Even years later cruising the radio dial on clear nights anywhere on the Great Plains, I could pick up the voice of a silver-tongued devil, seemingly from the farthest reaches of the universe, with news about the contrails and other ephemeral or unexplained phenomena in the night skies, what might be at home in the world beside or beyond this one, a voice audible only once the noise of the day quieted down. Art Bell's show *Coast to Coast* broadcast through the night from a trailer in the Nevada desert, a place called Pahrump in Nye County, so his slogan, "Broadcast from the Kingdom of Nye," was only half in jest since Bell took an apocalyptic view in confronting what he saw as the end times, always nigh. His voice had just a hint of a plea in it, not the paranoid defensiveness of the conspiracy theorist, harangue of the evangelist, or complacency of any majority presumption, but the tone of a genuine seeker. I could listen for hours, like Eve to the serpent at her ear. His interviews and talks were all about psychic phenomena, the occult, UFOs, alien abductions, mind control, the discrepancies in accounts of what happened or did not happen on the grassy knoll in Dallas when Kennedy was shot, the hushed-up ET landing at Roswell's Area 51, global warming early on, whether it was really happening or a sign of "the Quickening," and who really controls the internet, how much do they already know, what has been revealed, and who is watching, all the mysteries easily ignored, discounted, or suppressed in the full light of day, but looming sinister as a voice in the dark overheard by the sleepless and distressed on the outskirts of any blue rodeo, out on the road with work that doesn't get them home every night, or ever, especially out on the plains, dominated as they are by the enormous sky and so few natural obstacles to inhibit or even slow the outward pulsations of radio waves and their spread of conspiracies of religion, physics, and politics.

Bell interviewed all the speakers, expert and amateur, engineers, astrophysicists, meteorologists, cosmologists, believers, unbelievers, all claiming or trying to tell the difference, at 30,000 feet or from video shot from God knows where, between contrails of exhaust with traceable mechanical causes and chemical sources, and those calling for some other kind of explanation that then opened the floodgates to a wild diversity of interpretation and related stories that circulated through the night air. Suknaski adopted the jet contrails conspicuous over Wood Mountain and all over the Palliser Triangle skies into his conceptual art gift exchange every year with the Winnipeg artist Mike Olito. In a letter in December, Suknaski would enclose a drawing he'd made of a triangle starting at the point where he happened to be in the world, which he would then connect by a line to wherever Olito was on the map, and then connect the two points to a third point—Havana, Buenos Aires, Moose Jaw, Mankota, St. Boniface, Dallas, or Dodge. In a caption, he would write a justification of that third point and make the triangulation of stars his gift, writing "I give you all the constellations of stars within this triangle on Christmas night," something like that. And Olito would reciprocate in kind or with an answering concept, and ever since Suknaski told me about it, and even before I actually read *The Palliser Papers* or gave serious thought to the profound significance of the triangle, the geometric form and geographic territory that maps my coordinates, I slipped into a habit of locating myself at the point wherever I was, Zanzibar, Orlando, Bracebridge, Rivière-du-Loup, Miramichi, and connecting it to some point within the Palliser Triangle—Mom in Assiniboia, Dad in Swift Current or Cantuar, Suknaski in Wood Mountain—and then I would amuse myself with choosing the third point, any place in the world where I'd been, or where I'd never been but imagined a connection through someone I'd met and wondered about, such as Karl, or some place I'd heard of in a song, Sudbury, Kansas City, Nashville, St. Louis. The stars inside my triangle would be my gift to somebody, anybody who wouldn't think it silly (all too few), and Suknaski told me he'd got the idea from lying in Tonita's pasture on lazy afternoons when he'd been told in no uncertain terms to stay out of trouble, so he watched the contrails criss-cross the sky, everybody going somewhere else and passing over Wood Mountain, and they gave structure and destinations to his wayfaring, he said, a way of mapping it across the sky, always at least one coordinate on the Great Plains or one line crossing over them, the way to locate yourself anywhere from there, so you would always know where you were, which my mother told me to keep track of for myself. "It doesn't matter if I know where you are," she would say if I phoned home. "What matters is that you know where you are." Her words sent a chill up my spine as I realized I was on my own and should not look to her or anyone else to know where I was.

On the contrails, Bell was noncommittal about all the theories he entertained, usually. He made his libertarian views known from time to time, his support for the gun laws, for example, but he did not necessarily go along with all the conspiracies that pulsated on his air waves. His contract with the people he interviewed and the listeners who called in, likely the key to his popularity and high ratings, was to hear all that people had to say without ridicule or judgment. The plea in his voice I imagined was the sound of his straining, which the listener then began to mimic, to understand what people were saying about what they thought and how they arrived at that far point. Was it the truth they had arrived at, or was it just the story told to protect themselves from what was too terrible to look at or even contemplate could exist? All this Bell would then retail, some recountings of sightings and testing and theorizing going on for hours into the night and continuing in repeat appearances of the guests over several broadcasts, daily, weekly, monthly. I found it riveting though never entirely a believer, since I had decided pretty early on that things are all too complicated for any single person or idea to trace let alone orchestrate and control, even from 30,000 feet or more. To think all this was carefully planned made me shudder and then laugh, and I dismissed the idea with relief and a dose of my mother's self-certainty that we knew what was what. But still, I had to admit Bell tapped into a cosmic shadowland of fears and wishes of the America that believes the world, even the universe, is talking to it, sending messages that malignant forces amplify or obstruct or devour completely in the transmission, that run interference to disrupt the signals only the most technologically adept and equipped might decipher if the noise of the day is sufficiently toned down. It was the sound of paranoid America, and the names of his callers and experts wafted away eventually, like the contrails themselves, ghosts before the insatiable need, sounded in the voices, of longing for the place not here that we never arrive at, that we dream can be dwelt in, where life lives and the answers are.

When I got back to the crew trailer from Karl's store, I immediately had to start baking or chopping something, so I didn't notice the pen I had bought was missing from my purchases. After an hour or so, I heard the softest little tapping at the screen door of the trailer and turned to see Karl standing there, smiling and holding up my pen. He had come over as soon as he realized he hadn't put it in my package. "But who is at the store?" I asked. He assured me it was no trouble. His wife used to help when he had errands, but she passed away last year, "so I just lock the door and put up my 'Back in 5 Minutes' sign. The part-time boy is busy over at Lyle's today."

It must have been that very pen that I used to work on my vocabulary all through that travelling harvest season. I must have had a dictionary in the trailer, too, because my journal is filled with definitions I copied out of the hard words in Margaret Atwood's poems in *You Are Happy*, far from happy words when isolated on my list: *ennui, impervious, suppliants, extortion, iridescent, forsake, wane, acquiescent, auguries, molten, distended*. How do people know these things? I wondered, as I laboured with the dictionary on top of the cutting board among my knives and potatoes. It was the only book of poetry I had with me then and by coincidence I would still clutch tightly when everything went flying after the events in the corral. Eventually, the poems gave me the same feeling I had about my mother not saying something, withholding a significance, something everyone knew yet escaped me in my ever-expanding ignorance. There might have been jokes and ironies I missed, not to mention the happiness, because of not having the vocabulary to be sure of what was being said. I later took the idea of second-person narration for my "Legend of Ruined Children" from the title, as I think I might have mentioned somewhere, selecting the "You" in "You Are Happy" as an invitation to occupy that vacant pronoun that conflates the writer with the reader, both happy, or convincing ourselves we are despite all the ennui, whatever the cause, or despite coming upon a deer carcass tossed in a ditch, missing its head, that image far more lingering and ghastly than if only the head was left, the severed head of wildlife familiar in my world to the point of being invisible among all the glassy-eyed mounted heads with majestic antlers presiding over the Elks or any community hall.

The trouble with the heads of taxidermy, severed and stuffed, why they are so hard to look at, I thought, is the confusion of seeing the animal in its dead and perfectly preserved state, eyes and fur, horn and tooth and claw, that makes it look so alive. Yet its lifelikeness depends entirely on the animal's annihilation, possibly at the hands of a hunter who can't be bothered to carve up the meat and so leaves the carcass in the ditch, a hunter unworthy of the sacrifice of a life, and who tries to compensate by making that trip to the taxidermist. Another kind of imperial nostalgia. Longing for and reproducing the life of what you've just killed. To look that stuffed animal in the eye is to look straight into a contradiction, alive and dead at the same time, and hence the prominence of the antlers or horns, celebration and veneration of the tips of the horns at a safe remove, the animal now a bit of heaven. More down to earth than any mounted head or beast, strangely enough, are the ceramic or bronze horses, cows, buffalo, deer, and human figures cast by Joe Fafard at his workshop in Pense along the eastern line of the Palliser Triangle. Fafard's creatures are altogether more at home on Earth than the real thing dead and stuffed, even the few head of bronze cattle lazing around at the foot of the bank skyscrapers in downtown Toronto, those cows a bit larger than life size. We rely on the names Fafard gives his creatures, usually not in a herd but single and alone, such as Jeanette or Frieda Kahlo, Queen Elizabeth, Ma mère, Cree Man. Unusual is his sculpture of a buffalo basking in a full setting, domestic and wild at the same time. A large cow or bull—it has horns, but is that a sack of testicles or a bit of udder bulging out from beneath its girth?—sits contentedly on the triangular top of a three-legged parlour table that is also a pasture, tufts of grass forming a fringe, like a tablecloth, sticking out from underneath. Looking at the whole thing becomes awkward when your eye trails downward and you realize the table, a triangle on top, way down at the bottom, has four feet. The confounding disjunction of three legs ending in four feet confuses the eye, and therefore perception. We look from above, as if we are gods, casting it as a vertical top-down construction.

The buffalo is unconcerned, likely unaware of trouble approaching, while beneath its horizon, under the surface pasture of the tabletop where it lies, on the other side of the world, a small lunar orb dangles on a string, invisible to the buffalo, for whom nothing is amiss. The dangled moon has set, and the break of a new day is imminent, while farther down, on the lower shelf of the table below the moon, two triangles of rungs are fitted together to make a square with four corners and four feet that call for the fourth table leg that is missing. On that lower shelf is a small galleon ship with a central mast and sails perhaps just filling with propelling winds. Some kind of coating on the shelf rungs conveys movement, making the ship seem to ride the ocean's waves, in contrast to the stillness of the resting buffalo and the moon in the higher spheres. The title of the work is long and tells a whole story: *The Evil Moon Guides the* Santa Maria *to the New World*. The three-tiered construction of the parlour table places the buffalo on top as a kind of god in heaven and makes the triangular surface the Trinity, in a Christian view. The moon dangles below, about where the fourth leg would be, its face pocked by the shadows of evil. What can we call this middle lunar sphere if the buffalo's earth is the heaven on top? The whole work is an alternative order, a reordering. Maybe it's what Fafard imagined existed before the *Santa Maria* docked, when the buffalo was the Manitou and life on earth was sacred, and heaven wasn't imagined to be the hereafter, always somewhere else, but here and now in the present of the buffalo and all the beasts of the field. Fafard's lower shelf is placed where hell would be in the Christian order, on the lowest level, the plane where

Columbus's third ship—puny in comparison to the buffalo in heaven—sails inexorably toward the end of the world, at least from the perspective of the buffalo, were it to peer into the abyss opening beneath, to foresee what the ship's arrival might mean for its kind.

Of course, the buffalo does not look down, nor could it see into those depths at the end of the world, and I notice how Fafard, in addition to rearranging heaven and earth with this sculpture, locates the moment before the impending catastrophe when the heaven presided over by the Buffalo God might come crashing down, taking the animal by surprise, in the arrival of the ships. Those aboard were likely thinking they were sailing toward a new world, and this sad prospect, knowing what we now know, casts the buffalo as the incarnation of melancholy on the Great Plains, the creature sacrificed to the expansion of Europe, the sheer physical power and energy that the colonial intrusion required and what it destroyed, what was risked and thought worth the risk. Then again maybe the discrepancy between the three legs and four feet of Fafard's parlour table poses a visual challenge to any vertical vision of the world with heaven on top, the three-cornered surface insufficient in relation to the four corners of the Earth, the four strong winds, the four elements of earth, air, fire, and water that correspond with the four humours—sanguine, choler, phlegm, and melancholy—that served for over 1,000 years as both more and less than scientific medicine does in treating tremors and disturbances of the mind, our melancholy, especially in relation to the places the mind occupies, where it goes when lost, and the alterations that shape and follow those troubles in the firing of bronze and composition of stories.

On reflection, the missing fourth leg of Fafard's parlour table might point to the space or territory overcome in the colonial expansion, a transformation by which time also is reconfigured as unidirectional in the forward movement of progress from the Old World to the New, from land into territory, and then property, and every last plain and tree, river and rock, is subjected to the geometry of the surveyor for the erection of fences, borders, walls, for the disturbances of plows, borings of mine shafts, terrors of the bulldozer, tombs of asphalt. The lower shelf of Fafard's parlour table, meanwhile, appears to slope down toward the viewer, toward the unanchored fourth foot of the three-legged table. That's the slippery slope we occupy, our slide down to hell all but assured. To save us, the table will have to be toppled, for this is the opposite of a bull in a china shop. Not the bull but the parlour table is out of place, vertically flimsy, unstable, absurd on the windswept horizontal plains. To maintain it upright, that fourth leg would have to be built, new construction to support the fourth foot—the work of a Nimrod.

Except for about 1,000 individuals, including a lone bull that strayed in from Montana and was photographed at Wood Mountain in 1935, the entire buffalo species slid off, were chased or shot, stampeded into pounds, off jumps and cliffs, and the Indigenous peoples who lived by them similarly were driven onto reserves to the northeast, Carry the Kettle and elsewhere along the rim of the Qu'Appelle Valley, and the same fate of dispersal has been met by most of the offspring of the settlers who displaced them on the Great Plains, the homesteads within the Palliser Triangle abandoned or lost after the prolonged droughts of the 1930s and successive concentrations of land ownership that have not abated to this day. Where once there were 100 farm families, now there may be just one. The population density is indicated on maps as "sparse," numerically as 0.4–<10 persons per square kilometre on the Canadian side. So the deaths within a single month in 1979 of Johnny Bradley and my dad were a demographic decimation in addition to everything else they were. I myself left in 1988, the three exits together representing one-third of the population of, say, Bradley's home quarter within nine years. Just the year before, in 1987, geographers Frank and Deborah Popper published their essay "The Great Plains: From Dust to Dust." Their research showed hundreds of American counties on the

Great Plains with no more than six persons per square mile, many with fewer than two. Although overall North American population levels, including those in Saskatchewan outside the Palliser Triangle, are holding, largely through immigration of people fleeing conflagrations elsewhere on the globe, evacuation of the Great Plains continues, fluctuating only in dispersed localities in varying responses to the dominant boom-bust economic cycles of resource extraction, agriculture, and ranching. That depopulation is what prompted the Poppers, like Johnny Bradley and my dad, to attempt a re-envisioning of the plains as a "Buffalo Commons." They were trying to imagine the viability of reconnecting over 400 million acres of wild grasslands, much of them abandoned or about to be, that occupy the geographic centre of the continent from the apex of the Palliser Triangle at Manitou Lake and extending south as far as the deserts of Chihuahua in Mexico. The Poppers thought of trying to re-establish continuous ecological corridors large enough for buffalo herds and other native prairie wildlife while at the same time restoring the health and sustenance of human communities that persist there, however sparsely populated. Many plains peoples, as the Poppers readily acknowledge in their subsequent article, "The Buffalo Commons: Metaphor as Method," published in the *Geographical Review*, reject the idea of the Buffalo Commons, disliking especially the "commons" element because of its association with collectivism and its presumed lack of individual freedom and choice believed to be guaranteed only by privately owned property. The Poppers defend their terms as effective in generating discussion of alternative futures for the region, even if private rather than communal ownership of property, or some combination of the two, which exists even now, is adopted in the end.

"We conceived the Buffalo Commons in part as a literary device," they write, "a metaphor that would resolve the narrative conflicts—past, present and most important . . . future—of the Plains." Their metaphor was drawn "from a narrative about how the region was shaped" and intended to help "move the story past nostalgia to make understanding of place a cutting edge means for adaptation." They see "a growing recognition that the idea of the Buffalo Commons makes environmental, economic, and perhaps most important, imaginative sense—that it suggests plausible options for many places, choices other than casinos, prisons, hazardous waste, agribusiness, or continued long-term decline. We confidently expect the Buffalo Commons to keep acquiring the muscle of reality," they write, even stating that "the question is no longer why or whether the Buffalo Commons will occur, but how."

The Poppers selected the metaphor of the buffalo because it already serves as a symbol in the West given its role "as symbol and sustenance for both Native American and Euroamerican populations in the Plains," which suggests it can bear the yoke of the racial and ethnic as well as economic reconciliation needed but hardly imaginable otherwise. "Buffalo shaped the landscape with their migrations," write the Poppers, "trampling and rolling, loosening soil, bringing along other wildlife. Migrating across the Plains, they presented a visual point on the horizon that broke up the meeting of earth and sky. They signified the landscape and culture of the Plains. [Yet t]heir fate served as a warning." These two sides of the word *buffalo*—sustenance and its near extinction—make it an ambivalent symbol and premise, the negative side pointing to inevitable decline, yet stimulating motivation to do something about it, the positive side stirring romantic desire in cowboys such as Johnny Bradley and Dad for the unfenced plains, and generating the very image of freedom from constraint, making the word *buffalo* the means to contemplate the decline yet bring to mind possible remedies. The Poppers use that word *buffalo* as I do, instead of the more accurate *bison*, as they explain, because it is more familiar and "taps" a richer array of "allusions." The word *commons*, more controversially, makes the land a shared resource like air or water because, as geographers, the Poppers define the natural environment as social and public, not solely individual and private, whatever its ownership arrangements. The problems affecting the Great Plains cross international borders as well as private property lines, and both kinds of boundaries might be non-viable to maintain, in some cases too expensive, like the southwestern Saskatchewan part of the Palliser Triangle that is now Grasslands National Park, so designated by a Conservative government that was averse to public ownership but stepped in as the owner of last resort when retiring or dying or broke ranchers found no buyers, and the disappearance of the landowners or holders of the leases threatened to leave it untenanted, and the large territory, not to mention the border itself, vulnerable to encroachment by elements foreign, criminal, unimaginable.

Fully acknowledging their term "Buffalo Commons" was a mere literary device, the Poppers describe their method as a purposeful release of words into the wild, an ecological move with not only geographic but also literary significance. They waited to see how the term "Buffalo Commons" would fare, like watching whooping cranes first totter on spindly legs and then thrive on their way back from the brink of extinction. Despite bitter disparagement and rejection, especially by those overly alert to the slightest curtailment of private property rights, no matter how literary or provisional or abstract, the Poppers list the Grasslands National Park, the U.S. National Bison Association, the Inter-Tribal Bison Cooperative (a consortium of forty-four Native American governments), the Buffalo Commons Storytelling Festival at McCook, Nebraska, hundreds of articles and books, fact and fiction, including a novel with the title *The Buffalo Commons*, thriving stock production and robust tourism initiatives, especially in North Dakota but also in Yellowstone National Park, where in the first six months of 2015 five tourists were injured, none fatally, when backing up close to park buffalo to snap selfies, and took the horns in the back, in the side, and elsewhere, yet lived to tell the tale that is convincingly illustrated by the pictures circulated around the globe.

"A useful geographic or regional metaphor," write the Poppers, "has to be open-ended, multi-faceted, and ambiguous" to allow for the broadest range of interpretation and response. The metaphor should be more allusive than programmatic so it creates "a place apart, space for reflection" that "works especially well in times of great change, disorder, or disjunction." The Poppers go on to cite the "metaphor of Silicon Valley for the computer-driven industries of the San Francisco Peninsula," the now indispensable term casually coined "in 1971 as the title of a trade press article on the growth of the semiconductor industry in the overall Bay Area." I could cite, too, the still fanciful "Ring of Fire" of northwestern Ontario, where a find of mineral chromite was named by an investor and devotee of the country and western music of Johnny Cash. Already 35,000 claims have been staked in the lands encircled by the Ring of Fire, and seven or eight First Nations bands or tribal councils are equipping themselves to control, or at least benefit from, or at least minimize the damage that might be done in the construction of infrastructure and the circulation of wealth to be generated, which all levels of government, not to mention stock markets and all their dogs, are salivating over, despite the lack of actual flames or a single speck of chromite materializing to date. The most ambivalent of forces, fire, evokes both the pleasures and the dangers of love, and that doubleness rings out in the refrain of Spanish fanfare by raised trumpets of brass quite at home in Cash's country song. The ring is the wedding band that encircles and defines the bonds of love, and at the same time it's a constricting, even choking, device that might have a suffocating effect, just as the miners, investors, and Cree and Ojibway peoples of northwestern Ontario might flourish or fail beyond their wildest dreams or worst nightmares in the mining of chromite.

Paul Rickard, the Cree director of a documentary series called *Ring of Fire* made for APTN, the Aboriginal Peoples Television Network, told me he and the local people, Ojibway and Cree, whose lands are touched by the Ring don't use the term "Ring of Fire" but have coined what he called a hybrid Oji-Cree phrase. I spell it phonetically as I heard Rickard pronounce it, *shue-lee-yawn assin*, which translates as "money stone or rock," the last word, *assin*, also lodged in my town of Assiniboia, the "stone" or "rock" part of its name referring to the Stone Sioux who originally lived there and cooked with hot stones. We laughed, Rickard and I, at how, in spite of the attempt to distance themselves from the colonial language of English and the country and western song, the Oji-Cree word for the Ring of Fire makes another kind of link to it in the word *shue-lee-yawn*, or "money," which remembers the name of the singer, Cash, who made the song famous and beloved.

Coming up with a good metaphor is not exactly the same as ensuring a good outcome, as the Poppers note, and the outcome of both the Buffalo Commons and the Ring of Fire remains to be seen. Only the ambivalence of a term invites the many perspectives needed to activate and allow it to flourish in shaping the space that the metaphor calls into being. The Poppers note, too, that more rigorously postmodern or deconstructive geographers would concern themselves at the outset with exposing how a metaphor is both used and abused, how it "shifts over time and operates to naturalize power relationships" and in the process can justify exploitative, oppressive, and even violent values. They cite the questions raised about who and what the term "Silicon Valley" leaves out, for example, just as we might be anxious about who and what will get burned as the mining and marketing of chromite gets under way in the Ring of Fire. And here the Poppers' metaphor of a Buffalo Commons, now blowing in the wind, now smouldering underground beneath the Great Plains, both resembles and departs from the yet to be ignited Ring of Fire that brands and reduces a territory to the source of one mineral. The burning into flesh of the mark of ownership, the ranching form of branding, might become obsolete on a Great Plains held in common, its plants and animals, water, weather, and skies valued as priceless, as habitat and home that connect communities of humans and animals with the land rather than as extractable and mobile products, separately priced resources, or parcels of square footage to circulate and overwhelm Indigenous life and values.

In their article on the history of branding, theory and practice, in the *Journal of Historical Research in Marketing*, Wilson Bastos and Sidney Levy liken branding to naming. A brand starts as a sign, they write, "a way of denoting an object is what it is," which then becomes what is named—"a steer, a slave, a prisoner, a detergent"—their telling list tracing the transformation of branding from its origins in the stigmata of ownership of animals and humans into a seemingly benign mark of propriety in the marketplace. "The brander is often regarded as superior to the branded," they concede. Branding has "strong roots in human motives for power, conquest, and domination," they write, before going on to track its core association with fire and burning, as in the Ring of Fire. Bastos and Levy find the origins of the word *brand*, among other ancient sources, in a translation of a play by the Greek tragedian Euripides. In *The Bacchae*, the brand is linked to the deity known as Bacchus or Dionysus, the god of wine and intoxication as well as of writing. The god's mother, Semele, is referred to as "the brand" and "Lightning's Bride" because she dies in a lightning bolt when her wish to see the face of Zeus in all his glory is granted and she accepts the condition that the vision will destroy her. Their child, Dionysus, survives when he is ripped from her belly at the very moment she perishes in fire, the mother becoming what is sacrificed in "the brand." Semele gives birth to the "lightning-bearing fire," according to an alternative translation consulted by the authors, and they link this usage to the metaphor "firing up," giving life to something, an engine, a campaign, a story, or a song. Not only through ancient literary transmission, but also through the root words in English, the brand is linked to flaming torches and hot irons, and to passionate motivation, even sexually expressed desires, "fire in the belly" for our cause, without which not much is to be done beyond mere subsistence.

Fire is warm and comforting, write the scholars, in their search for the life-giving origins of branding, perhaps to justify marketing's embrace of a term and an activity with marked painful and exploitative associations. Fire lights the way and characterizes people who care strongly about their ideas and feelings. The "brand new" object or idea still sizzles with "the heat of its creation and freshness of its information." But fire is also the destroyer, of course, and they do touch on the "firebrand," the "piece of burning wood" and its afterlife as the metaphor for the "agitator" who creates "strife and unrest in aggressively promoting a cause" to the brink of what resists it. Bastos and Levy go on to enumerate how unacceptable individuals or their effigies are burned at the stake. We speak of a "fiery temper," of "getting fired from a job," and there is the gesture of brandishing, to wave something menacingly, a weapon, or to display wealth and well-being with ostentation. In short, its origin in fire accounts for branding's intensification of significance well beyond the utility of the thing branded, cell phone, waterfront property, or shoes. Branding "generates feelings of partisanship and opposition, of power and excitement," the authors note. It commands conformity and at the same time "arouses criticism and resistance against its domination."

The section of the Bastos and Levy article immediately following this review of fire and lightning in the origin of branding is titled "The Early Days of Modern Branding," but I am disappointed to find they move on to commercial marketing and even branding's displacement of the term "marketing," along with the corporate department formerly called Marketing, instead of exploring branding's sources in and resonances for the country and western world of branding cattle and other livestock, about which they have little to say, despite their setting at the University of Arizona in Tucson. Still, it's telling that something as thoroughly country and western as livestock branding, its centrality and importance until recently in the Americas, North and South, goes without saying in a history of the very world of commerce and consumption to which the brand has migrated in the formation of an economy that has not been insignificant in depopulating the Great Plains, increasingly uninhabitable as much by people as by buffalo. Wherever the Buffalo Commons has got to by now, by the wayside for the time being of pipelines, yes or no, now or never, I have to hope it has legs, since it so fully answers the cause of reclaiming the Great Plains and putting us all on a more secure and life-giving footing, Indigenous, immigrant, and settler descended.

All through that travelling harvest season, I picked up radio signals from across the plains, and one night late, the volume down low in my tent, I tuned in to Austin, Texas, while fiddling with the dial, and part of a chorus caught my ear, and I zeroed in. It was a whole show about somebody named Gram Parsons. He was accompanied by the angelic harmonies of Emmylou Harris, their voices wavering through the radio night air, something about a return of the "grievous angels." It was a campus radio station playing a new kind of country music linked to Parsons and The Byrds, and The Eagles, that was getting airplay on rock but not country stations, until the deejays caught on, and they were just then catching on, that the music was mixing rock and country in a new way, like "Desperado," the words written by urban cowboys Glenn Frey and Don Henley in Los Angeles, the loneliness intensifying, cutting a deeper and more jagged line between country life and city lights, what cut right through everybody boarding a bus or swinging up into a transport truck or hitching a ride to get out of Dodge and go where the work was and a living could be made. That's when I fell in love with radio, too, the selection and introduction of the songs by someone else who shared something more than a song, the beats and grooves we all heard together, and heard at the same time all over the country, the sounds wavering through the air to be picked up by who knows what random and remote but now receiving and connected minds, and it made me homesick for my dad's world of Hank Williams, the honky-tonk, so

lonesome I could cry. They went on and on about Parsons, how
his father fought in the Second World War and was at Pearl
Harbor, and then killed himself two days before Christmas
when Parsons was only fifteen, and how his mother remar-
ried but then slowly drank herself to death in the early 1960s.
They played the song Parsons wrote about her, "Brass Buttons,"
which for me recalled my own mother's love for the fashion
found in the *Ladies' Home Journal* that Mom would sew for
herself, and how we tried on all those clothes when she was out
of the house, each outfit a perfect story with a colour picked
out from the printed fabric for matching shoes, purse, gloves,
nail polish, lipstick. All this washes over me, the special bond
Mom and I shared before our fight over writing and her compromising gifts of the tea towels, how we had exchanged knowing looks and laughs about how she always wanted to know
what I'd had for supper no matter where in the world I went,
how many bulls I wrestled, deadlines I met, books I read, jobs
I landed and left. What was important for her was what did
you have for supper and how did it get to the plate, not a triv-
ial way of recording the days, as I was learning even then. It
became the knowing joke between us about how much work
and calculation go into getting food on the table when everybody just orders up and chows down without a thought about
who made or grew or slaughtered it and at what cost. Mom
must have been pleased when I got the crew cook job, though
she never said anything. All through those late radio nights,
and with my own family's disintegration going on without me,
I was preoccupied with the story of Parsons and how he made
those songs out of it, and I strained to hear more and more
of his song "Hickory Wind." I could pick up the Austin signal
for quite a while, but eventually had to cruise the dial to find
another station playing his *Grievous Angel* songs, until I put
together why his name was so much in the air. He was already a
legend and a dead man, his album coming out in 1974, the year
after he died, and credited with setting the stage for the fusion
of country and pop rock by The Eagles.

Parsons was pronounced dead at 12:15 a.m. on September 19, 1973, when his friends found him apparently asleep but unresponsive. He had taken an overdose of morphine although already drunk on alcohol, and we will never know for sure if he intended to die or if it was an accident. I read he began to use heroin and cocaine while staying for a brief time somewhere in France with Keith Richards of The Rolling Stones. He introduced the Stones to country and western music, and they thanked him with their song "Wild Horses" and by introducing Parsons to heroin, as the story goes. After his death, his body went missing from the Los Angeles International Airport, where his stepfather Bob waited to collect it. Bob was in line to inherit Gram's share of the Parsons estate if it could be demonstrated Gram had been resident in Louisiana. But the stepdad had neglected to invite Gram's friends to the burial in Louisiana, so they borrowed a hearse from their friends—and you have to wonder who has friends with an extra hearse in the driveway, but anyway—and snatched the body, I don't know, maybe from the tarmac, loaded it into the borrowed hearse, and drove out to Joshua Tree National Park, claiming Gram had said he wanted his ashes spread there. They tried to cremate the corpse by pouring four or five gallons of gasoline into the coffin and then throwing a match into it. Instead of a purifying fire to fulfill their revered and talented friend's wishes, there was a huge explosion that attracted wardens and police officers, who gave chase, but the thieves escaped through the woods and across the desert, and when the law finally caught up with them they were charged only with the theft of a coffin, which must be a dusty statute, and fined US$750, since the theft of a corpse is not a crime that occurred to the lawmakers, even in the United States, to write into the books. Thirty-five pounds of charred remains were eventually sent to Metairie, Louisiana, and buried in the Garden of Memories Cemetery, and presumably Bob the stepdad got the inheritance, and Gram's friends later marked the cremation spot in Joshua Tree National Park with a concrete slab next to an outcropping of rocks that hikers then named The Gram Parsons Memorial Hand Traverse. To this day, pilgrims make their way to this unofficial site to write their messages of sorrow at America's loss in the perishing of the singer who dreamed of a cosmic American cowboy music that would bring into contact traditional country, the heart-rending bluegrass of Kentucky and West Virginia, rhythm and blues and soul of the African Americans, Scots and Irish folk songs, and rock and roll. Parsons was the cowboy who lived fast, died young, and left a charred corpse, in the words of the travelling theatre of musicians and devotees who took Parson's album on the road, calling their show *Grievous Angel: The Legend of Gram Parsons.*

Across the Buffalo Commons, so many people had died or left the Great Plains by the time of the Poppers' writing in 1987 that the ratio was down to two persons per square mile in the United States, and it couldn't have been much more than that ten years earlier when I went through with the custom harvest crew, two being the minimum needed, at that time, for human reproduction. Private and corporate ownership of the land, profit for the few, hard labour with low wages and no benefits for merely operating the machinery of grain production, oil and gas extraction, mining, or ranching, and competition for even that seasonal work and for the women who might serve in such a life, hostilities sustained at high tension in the scramble to make money before prices crashed or storms blew in or machines broke down, it doesn't leave much left over for planning ahead even nine months, let alone what's involved in raising even one child to the age of responsibility and making a living of her own. A few of the combining crew members brought girlfriends or wives, a few enterprising women followed along in trailers or stopped by on weekends, and I heard women sometimes showed up in the bars, some with small children tagging along, but mostly it was a world of men, jeans so caked with dirt they'd stand up stiff in the corners on their own long after they were peeled off and their inhabitants had crawled into the bunks to sleep.

SUICIDE NOTES

Eventually, like all the others, settler and Indigenous, I also fled, suicides and corpses piling up, leaching into dreams. Then in 2003 one of my brothers bought the farm, as we say, succumbing to the losses and adding to ours in the evening of the June solstice, when he traded the shortest night of the year for the long night of the dead by running a tube from the exhaust of his half-ton into the air vent of the cab, and sealing up the windows, and then waiting with the engine idling in the coulee that runs through the yard of the Morgan home place, waiting for the balm of oblivion, heaven, the trigger in his case being money troubles, overwhelming arrears of taxes owing and borrowing for seed-cleaning machinery at the very moment when the West Coast grain handlers went on strike, and their bosses held everyone hostage for the longest time to save a dime and turn us against the working class, and that prolonged struggle clogged up the movement of grain for months all across the prairies, cutting off the cash flow he needed to meet the payments by the skin of his teeth, and all other job prospects drying up just then, the usual abusive boom-bust cycle, his indebtedness also partly the result of impatience, not to say indignance, at what we considered the systematic theft of the surplus value he generated for his employers, one after another, along with his repeated sporadic use and abuse of drugs and drink just to get through the day, then the night, we'll never know all of it, despite his thoughtful detailing of each job and each woman and child and every debt and repayment and fine and backsliding that followed each stretch of abstinence. It was all there in an eloquent letter he wrote, five pages long, single spaced, and he could have kept on writing, on and on, past all bounds of prudence and propriety, if only he would have. We were all good readers, and I've made my way through sentences much longer and more convoluted. To keep writing would have been better.

My brother used to say with a laugh he didn't think the capitalist system was working all that well for everybody, and in fact that is precisely how it ensures high profits for the few. For most, he thought, capitalism was *The Road to Serfdom*, the destroyer of the commonwealth, in spite of what the book of that title claims to the opposite. Not only that book came into his hands somehow, but also once when flush he went out and bought *The Collected Works of Karl Marx and Frederick Engels*, the complete set bound in calf, which he might or might not have read cover to cover but for sure dipped into enough to acquire a certain vocabulary and understanding of his place in the scheme of things. He was a ragged-trousered philanthropist, he said, after reading the Robert Tressel novel with that title, both dangerous and ridiculous, made a fool when he was forced to donate to the rich the surplus value of his labour. For him, upward mobility amounted to racing his co-workers to the tops of telephone poles when he worked as a lineman, his climbing spurs and holster of tools jangling, and up on top he would do his wiretapping, listening in just to show he could, yelling "You should hear what everybody is not saying!" and then just as fast swing back down, jump into his truck, and drive to the next pole on the work order, the poles climbed and miles travelled only breaking his back and making him sing "I've got a weak back / Happened about a week back" to anyone who asked how he was doing. None of it, all that work and energy, jokes and pain, it never added up to quite enough, and eventually the work my brother did with such gusto and good humour he resented for wearing him down with only the sensation of climbing up, only seeming to hold out the potential for success, real enough but always only potential for all the dead ends he ran up against, just part of the forces marshalled against him, or any cowboy unhorsed, disowned, and put out of the house. Desperado. The main thing that connects us now, I thought from afar, are those words of disconnection. What everybody is not saying. In the shack of his things, I regret to this day not having had the presence of mind to search for the *Collected Works* or any other remnant of his working man's library, not entering his shack beyond the kitchen table where he'd left the letter. And hearing no report of the *Collected Works* being found among his things, I supposed he had sold them, such a valuable commodity would bring in cash, his life being full of such ironies as much as tyrannies.

His truck was hidden from the road winding past the collapsing farmhouse already covered with lichen the colour of rust and tottering precipitously like a shipwreck after the waters have receded, unmoored from its stone foundation, crumbled to loosened and broken stones, the mortar long since disintegrated. The truck was just visible from the opposite direction, from the field beyond, a piece of the original quarter proved up by Pop Morgan, who like my dad and brother was loved by all, and Pop sang like the Welshman he was and taught us his strange language, the names of his brothers and sisters left behind in Wales, enchanted words and names that filled us with a joyful sensation that our kin are everywhere, lost and found. My brother's truck could be seen from the northwest, if I am not disoriented in memory, the Morgan land then farmed by John Colpitts, son of Willard who stood up as the best man at our parents' wedding. John was like a cousin or brother to us, and he was out with the harrows since the field was fallow that year. When John glimpsed Curt's truck, he recognized it right away, but saw it was still, having run out of gas, my brother's body slumped behind the wheel, a silhouette lit up by the rays of the morning sun. John thought to himself, he told someone later, as his eyes followed the tubes and rigging from exhaust to vent, and the duct tape framing the windows, I don't think we have to worry about Curtis anymore. And that's how we learned how much John had worried about our brother, who nursed a desire to buy back the farm, to redeem it and himself somehow, for raising horses and leaning into the winds, rebuilding the house so we could all come home to him and to Dad and to Pop, once each year, while his life in the meantime was increasingly beggared and misshapen, falling short and falling apart, taking the blows, grief and shame at losing the farm that had fed the dream that destroyed the buffalo and crowded out the Assiniboine, the debts piling up and history bearing down, and then the anchor cut loose when Dad died, my brother having met up with Dad at the bar of the Healy Hotel just after Johnny was killed, in those weeks before April 1, 1979, and their eyes met over their beer, and Dad seemed to ask something of him, and my brother struggled with an inchoate request or reply of his own, the words pressing up against both their throats, never taking shape or finding their way out, and Curt said he felt a tether broke, and Dad was already slipping over the great divide, no weight sufficient to steady or hold him back.

A handwritten note on loose-leaf was found on the dashboard of the pickup. The note directed the finder to a much longer letter left on the kitchen table of the small house in Cabri where my brother had set up housekeeping, a shack really, and it's gone now, but he was fixing it up, and it was home by virtue of its provision of shelter near the home place. The letter is addressed to no single reader, my brother by then being, though on good terms, to some extent also estranged from many ex-wives, girlfriends, three children. He was our Henry VIII. He didn't kill them, the wives, but they left him to save themselves, or he left them for work somewhere else or to chase his homesteading dreams. Who was speaking to whom in those domestic entanglements we didn't necessarily know or keep track of, but in a family scattered to the four corners by a rifle shot fired so long ago and now disinclined to look back or into the wells of sorrow deepening everywhere on the plains, each grasping at farther shores, we didn't find ourselves able to offer a hand to our brother, who had circled back in his distress and floundering and never again fully recovered his balance. And if his final letter had been addressed to someone in particular, the rest of us surely would have taken that as an excuse not to read it, fearing his sentimentality two centuries old and three miles deep, fearing also his reproaches, surely justified, but there was none, only his self-blame and conviction he was finally taking responsibility for the way things had gotten all balled up. He went on about how amazing his family was, his children astounding him, how much he loved and admired us all, how lowly a worm he felt himself in comparison no matter how many workdays done, time sheets punched, wages earned, cheques cashed, bills paid, groceries bought, children born, laughter spread, stories told, for he was quite as hard a worker and jokester and storyteller as Pop and Dad.

There's a reproach, I thought, in the lack of any, despite having his say in such a long letter, and I felt its lash in my inability, now without end, to be my brother's keeper. As for the words Curt finally found to compose his letter, which seemed to rush out of his pen in floods of feeling, they began and proceeded with an incantatory refrain of "Precious to me are . . ." that made him the object instead of the subject of all his sentences, one after another, which struck me as philosophically interesting, his grammar allowing for rearranging and therefore seeing things differently, and seeing different things, oddly, coming at him, the way things looked to him, and I wondered if that conflation of subjects and objects might be a distinguishing mark of the grammar and genre of suicide notes more generally, I mean when all boundaries collapse in on themselves, though I've only ever read just this one note and hope to read no other.

To my brother's point, the implication, intentional or not, and written in a shaking hand, was why should we have to choose between ourselves and our parents? Or between our parents, father and mother? For that matter, why do we so rigidly distinguish the living from the dead, and is that how it actually is? And for whom? Because that's not how it is for us. Divisions that only force us to value one over the other, father or mother, settler or Indigenous, past or future. Why must we choose either/or to make a sentence intelligible according to a grammar that instead should make room for all, and that most generously, rather than the other way around? Precious to my brother all such implications, treacherous and exhilarating, as precious as all the women, his attempts to find or make homes, families, children, his fear of not measuring up, his lines reviewing endless financial battles and embroilments, and he names names and quotes the exact words of the tax collector, with quotation marks, as if deposing in court or before a judge, his own words justifying his decisions in pleading reply, all for naught, but there laid out why he needed just one or two months more, and that time not available or extendable for reasons unbending or withheld, cruel either way. And even though my brother reunited with our dad in death, going to his grave on the Morgan home place, where both were born and all trials began, that letter, his suicide note, tore him from our mother forever.

Mom read the letter first and then tossed it aside, pronouncing it "All lies," distressingly, on the basis of a subordinate clause, a fragment of a single line in a work of portentous density, in which she is said, without reproach, to have thrown Dad out of the house. Until then, most of us thought this an uncontroversial detail, since she felt the back of Dad's hand at least once, though he might have been only drunkenly pawing at the air to keep his balance after staggering in through the back door, late, and they had words, and then Mom's eyeglasses went flying and broke apart across the floor, one of the tiny screws rolling under the sewing machine, which was all I saw from my upstairs perch crouched over the hot air register. If Mom really were a battered wife, then she was justified in throwing Dad out, we probably thought, but she never made that claim, and I think she wasn't, you couldn't say that about her or the situation, except to the extent the threat of violence is always there for all women, but instead she was adamant she gave Dad a choice, and he made his choice, and it was pointedly not her choice to undo the bonds that tied them together, as witnessed by God and Willard Colpitts and Mom's sister, Aunt Jessie. What might have irked her especially was seeing that phrase, "when Mom threw Dad out," which makes her the subject of the verb *to throw*, and to see it put into writing for all of us, where it rang with the truth of the last words of a dying man with no motive to lie or adorn the facts, and for my brother at the touch of a pen to put such words in a document that John Colpitts understandably felt obliged to share with all, a form of publication Mom lacked the power to censor or revise as we strayed back home from afar to mark the passing and countenance the shambles of our brother's life, forgive us our trespasses.

Among those of us gathered at the farm to retrace his steps in the coulee, to scatter and bury his ashes, were his three children, young adults by then, who held hands with each other in the centre of a ragged circle we made, stepping through thick clods of prairie grass in our dress shoes and heels. We encircled them—grandmother, uncles, aunts, husbands and wives, nephews and nieces, and all the children and children's children—as the sun tracked across the sky and the shadows deepened around us like crowds forming, multitudes, and I was startled to suddenly notice a mournful symmetry, something more than a kindred relation, between myself and my brother's oldest daughter, who shares my name and was then twenty-one years old, the exact age I was when my dad ended his life in the ranch house down the road from where their deaths, her father's and mine, now summoned us back to these forlorn fields. We also held hands, my brother's circle of kin opening to ours, ours to his, my niece's long white Welsh hair fluttering up into the wind like swallows, grievous angels, and we were bereft, knowing even the dead are not safe from what unsettles us here, what likewise unsettled the Assiniboine when Treaty 4 was signed on their behalf and without their presence and the creaking of wooden wagon wheels was about to drown out the thundering of buffalo hooves and all our extinctions began.

TRAVELLING THEATRES
OF THE GREAT PLAINS
AND THE ISTHMUS

As soon as we finished at Farnsworth, we headed over to Oklahoma, where we had work lined up to keep us busy for a couple of weeks. Then, on a rainy Saturday, we rolled out of Hobart and drove north into Kansas, where work was waiting for us around Selden to the northwest. Our route took us through Dodge City, and there was no way to avoid driving right through it on the short jog back over to Highway 83 north. I thought there would be some excitement or jokes about driving into Dodge and then getting out of it, sightings of Miss Kitty or Marshall Matt Dillon or something, but the radios went quiet, and I had the sensation the audio in the whole world suddenly went dead. We drove past silent lumberyards and equipment dealers and hardware stores, the drugstore, the courthouse, even a saloon, and it all seemed to go by in slow motion, in some other order of motion, people walking on the streets slowed down or broken up in time, and I thought it seemed that way because of how Dodge is normally just a movie or TV set, a coordinate on the map of our imaginations that studs the language, so everyone knows what it means to say "We have to get out of Dodge," the urgent need to avoid trouble by leaving, or "She never did get out of Dodge," or "There'll be trouble in Dodge," if you do or do not do this or that. So when we pulled into actual Dodge, all those ways of trying to dodge situations or get out of the way of the hammer or stampede, the gunfight at sundown, we found ourselves driving right through it and felt beside ourselves, unnerved, stilled, and maybe a little doubtful about who we were just in those moments, as if we suddenly became aware of ourselves as fictions. Passing the courthouse especially, which I think faced the saloon right across the street (or did I just imagine that?), was like finding myself in a pasteboard pop-up world, like a dollhouse or toy town, but life sized, as if suddenly we were driving through the essence of country and western, familiar and strange, where the law meets the outlaw trying to get out of Dodge, as if the founding myth of the West was a stage on which all the gunslingers got up, dusted themselves off, and walked around, and we were among them, actors on the set, dark strangers riding into town or heading out on a horse with no name.

We passed through Dodge, eventually, and it passed through us, seeming to take forever until the sound of the world, the engines of the vehicles we rode in, came back on like radio signals as we drove nearly all the way to the northern boundary of Kansas in Sheridan County, to the little town called Selden, where we got a sizable contract that placed us right at the crop-ripening line well ahead of the competition. From there, the crew boss could scout for work up in Nebraska once we got going in the Selden fields. The idea was to work steadily all the way north, arriving at and crossing the border just in time for the August ripening of wheat, barley, and rye around Assiniboia, including the crew boss's home place. Long before the drive through Dodge, as if at the bottom of the sea, on leaving Hobart, I thought of the Two Toms of Oklahoma City, my bosses at the fly-in Sportsman's Lodge on McIntosh Lake in northern Saskatchewan, where I had worked as a chambermaid the summer before. I had thought of calling them from Hobart just to say hello, but then feared that might be awkward for some reason, maybe they wouldn't remember me, or they wouldn't consider my job as crew cook much of an improvement in life, if it was at all, over the chambermaid I had been, even though "I was happy" and at home with myself, as much as could be expected, with a job and a crew, but that probably would seem so far beneath them, too remote, and I'd be especially hurt if they said anything discouraging, either one of them, even as a joke, and then the silence on the phone would be unbearable, and I'd blush as I hung up, and my good memories of them would be compromised, if not wiped out, especially if I thought the crew boss or Black Bart overheard while waiting in line to use the phone after me. I couldn't have known then that my job and travels into the heart of the Great Plains of America would soon give me another connection to Oklahoma, one that is still more vivid and had nothing to do with either of the Toms, though it did have to do with geography and class struggle in the travelling nature theatre depicted in *Amerika*, the unfinished novel by Franz Kafka, who had never been there but so well understood the promise it held for the resolution of dreams.

In Selden, I had to allow at least double the usual time to pick up groceries because the store had all its goods on tall shelves up to the ceiling behind the counter that ran the length of the store. I had to recite my list out loud and wait for the shuffling clerk, the old man who owned the store, Karl, who forgot and then remembered my pen and delivered it to my door, whose father had owned the store before him. I had to wait for Karl to fetch each item—cocoa, yeast, onion soup mix, tinfoil—which made my jaw stiffen with fear of his falling and my lungs ache for breath as he rattled a wooden ladder into position and climbed up, teetering a bit when he reached for a dusty can or package with his age-speckled hand, and then slowly climbed back down with only one hand free to hang on and steady himself. If I found this way of shopping to be exhausting, then how much worse it must have been for him, though he seemed to enjoy the company of even just one customer. There was hardly ever anyone else in the store, and Karl was pleasant enough, perhaps even thrilled in the reserved manner of the West, which can be next to impossible to detect. In my notes, I find my account of spending a quiet hour one day on the bench on Main Street in Selden, thinking how the stiffest competition in town was between Karl's store and Lyle's Meat & Grocer, and how fierce could that be since I learned Karl and Lyle were half-brothers and first cousins, and their stores shared one part-time employee, nephew to both, the son of their sister and the local farmer she married. The nephew ran back and forth across the street between the stores as needed. I bought meat and produce from Lyle, non-perishables and dry goods from Karl. The crew boss told me to buy from the local stores wherever possible, in towns no matter how small, and he would then let it be known to the farmers he was haggling with for work, and it would become a selling point in favour of hiring our crew over all others, appealing to the farmer's civic pride and desire to keep the store open by giving it our business. Slow as it was, shopping at Karl's, the quiet ticking minutes it took for Karl to rustle goods out of huge wooden bins or scale the higher-up shelves, was still faster than making the drive to the larger towns such as Hoxie to the south, or up to Oberlin in the next county, where there might have been more modern stores with larger selections of fresher foods. Once I gave in to the slower pace, I came to enjoy the break from the chuckwagon races to and from the fields. It was only when I happened to glance at the receipt from Lyle's one day, and saw the official company name was Rossmann's Inc., or thought that's what it said, that I then thought to ask Karl more about his family.

"How can you and Lyle be half-brothers and first cousins?" I asked Karl when I got up from the bench and went back inside his store.

"Well," he appeared delighted to be asked, "our father married sisters. First he married my mother, and I was born, and we were still living in Oklahoma then. But then my mother took a fall at work—she was a kind of actress for a little theatre outfit. She had to work on these high stilts that I could tell you about, oh boy. So after her fall, she couldn't work, and then she could barely look after me, and then she just got worse and worse, until she passed away, her bones crumbling to bits. She was an angel, my mother, though I barely remember her, just the few things people have told me. And then Dad and I were alone, and I was a motherless child, and Dad always said you would hear a song with that name on the radio around that time, and that was my song, so sad, he said. He had a good job with an engineering firm, you know, even without much education. But he found it tough and needed help to keep the house and take care of me, so he started courting my aunt, my mother's younger sister," and I nodded at the funny practicality of the whole thing, as it often seems in retrospect. "And my aunt," Karl went on, "she'd been working around, doing various things, but she hadn't married. Well, soon she and Dad got married, and along came Lyle's sister, first, and then Lyle. So my aunt's son Lyle is my first cousin, his mother being my mother's sister, but because his dad is my dad we're half-brothers too."

Wow, I thought. That makes perfect sense, but still seems strange. "And that kid you call your nephew, how is he nephew to both of you?"

"Well, yes," said Karl, "he's, I guess, my half- or step-nephew, and Lyle's," he hesitated, searching for the word, "he's Lyle's full nephew, the son of his sister."

"And your son in Alaska who flies over Canada, leaving a contrail over Saskatchewan when he comes home, what's his name, and what is he doing up there?" I pressed on, not sure myself why it all mattered but feeling that it did, even urgently. I felt propelled to pursue all possible connections, how each of us is related, one to another, as though, if taken far enough, we might all be related by the contrails of kinship when our paths crossed and we touched, however briefly, while occupying the same patch of land or sky, a tendency I got from my mother, who presumed she was related to pretty much everybody, and it was just a matter of time until the degrees of connection, closer and closer, would rein in everyone who had ever crossed her path.

Karl said his son was also Karl Rossmann, and he was not a passenger in the jets flying overhead but a pilot, and at this immodest statement Karl beamed, then tried to hide the pride he took in his son by looking down and shuffling his feet a bit. I assured him of the impressiveness of this fact and complimented him on having such a son, and I meant to ask more about his father and about Lyle, his cousin and half-brother, and how each came to have a store in the same town that made them competitors, but just then a woman about Karl's age came in looking to buy a pair of scissors, and the two of them were soon huddled before a wall rack of implements, indoor and outdoor, on the far side of the store. I checked the time and ran back to the crew trailer just in time to get supper on.

I never had another chance to ask Karl more, but then I couldn't possibly have asked the right questions, not yet having read Kafka's novel *Amerika*, the Great Plains as imagined by Europe, its central character named Karl Rossmann, the double of my Karl Rossmann, as I thought, my grocer in Selden, Kansas, who was really three Karl Rossmanns, counting his father six feet underground and his son 30,000 feet overhead, the pilot son based in Alaska realizing the lofty aspirations of Kafka's Karl Rossmann, by the way, for a profession to be known by, though barely sixteen years old when he is packed off to the United States by his parents because of a dangerous intimacy that sprang up between him and a servant girl in Prague, "who had got herself a child by him," as the translation by Willa and Edwin Muir puts it, their attempt to convey how the parents, if not the son, evade responsibility for his role in the affair. Like the character K. in Kafka's novel *The Castle*, Karl arrives in America full of hope for success, but through the chapters of his travels and adventures, beginning with the loss of his luggage after becoming distracted by forgetting his umbrella in the stampede of passengers disembarking at New York harbour under the benevolent gaze of Liberty herself, he experiences the rising and falling fortunes that Americans take pride in but that destroy no small number of them while deflecting attention away from the inherited privilege and wealth, not to mention the pecking orders of race and religion and ethnicity, that go into the making and unmaking of fortunes in a supposed-to-be-horizontal new world.

Young Karl gets his first job as a stoker of ships' engines even before leaving the ship, which, for all its fire and promise, does not get him far, and though he enjoys all the scrapes and compromising situations into which and out of which he gets, it soon becomes apparent he is working his way westward, until, in the final chapter—though the novel is unfinished—called "The Nature Theatre of Oklahoma" he is taken on, somewhat hesitantly, by an outfit called The Oklahoma Theatre, a working man's heaven that makes a time-limited offer to hire any number of people and even claims to have a place for everyone! After finally losing Delamarche and Robinson, two clowns who follow him from job to job, always showing up to drag him down and ruin his chances for advancement, Karl feels he is "entitled to apply for a job of which he need not be ashamed. . . . Even if the great Theatre of Oklahoma were an insignificant travelling circus," he thinks, "it wanted to engage people, and that was enough."

He is all but overcome, though, by the scale of the Nature Theatre when he steps off the train at the designated meeting place to a cacophony of trumpets blaring. Few other job seekers are in sight, and instead he sees crowds of women dressed in long, trailing white gowns with angel wings on their shoulders and standing on pedestals

> which could not however be seen, since they were completely hidden by long flowing draperies of the robes. . . . To avoid monotony, the pedestals were of all sizes; there were women quite low down, not much over life-size, but beside them others soared to such a height that one felt the

slightest gust of wind could capsize them. And all these women were blowing their trumpets.

Karl is trying to find someone to ask for information when he hears his name called out, and it bodes well that he is singled out and recognized by an angel. It is Fanny, someone Karl knows from his previous employment. She rather lewdly "parted her draperies" so that her pedestal and "a little ladder leading up to it became visible" beneath her flowing robes, and Karl clambers up to her raised level to talk. Fanny says she spotted him as soon as he stepped off the train and blew on her trumpet as loudly as she could to attract his attention, but Karl failed to recognize her or even consider an angel might be hailing him personally.

> "You all play very badly," said Karl, "let me have a turn." When he plays, many of the angels stop to listen, and Fanny exclaims he is an artist.
> "Ask to be taken on as a trumpeter."
> "Are men taken on for it too?" asked Karl.
> "Oh yes," said Fanny. "We play for two hours; then we're relieved by men who are dressed as devils. Half of them blow, the other half beat drums."

Kafka's literary executor, Max Brod, records the author, his friend, saying how this novel was "more optimistic and lighter in mood than any of his other writings," which are bywords for a dark and cloying absurdity. Brod dwells on Kafka's fondness for reading travel books and memoirs, saying Benjamin Franklin's biography was one of his favourites. Kafka liked reading passages aloud, and he always had a longing for open space and distant lands. Brod affirms the incomplete chapter about the Nature Theatre of Oklahoma was intended as the novel's conclusion in the resolution of all Karl's aspirations and desires. "Kafka used to hint smilingly," he writes, "that within this 'almost limitless' theatre Karl Rossmann was going to find again a profession, his freedom, even his old home and his parents, as if by some celestial witchery." As it is, the final chapter trails off after only about twenty pages, when the train, packed with new recruits to the Nature Theatre, sets out on a journey of two days and two nights to Oklahoma. Only then does Karl understand how huge America is, and a concern about the immense territory to be traversed in America has to be acknowledged in the incomplete or aborted journeys more typical of Kafka's stories than the reaching of final destinations, so much so that Brod's hint about Karl's ultimate arrival at a state of happiness and fulfillment is nearly impossible to imagine.

Judith Butler calls it a "poetics of non-arrival" that pervades Kafka's stories when it comes up in legal wrangling, to this day, over the question of where his archive belongs, the question of who owns Kafka, a Prague Jew who spoke Czech but wrote in German, and whose Yiddish was not part of his daily life, though it was the major factor of his fascination with the travelling theatre, which he longed for and even planned to follow but never did. A reviewer of his famous *Metamorphosis*, better known in English as *The Fly* from the film version starring Jeff Goldblum, noted something fundamentally German about that story of transformation, whereas another argued he found it typically Jewish. "A difficult case," Butler reports Kafka writing in response. "Am I a circus rider on two horses?"

Non-arrival is the predicament of Kafka's stories famous for depicting travellers who fail to arrive or whose arrival goes unacknowledged, unrecognized, or is misinterpreted. Messages also fall short, intercepted or misdirected from their intended receivers. Instead of the expected arrival of a traveller or message, the distance between departure and arrival opens up to the story and its wayfarer for travelling on and on, like my ride in the transport headed west toward the annihilation that is certain in a truck that never arrives or gets me out ahead of the impending disaster to keep it from happening over and over and on and on. And not only the travellers but also the messages, portents and warnings, the dispatches of angels, how many are written and sent, propelling the fantasy of reunion, children with their parents, the full scale of creative power needed to bring it about, how many are written and sent but whose arrival is uncertain or impossible to affirm, whether consumed by ghosts gathered in the distances, along the road's shoulder, then dispelled into thin air like contrails?

Kafka himself didn't get far, at least not geographically, and he took no territory as a writer, as we see from the legal dispute over where to reposit his archive. He lived briefly in Berlin, but otherwise travelled outside his hometown of Prague only as far as France and northern Italy, never really getting out of Dodge, so it is not surprising his geography of the United States was comically way off the map. On the train to Oklahoma from New York or Chicago, Karl Rossmann has the impression of passing mountains and valleys like the Alps or Rockies, not the Alleghenies or Appalachians. And similarly, in the fragment of *Amerika* that Kafka completed, the Nature Theatre that hires Karl is more awesome, more sublime than any other he has encountered in Europe, of unfathomable proportions and stupefying bureaucratic complexity, to the extent that its own nature as an enterprise is so vaguely outlined from the partial and ground-level perspective of young Karl, as he sees it, that the reader can be forgiven for suspecting his journey is grimly prophetic of later trains herding passengers to ghastly destinations, which Kafka could not have known about since he died of tuberculosis in 1925.

Suggestive but also incomplete is the story of the trumpeting female angels and the non-arrival into the story of their male devil counterparts as described by Fanny, whose ranks Karl aspires to join and who might have spelled triumph or trouble for his story's resolution on the Great Plains, then resounding with those drums quieted by law and now pounding again with Indigenous beats. We know Karl is taken on as a minor technician of some sort, or a technician's assistant, though he tries to pass himself off as an engineer, just like the father of Karl of Selden did when he got work as an "engineer" without the formal education of an actual engineer. Kafka's Karl wants to become an engineer, or partially trains to become one, or thinks of doing so while at school back in Prague before he is distracted by the servant girl. But it was only long after I met Karl Rossmann in Selden that I read Kafka's novel *Amerika* and wished I had asked Karl about his mother's name. Was she Fanny, and did she perform as an angel playing a trumpet in her job with the Nature Theatre of Oklahoma, and was that why she took a fall from high stilts when a wind blew in and toppled her or she lost her balance from parting her skirts once too often for friends to climb her ladder for a visit? Or was Karl just using a figure of speech when he referred to his mother as an angel? If his parents were, in fact, the people Kafka wrote about, fantastically, from the other side of the Atlantic and the fact/fiction divide, Fanny might have been injured in a fall from her pedestal just as Kafka's Karl began his metamorphosis into the father of Karl of Selden, Kansas, by climbing her ladder for a second visit, and maybe they begot Karl the grocer before a big wind ripped down tornado alley and sent her crashing to the ground, breaking her bones. From the scant details Karl gave me in Selden, for all I know his mother might not have been a regular angel at all but someone who usually worked in the Props Department serving the bona fide performing angels, who got a break one day to mount the stilts and blow the horn of an angel who called in sick, and that's when she happened to see Karl the father of my grocer in Selden when he stepped off the train and recognized him. There might be any number of ways she fell and broke her bones and died too young, leaving her baby Karl an orphan and her husband Karl a widower.

My own dad's first job in Assiniboia, the job Dad took after selling the farm and moving his family into town nine days before I was born, was at the Co-op lumberyard, and there he fell from a ladder one day as if to register in pain and muscle and bone his fall and general downward mobility from landowner and farmer to hourly wage worker, later stocking the produce section of the Co-op grocery store after his injury, and then taking on additional part-time janitorial work, maintenance, and bartending at the Elks Hall, and everyone said he was never the same after his fall at the lumberyard, and it was suspected he drank partly to numb the pain in his weakened back while calculating what would be needed from him for how many years to feed the greedy mewling mouths of more and more children every year up to the number nine.

Why no one else, no other writer to my knowledge, among the German settler descendants of Kansas, Oklahoma, or any other immigrant settler on the Great Plains, has yet gone to the trouble of imagining the continuation or resolution of Kafka's *Amerika* I can't say. It's a story that invites, even begs, for completion, and my own attempt is no more a confabulation than the western pulp fiction Kafka surely read in German written by Karl May in the 1890s depicting the American West that was already disappearing and that May never travelled to but led readers to believe he had. Is Kafka's Karl Rossmann the father, as I propose, of Karl the grocer in Selden, who befriended me and delivered my pen to draw what connections I would on the ground or the page or in the sky over the Great Plains? Is my reconnection with Kafka's Karl in Kansas any more preposterous than the actual thriving of Nemsi Books, the South Dakota publisher that exists almost solely to publish May's books to this day, the westerns and travellers' tales translated into English for the benefit of the children of German immigrants to America who no longer speak or read German? Meanwhile on the European side even now the yearly Karl May Festivals in German towns attract hundreds of thousands of his readers, who can recite the lines of his beloved characters, the nonsensical Apache-cum-Plains "Indian" leader named Winnetou and his blood brother Old Shatterhand, a German immigrant stand-in for May himself, who wrote the stories shortly after Buffalo Bill Cody arrived in Munich in 1890 with his Wild West show that "featured two hundred cowboys and Indians, Sioux Ghost Dance performances, and reënactments of the battle of Little Bighorn with 'the people who were there!'" as reported by journalist Rivka Galchen. Strangely, May avoided the shows and even defamed the Wild West players, who nearly included Chief Sitting Bull, claiming they were "outcasts from their tribe" starring in "vile, lying roles," according to Galchen's article in *The New Yorker* in 2012. Meeting actual Indians at that time would have been awkward since May did not speak any Indigenous language. He even accused Buffalo Bill Cody of causing the "deaths" of two fictional characters in his novels, Old Firehand and Old Surehand, who had to be killed off because of his readers' exposure to the travelling theatre performances of actual historical Sioux in Germany. May's status as a confabulator is only enhanced, writes Galchen, when in an interview May described in great detail two books he said most influenced his writing, though neither book turns out to exist. Despite this, Galchen asserts that "both almost certainly were big influences on him."

What are my modest speculative trespasses into fiction in comparison? May's non-fictional autobiography, *My Life and My Efforts*, reads like "a defense statement in a trial," as Galchen describes it, but is designed to foment conflict and confusion among those who will judge May. The charges against May of dishonesty and misrepresentation are turned back on his accusers: "Are there not almost innumerable fables and fairy-tales, my opponents have built up around me? And whenever I protest against this, I am believed just as little as some people believe in fairy-tales. But as for every genuine fairy-tale, there will finally come a time, when its truth will be evident, so all of my truth will eventually become evident." And, in fact, the correction of May's cowboy and Indian stories in light of historical records and eyewitness testimony is precisely what seems to engage and activate his numerous readers and fans, whether they seek to debunk his claims to authenticity or validate the admirable aspirations of his westerns to find grounds for social unity between settlers and Indigenous peoples, the dream those stories keep alive even while ruling it out.

I tore myself away from Selden with some difficulty after we packed up and rolled out on Highway 83 north through McCook, Nebraska, where the Poppers report the Buffalo Commons Storytelling Festival takes place, or took place, and then we turned west again to a place called Madrid, the name I did not recognize at first, now hard to believe, because of the way it was pronounced there as MAH'-drid, with emphasis on the first syllable, and the second swallowed, nothing like the more familiar Meh-DRID', as we say up north when referring to the capital of Spain. Well, I've "Never Been to Spain," Hoyt Axton sang, and no need to go there, he might have said, since Don Quixote famously can't or won't distinguish between fact and fiction, that's the whole joke and problem he brings into the heart of America, the Great Plains, the original of the cowboy naturalizing the Spanish brass fanfare that blasts out in Cash's "Ring of Fire." It was because of the drawl, I thought, as I studiously acquired it in Madrid so I could be understood by the locals. We levelled the trailers at the edge of a kind of fairgrounds where we could see the rodeo was held at another time of year. Our crew and two or three others circled our vehicles like wagons around a shabby, broken-down corral with three horses in it. Part of the corral fence was made of wooden posts greyed and worn smooth, but some were jaggedly broken in half, or burned, as if they'd been struck by lightning. The burned and broken posts were strung together by extra tangles of barbed wire wrapped around them, some joined to parts of still-good posts and tied up together, so I remember the whole thing was cartoonish, like scribbles in barbed wire, with the odd burned post sticking out, only some set down on or into the ground. The horses appeared to be neglected, too, and ran up to the fence whenever we approached or walked by, as if to ask for something, or as if they wanted to escape to any place not there, and it was all I could do the whole time in Madrid, several weeks, to keep from unlatching the gate to let them run away free. The smaller pony had open sores on his neck and scabs on his front forelock, maybe from being crowded against the barbed wire by the two larger and more dominant horses. I thought about asking who was supposed to be looking after them, if anyone was.

I wrote in my journal at the table in the trailer in the bits of time between meals and trips to the field and loads of laundry, and one day early on at Madrid an extremely clean-cut guy named Frank rapped at the door in the hot mid-afternoon. I had just been thinking about starting supper, the horses barely stirring outside in the heat, and I was a bit anxious about the interruption. Frank held a New Testament along with a pen and notebook in one hand, and said he'd seen me through the screen door, and since he was a writer, too, he thought he'd say hello. "The unrecorded life is not worth living," he said, then named his source, Aristotle or somebody like that. Or that's who I thought at that time, what Frank might have said, and only later I learned it was Socrates who said it, and still later I found he wrote nothing down, it was Plato who wrote, so you don't have to go to the trouble of correcting me, I know, I know, but I am trying to depict who I was then, not what you know now. In the moment, I blushed to think Frank caught me thinking my life was worth recording, but we talked for a while in a friendly way. He said his crew, parked across from our trailer on the other side of the corral, was still waiting on a contract, so he had time on his hands. When I told him about my secret desire to free the horses, he told me there was a rough-looking hired hand everyone called Coyote, or sometimes Coy Boy. Or sometimes just Boy, he mumbled the last name, probably embarrassed at the condescension and disrespect it showed. Frank said Coyote filled the water troughs and chop pails, but he must have been doing it so early or late that I hadn't ever crossed paths with him or even seen him through my window. Frank said his crew across the way were all wondering who I was, so I quickly overstated my family connection with my own crew boss to discourage any undue curiosity or forwardness. About the New Testament in his hand, he asked if he could talk to me about it, the Book of Revelation. Then he asked directly about the state of my soul, and where I was in regard to His plan for me, and I made excuses about my plan to get supper going, and our talk dwindled out, and eventually he left. I wished I hadn't, but I detected a hint of menace in the way he seemed to point out how vulnerable I was to the leers and questions of the crews around the corral, and then immediately switched to the matter of my salvation, as though the two were related, the danger I was in and the salvation he offered bound up in a creepy little package, like the tiny New Testament in his hand.

I think I was firm enough, and in the days following busy enough, that Frank did not bother me anymore, yet I ached for the plight of the horses in the corral, which distracted me from the other crews camped out around it, who soon enough got their contracts and went to work or left empty-handed and chased other contracts elsewhere. A few years after the events in Johnny Bradley's corral, I myself chased a cowboy all the way to Nashville, driving my second-hand Pontiac Sunfire down to see him during my vacation from the radio station where I was working by then. I stuck to the main interstates for speed and stopped each night at a Motel 6, delirious at my getaway and achingly anticipating my romantic destination. I found Nashville a small city at that time, what I saw of it, a little seedy and a little foreign, like Moose Jaw. Chase was waiting tables at a bar just a few streets off Music Row, and, as I might have expected from any number of country songs I sang with the radio or my tape deck all the way there, he was not as happy to see me, though he hadn't said anything on the phone ahead of time to discourage me from coming, or if he did I hadn't heard it. Maybe he thought I came from a world he was trying to escape in chasing his dreams, or maybe it was for some other reason. I was crushed and at a loss what to do in Nashville if we weren't going to be in love. Somebody said Dwight Yoakam was down and out there at that time after he was turned down by the country music establishment and before his honky-tonk revival with Buck Owens. Only later did I remember seeing a handsome cowboy with feathery hair like Dwight's wafting out from under his hat, eyes all pouty and watering. He was sprawled on a bar stool where Chase waited tables, and I noticed him because I had to step around his guitar case on the floor in making my humiliated retreat, and I couldn't help but notice his extremely tight jeans with a rip in one knee that looked like trouble and wasn't yet recognized as style. Cheap rhinestones studded his jacket, and he wore scuffed but fancy white and black tooled boots, and he was sullenly nursing a drink as I went by in a blur, guitars, Cadillacs.

So long, Dwight! I had thought Chase and I would hang out at recording studios in Nashville, if only to wash the floors the way Kris Kristofferson started out, or fetch the coffee, and I was quite sure the country and western world would take particular notice of us, seeing we were their kind of people, and they would invite us in for our talent and longing, which they would recognize. Crystal Gayle was nowhere in sight, but I did see Dolly Parton's name in lights. Chase said with a snobby tone that Nashville is full of names spoken with reverence, yet known by only a few, the most serious and talented songwriters, drummers, fiddlers, guitarists, producers—all that heightened my sense of isolation and distance from him and the whole country and western world even as I clung to it for dear life. Chase was figuring out who was who, and he was on the lookout for some unspecified serendipity, what fame seems to rest on, and I could see he wished me gone, and the whole thing, whatever it was, all the unwritten songs looming between us and both of us feeling more than we could say.

I left Nashville in tears barely twenty-four hours later, not in love anymore, and several years after that I received a long diatribe of a letter from Chase, which I burned, and couldn't for the life of me figure out why he was so angry with me. He claimed to feel deceived, as if I was only pretending to be the person he thought I was. "Hey! I'm that girl from the north country," I sang. And no more a true love of yours. I was counting it all up through my tears as I drove back through the tobacco and cotton fields of west Tennessee, all my heartaches by the number, and I wailed that old Ray Price song without knowing Dwight would soon make it a country hit again. There are more stars in the sky than the millions we can see, I thought, and all thousands, millions, of years old, and gone, but still they shine and flash as they crumble and fall before our belated eyes down here on Earth. I was already ascending the plains and merging onto the I-55, soon nearing St. Louis, when the songs trailed off and I became aware of being unable to get off the road, though my gas was low and I had to go to the bathroom. I'd see a sign for an exit with gas and think, okay, I'll take that one, but then my elbows seemed to fill with cement, and I wasn't able to flip on the signal light, let alone turn the wheel, even slightly, and I must have driven past half a dozen exit ramps like that until I became alarmed, and St. Louis was in my rear-view mirror. I was running out of gas yet couldn't get myself to stop. I wasn't thinking at all clearly about how bad it could be to run out of gas on the shoulder of the interstate. Not that bad. Somebody would help out. There were trooper patrols everywhere, although they'd probably disappear the minute I needed them. But I felt my situation to be more than at risk of running out of gas, more like I was about to fail in making a curve and drive off into thin air, or plunge into some ravine, not puttering out along the roadside to wait passively for help, and the thought of having to explain myself to a state trooper or anyone else was almost as horrifying as flying off a cliff.

Finally, somewhere near the turnoff for Jefferson City, I inched my way over to the exit lane and then the off-ramp with the most rigid exercise of willpower, slowly slowing right down, decelerating almost imperceptibly, so my foot didn't know what my mind was thinking, or vice versa, and I forced myself into a situation of having to get out of the way of the traffic bearing down on me, despite feeling like someone else was holding the wheel, and I had to wrest it from hands stronger than mine. When I saw a Motel 6 sign from the exit ramp,

I knew if I could get stopped there for gas I wouldn't have to get back on the interstate that day. I stiffly veered off and slowed down to the pumps at a gas bar with a diner, even better, whose parking lot connected with the motel next door. I could even see the ramp leading back onto the highway, so I calmed down about being able to get back on the road, if I could, after a night's sleep. I spent all the rest of that night quelling the panic in my throat and working out the next night's stop on the map so I would have something to aim for and time to talk myself into taking the exit. I was filling with awareness of the serious danger I was in, of what could only be called involuntary suicide, but why exactly I could not say, such a jumble of things I was almost numb. All the parts of me seemed to have become disconnected, disarticulated, not talking to each other. Hadn't I been let down by guys like Chase and lived to laugh about the sorry state romance leaves you in, time and again, yet here I was wanting to fling myself off a cliff and trying not to. For that whole trip north and west, I felt chased by Fear, somehow entranced, all through Missouri, Kansas, and into Colorado, as though I'd slipped into a sixth gear I hadn't known about, suicide gear of the death drive, I riffed on the idea ghoulishly, and maybe this is how it happens, how it happened with my dad. Maybe he was just feeling blue, like me singing the country and western blues, and then the tremor went through him, his hand twitching, but it was on the trigger, not a guitar string or steering wheel or his AA pen writing a letter home, and then he was gone by that shaky hand, the end of a story that could have carried on, and gone elsewhere, and been otherwise.

I could have turned north onto Highway 83 and passed right through Selden again to say hello to Karl, but I was in no condition for two-way highway driving, the slowness of it, getting stuck behind combine crews or tractors, and I thought, in Colorado, the mountains would finally stop me, force a decision and a destination and an arrival somewhere. I could only get myself to exit for nightly stops with the most careful planning ahead, intense concentration, and physical effort, and I felt my skin had filled with a membrane of lead, my brain and the pathways of my thoughts crusted over by something just as rigid and final. There was no one to call, no one to cry out to. If I had reached out to say "I'm afraid I'm going to kill myself on the road," how would I even say that out loud? What could the person say but "Well, don't" (I laughed sadistically to myself). You drive yourself all the way to Nashville, and you can't drive yourself back? Get a grip, sister. There's no one else who knows where you are, so you have to know where you are and deal with it. I was writing it all down in the motel rooms at night, whining and wailing my country and western lines,

Lyin' face down in a motel bed
Goin' over and over all the things that you said
Car doors slam in the parking lot below
But I can't even get up
I can't seem to go

Now that I been to Nashville
I know why they write those songs
Draw you in
Let you down
And baby I might sing about it
But Nashville's not where I belong.
(Don't know where I belong.)

Drove down through the badlands, the hard Missouri rain
When I finally found you it just wasn't the same
Tires crush the gravel as the cars turn to go
Everybody's checking out
But I can't get out of bed
I can't seem to go.

I came too far south
And into the past
After all the miles between us, I should've known it wouldn't last

Traffic roars by on the interstate below
Everybody's moving on
But I'll just lie here awhile
I got nowhere else to go.

> Now that I been to Nashville
> I know how you wrote those songs
> Drew me in
> Let me down
> Now baby you can sing about it
> Nashville's not where I belong
> (Don't know where I belong.)

So now that I been to Nashville, I wrote my own sad song—
could not keep from writing it—though I never could decide
when the chorus comes in or if it's repeated after every verse.
I'd have to play around with the melody and then the bridge,
whatever it would be, although even saying that makes it
sound like I'm a player, like I know how to compose music,
which I don't, and only hope, hopelessly, that Joni Mitchell or
kd lang might pick it up, in my dreams, and figure out how to
get that song to sing.

Denver when I reached it was a new problem because I
had to decide whether to go north or south the next day. North
toward the forty-ninth parallel and home, where I'd have to
explain why I was back so soon, time heavy on my hands
before I was expected back at work, or south to Albuquerque,
where I felt sure I'd be able to stand on level ground. But I could
only get there along the treacherous winding road where the
mountains rise up, not too gradually in places. I didn't feel sure
I could make all the turns, not sure I wouldn't do a *Thelma
and Louise*, in spite of not wanting or meaning to, though that
movie, shot farther west in the more extreme precipitousness
of Utah, had not yet been made, and when I saw it I thought
the director had been with me on that drive west and had to
turn away my eyes. At a diner, I ordered a Western sandwich,

wondering if it was a Denver there, as it is in Assiniboia and as far east as the Ring of Fire, which made me think how the names we give to things say what is not there, like the name Assiniboia for where there are no Assiniboine people left, in Denver no Denver, and the grievous angel of Gram Parsons alive only on the radio once he's dead and gone. The name of what is not there, what we do not have, what we exclude or eliminate, the way country music circles around and around the losses, the loneliness of it all, the driven road and lost highway, trail's end, ever-expanding solitudes filling the vastness of the plains in songs about who's gone, what's left behind when we ride off alone and along. Neither a Western nor a Denver sandwich seemed to exist in Denver, and I've since measured my distance from that city by the name given to the fried egg and ham sandwich with onions and green peppers and a dash of cayenne pepper, Western or Denver. In the east, it's a Western, in the northwest a Denver, but in Denver itself the waitress looked at me with incomprehension, so I asked for a fried egg and ham toasted, and that got results.

Distracted by my sandwich, what to call it, and the implications for knowing where I was and what I was longing for, I failed to make a decision about turning north or south, so once back on the road I quickly missed the northbound exit at the interchange and found myself merging with the southbound traffic, and that's when I might have been at the greatest risk, not really making decisions and the world turning to dust. But I was wailing "Now That I Been to Nashville," the lyrics as I'd written them out on the Motel 6 stationery, that original manuscript in my files somewhere. I later typed it up, which shows I did arrive at a typewriter and a solid surface of a desk or table somewhere, eventually, though not for long, and I was unrecognized as usual. I did make that choice in the roadside motels to pick up a pen, it's now safe to say, but on that drive south along the narrow ledge where the plains rise into foothills with sharp steep inclines and cliffs, winding around bare rock faces, the car swaying this way and that,

I only tried to keep steering within a very narrow range, and that gave me a feeling of hard-won control. I cranked up the Pointer Sisters singing their "Fairytale" live in San Francisco and laughed to hear them open their show by asking permission to "sing some country music here in the Opera House tonight. The Pointer Sisters love country music."

It took all of a long day to get to Santa Fe. By dusk, the curves in the road sharpened and became more frequent, slowing me down even more with the desert taking on streaks of purple and pink in the rough two-way traffic. I slowed down only with great effort, since now my foot felt like lead, and from time to time I had let myself get going too fast and then had trouble letting up. I heard reckless cackling close to my ears and was terrified. More than once I closed my eyes, feeling myself bolting through the air and not expecting to land, ready to give it up, and then my eyes would open, and I'd catch myself, and this continued all the way to the outskirts of Santa Fe, where, thankfully, the cars in front of me slowed to a crawl, and so mine had to. When I took a deep breath, my chest hurt. At the first roadside motel inside the city limits, I pulled over and got a room where I could park right at the door, then sat shaking and chilled on the flowered bedspread for that night and a day. My jaw was locked, seized up. Muscles in my face, neck, and back felt dry and about to crack. Okay, okay, I came to myself thinking. I can stay here for a few days and then get myself to the flat desert plain of Albuquerque, and I'll be safe there, no cliffs to fall off or leap from. I thought I'd knock around Albuquerque until I felt able to drive home, or I'd just stay there, since it seemed like a place where I could easily slip over the border into Spanish through the poetry of José Marti or Ernesto Cardenal.

The attraction of Albuquerque was not only the flat desert and lack of cliffs to slide or drive off. I associated it with Margaret Randall, the poet and writer who was a U.S. citizen, although Albuquerque might only have been the place she escaped from, becoming a Spanish person in Mexico and Cuba across the Gulf and back to Nicaragua, the most triangular country in the world, where I first came across her book *Sandino's Daughters*, a transcription of the stories of women who dropped everything—children, jobs, husbands—to join the guerrillas who trounced the dictator Somoza, ran him out of the country, in July 1979, at the very time when I was out of my mind with grief and suffering the general loss of direction I've been trying to recover from ever since. I can't remember if I met Randall in Nicaragua when I went there with a trade union delegation in 1981, or whether I just thought I did, since I've seen her on film and news clips and at that time had read some of her poems and other writings. I've already said how I joined up with pretty much any carnival crew or travelling troupe leaving town after my dad died, just to get out of Dodge, and around the same time I took up with Suknaski I became quite fired up by the Sandinistas, mostly, I thought, from reading José Marti and somebody called Immanuel Wallerstein, who makes modernity and colonialism two sides of the same bad coin, everything "modern" and "new" contaminated with the colonial incursions and plunder, and all they entail, the writings of both poet and political scientist motivated by the general sense of being always in a state of emergency as the refugees flooded into even the smallest towns of the coldest, most remote northern provinces, all of Central America descending into civil war and spewing their peoples at that time. The United States, still sore from its losses in Vietnam, kept supporting the wrong side in the countries of the isthmus, the side turning the guns on its own people. So I joined the trade union delegation despite belonging only to a union local without any particular interest in my eyewitness testimony of what we thought the Sandinistas were trying to accomplish for the poor and the labouring classes. I was given a letter with general greetings of solidarity and maybe a couple of hundred bucks toward my fare, for which I was thankful.

All the way south to Albuquerque I was grasping for an explanation of my terrorized state. What was threatening me, and why did I feel like I was fighting for my life? It was not just that my heart was broken. There was something darker in finding no way to occupy myself on the plains I grew out of and longed for, except to drive through them and be gone. Small dust devils whirled up in the ditches and along the shoulder. The road does not permit stopping to think or dwell too much on these questions—that was the insight, if you can call it that, of Kerouac's pounding prose of the rolling road, and it's more or less what I was experiencing, as I eventually understood. Wanting to abandon the journey but at the same time knowing there is no stopping on the shoulder. No stopping, period, even though I found myself unable to ignore my lack of an alibi for being here or there, it being of no consequence, domestic or cosmic, if I just drove off the map entirely and disappeared into the sand and sage, good riddance, bon débarras. Overwhelmed, smothered, by turns ignored and bossed around by my over-large family, breaking the bonds (Get out of Dodge!). Did it matter what I was doing? Whether I went north or south? East or west? I couldn't tell, suspected it didn't matter, though I only wanted to be in the desert triangle, despite having nothing to do there, and at that moment I sank with the certainty there was not a single person who knew or cared where I was or where I was going, not a single bond to grasp onto, no sister or friend who would steal my corpse and know my final wishes and carry them out in defiance of the law, borrow or steal a hearse, and then I was touched by my dad's despair. I felt it on my skin and hair like chalk, not self-pity, just the reality of our solitude, visceral. Did his hand tremble inadvertently, and what could my mother be meaning to say or hold back, and is it all going to be this unendingly ghoulish, on and on? Wouldn't the Assiniboine have done better with all this land, the Great Plains and its sky manifesting the Manitou, the Buffalo God? The silences and withholdings of the living, uncertainties that make life a hesitation of doubt, stranded between stone outcroppings and the blue yonder, driving south, to some kind of refuge, heaven. North versus south, north linked to my mother and the tea towels, making a family of my own to ruin, south another kind of trouble and loyalty to my father, embracing the blown-apart absurdity of things, off the grid, recomposition, tracking a redrawn land that might never exist. I sought a landscape of loneliness where my solitude would have the room to expand to its full magnitude, the full measure of just how great was my pain, by then a little larger than the Western Hemisphere. The story I was coming up with, the story that was affecting my driving and threatening the likelihood of ever leaving the road or arriving at a destination, let alone Albuquerque, would have to be as huge, and in the end has taken ten times longer than all the voyages of Columbus to piece together.

I had not the wherewithal during the drive to answer my question of whether I meant to live or die, in so many words, or even to focus on it for long. I began to relax a little at the motel in Santa Fe as the waves of exhaustion washed over me. I was so tired I took a hot shower and fell into bed, resolved to resume the inquisition of myself the next day. But in the morning, I asked the man behind the cash register at the pumps what was the best way to drive through Santa Fe to get a sense of the place, see the famous pueblo architecture, having forgotten, by then, my plan and even the problem of choosing between life and death (that's crew cooks for you).

The gas jockey looked at me with sparkling eyes and then glanced slowly over my whole car. "If that's what you're driving, lady, I don't think you can afford to look at the architecture in Santa Fe."

"What?"

"No, I don't think you can drive down those streets. This is a place for rich people. They might run you off or send the police to chase you out of town." But then he winked and gave me directions to an open-air market near the untouchable art galleries at the city centre. "You won't be able to buy more than a cup of coffee," he yelled cheerfully as he waved goodbye.

I found the market easily, and, yes, it was beautiful, and the low-rise adobe imitations of Pueblo Indian architecture were gorgeous, though I wondered how many Pueblos could afford to drive through the city, let alone live in those houses of imperial nostalgia. The city looked like a vaguely familiar painting that I stepped into from the car. The market sold hot chili peppers strung in long strips and a sweetgrass-smelling incense that I was still burning years later when U2's *Joshua Tree* album came out, and I listened to it over and over, thinking of Gram Parsons and the sadness of Emmylou at his mysterious death, botched cremation, and officious interment outside New Orleans while I breathed in the desert and the sagebrush that seemed to be what I was then looking for.

I dawdled around the market stalls and talked to a few of the vendors until I became aware of a voice urging me on, to get back on the road, move on to Albuquerque, that's where you should go. This place is dead. Stopping there was threatening, forgetfulness and death, and I was only saved by that voice that knew better than me what danger I might be in if I didn't keep moving. Luckily, I remembered to ask, before driving off, where to buy recorded music for the road. Directed down the street to a shop, I set out on foot, slowly feeling like I was in control now, winding downhill like an awakened snake gathering speed as it sloughs off another skin. The first album I saw was *Grievous Angel*, still a big thing and a collector's item around there, and since mine was worn out to the point of skipping on the songs I played the most I bought it on cassette along with a few other tapes, and then I walked a little farther to a lunch counter around noon. The streets were all but empty, and the place was giving me the creeps, like Dodge City, as if I'd stumbled onto the scene just before or after the gunfight, or the instant after the imperial aliens had come and gone with their human cargo, the children. Lunch cost quite a bit, almost twenty dollars for a sandwich, though a very good sandwich, but still. By the time I finished eating, I couldn't get out of Santa Fe fast enough, though I drove out slowly and with deliberate care up and around the hills and onto the highway toward Albuquerque, not so far, even at a speed that allowed me to concentrate on the spectacular purple desert. A duet by Parsons and Harris gave me courage and filled me with confidence that I might even be able to drive home eventually, a song with Old Testament–sounding lyrics I hear in most songs by Emmylou, "In My Hour of Darkness," which calls for "speed" despite a slow tempo and mournful melody that put the brakes on the idea of speed and stalled any progress. So I thought "speed" might mean certainty of reaching the destination rather than quickness in getting there. And then I thought maybe the slowness that conflicted with the repetition of the word "speed" was the poetics of non-arrival that I was living during that whole long travelling road show. I sang that chorus under my breath and then rolled down the window and sang it at the top of my lungs, even as I slowly became aware, like a cloud passing over the sun, that I was on the very route William Walker took when he left Nashville in the 1850s, heading west to cross the Mississippi at Memphis instead of St. Louis the way I had gone, but then angling south on the same side of the mountains between Santa Fe and Albuquerque, the very road I was on. He would have gone straight through Albuquerque and along the Rio Grande all the way down to El Paso and then crossed over to Juárez and west again to Sonora, a stranger riding into town, to hear the Nicaraguan Ernesto Cardenal tell it in his poems published in *With Walker in Nicaragua* and *Zero Hour*. "Nobody was his friend," Cardenal's poem says, "and I don't remember ever having seen him smile."

Walker's plan, swiftly carried out, was to invade and occupy Sonora and offer titles to the land to Americans. Before long, about fifty-seven Californians rode down across the desert to take up what was not Walker's to offer. Cardenal's poems tell how Walker, in another correspondence with my flight from Chase, had left his fiancée, a deaf and mute woman, back in Nashville, where she was soon stricken with yellow fever and died alone, among other details that flesh out his character as far "beyond the reach of human communication," according to Stephen Henighan, who tells the tale in his book *Sandino's Nation*. Walker was still in Sonora in 1855 when Captain Palliser was building support and raising money back in England for his expedition that would offer Assiniboine, Cree, and Blackfoot lands to settlers from Europe, Quebec, Michigan, and elsewhere. In Walker's case, one of the Nicaraguan factions competing to build and control an overland route or a naval canal to link its Atlantic and Pacific coasts hired Walker to bring a mercenary military solution to their dispute. There was money to be made by offering such a route from the hundreds, if not thousands, of Americans, crazed by gold rush fever, who wanted to get to California without risking the dangers of crossing the Great Plains territory defended by increasingly aggrieved Indigenous peoples who lived there. A southern route severing the hemisphere, whether by a canal or a road to shorten and ease the portage, was planned to cross through Nicaraguan territory. Walker and his band were hired by the Liberal faction to attack the city of Granada, stronghold of the Conservative faction on the shores of Lake Nicaragua, as Henighan tells it. Walker duly launched his assault on the farms and homes of the ancestors of Ernesto Cardenal living around Granada, but as soon as the gunslinger accomplished the job he was hired for he turned around and betrayed the party that had invited him into the country. He appointed a puppet president, then installed himself in the office, declared English the official language, appropriated the land, as he had in Mexico, reinstated slavery, and aligned his new country with the slaveholders of the American South, especially western Tennessee.

Two thousand grants of Nicaraguan land were made to U.S. settlers, who poured into the country, or were supposed to, or were about to, and President Walker is quoted as saying, "With the negro-slave as his companion, the white man would become fixed to the soil; and they together would destroy the

power of the mixed race which is the bane of the country."
But by the time Palliser and his expedition gathered and set
out from Fort Garry, or Winnipeg, in May 1857, Walker's fortunes had gone the other way. Walker was one mean outlaw
cowboy, as illustrated in the story of another Granada family, the Corrals, who beseeched him to commute the death
sentence he had pronounced on one of its members. Walker
responded by decreeing their kinsman would not be shot
at noon, as originally scheduled, but at 2 p.m. By this time,
even poor and non-aligned Nicaraguans were roused to beat
Walker back and out of their country with guns and sticks and
stones, and finally he was forced to surrender, escaping death
only thanks to his evacuation by a U.S. naval officer. Walker
set out for the territory again a few years later, but in 1860 the
British turned him over to Honduras, where he was executed
by firing squad. Those gunshots at the devil would have been
still ringing in the air when Palliser, along with the loyal but
shadowy John Sullivan and the resurrected Dr. James Hector,
docked on the Pacific coast of what was then still the Gran
Colombian territory of Panama for the short traverse of the
isthmus by stagecoach and canoe piled high with the buffalo
head trophies and hides stuffed in among the written reports
and scientific gauges and measurements that made up their
luggage, and then boarding a steamer back to England on the
West Indian side, as Palliser had hoped.

So long after the Central American countries gained
independence from Spain in 1821, Nicaragua and the others
were still riven by battles over where to build a passage over
the isthmus or dig a canal through it and to whose benefit. A
canal that was the completion of the colonial dream, British
and Spanish, and the French were in there, too, of reaching
the Indies, East and West, by sea routes through the Americas,
until finally in 1903 President Theodore Roosevelt, fresh from
his widely publicized ride along the forty-ninth parallel from
the Cypress Hills to Wood Mountain in a democrat, the horse-
drawn buggy so called, I guess, because driver and passengers

rode on the same level, took the bull by the horns and invaded Gran Colombia to carve out the territory of Panama, a newly made-up country whose sole reason for being was to host a canal through the isthmus with U.S. money to ensure American control over the passage linking east to west. By then, the governing classes of Nicaragua had completely lost track of their own interests, let alone those of a nation in whose name they claimed to act. Even the completion and opening of the Panama Canal in 1914, amid the groans of the dying empires of Europe that momentarily distracted the attention of the colonial powers, did not stop the bitter fighting in Nicaragua, until the fatal year 1979 and the routing of the dictator Somoza, the final offensive beginning in early May, just after the lonesome gunshot fired on Johnny Bradley's ranch on April 1st, and it's hard to avoid the speculation, if not the conclusion, that my dad's gunshot was like a starter pistol that somehow the Sandinista cowboy rebels, high up in Sandino's mountains, heard, or sensed, and took as a signal that it was time to surprise Somoza's army and National Guard, ferreting them out wherever they swaggered or hid, and they knew, come July, when Somoza fled the country, Nicaraguans might finally be able to begin making their own plans that would not depend on Christopher Columbus, the evil moon that guided his ship, the *Santa Maria*, or the thieving schemes of cowboys riding in from Nashville and Albuquerque and Sonora.

I am as surprised as anyone that the Panama Canal turns out to be the colonial wound at the heart of the story, where the tips of the horns tore the fabric of so many lives and not only in Bradley's corral. The schism of the Americas allowing ships and cargo to pass through on the way to elsewhere, Europe, the Orient. Of course, I know it's outlandishly paranoid to make these connections, as though some kind of logic were at work, some designing hand weaving the stories together, mine and those of the entire Western Hemisphere, but isn't that what the story and its telling are? The selection of significant events, silent omission of what you would suppress or evade, what escapes notice, impressing a beginning, middle, and end on the chaotic formlessness of things and unendingness of time, especially on the compounded disorder caused by the sudden disappearance of a grounding coordinate, like a parent, from a misbegotten ranch at the centre of a surveyor's triangle on the polemical map? Palliser, by the way, surveyor of the triangle and hunter of buffalo, turns out to be the prototype of the globetrotter whose work and pleasure created the need for a canal through the isthmus in the first place, easing passage from one side of the Americas to the other, and back and forth to Europe, Africa, and the Orient, where, let us recall, Columbus and his backers were only seeking access to spices to improve the taste of food and assist in its preservation. In my defence, while admittedly overly indulgent of self-regard in a few places, and at times small-minded and fanciful, my story departs from the civilizing mission of colonialism in that nowhere, so far, does it claim to work from an overarching scheme or plan, fully cognizant of my lack of an alibi and proposing no inevitability to events as they devolve in a spectacle of deshaping and ruin, loose ends everywhere. I'm not saying these events are connected, only that's how I put them back together after they fell apart and then crowded into my devising and telling of the story of experience on colonized territory in history.

I found Margaret Randall not at home in Albuquerque, or not resident there, though I did find a volume of her poems at one of the many outdoor bookstalls around the campus, which I recall being in the centre of a dreamy and sandy city I could have lain down to die in. After a few days, though, my vital spirits and sense of direction recovered as I climbed into the driver's seat again to make my way resignedly back north, even coming around the mountain passes, sharp and steep, along rivers gushing from the foothills and up onto the wide-open welcoming plains of Wyoming where the antelope dance sideways in unison, with a feeling of certainty that "Everything changes / The world is new / Love will come again," from

Chase's song about to break through. On through Montana past Hoyt Axton's ranch, my brother's cowboy hero, country and western royalty really, whose mother wrote "Heartbreak Hotel," which Elvis recorded, making Mae and her son fabulously well-to-do for a time until they lost everything. Yeah, water for my horses, the songs no matter how forlorn blew fear to the far horizons, the four corners, with their bluegrass twang of country poverty and cowboy regret sharpening the colours that danced on the blanched grasses and sands, and I could feel how country and western took in its hillbilly brethren, aching bluegrass, to form the dominant white ethnic music by the end of the Dirty Thirties, combining it with the guitar strumming that calmed the cattle out west at night, forestalling the stampede that would be triggered by the slightest unexpected cry, rustling of coyotes or wolves in the brush, the way horses will bolt at the rustle of a paper bag, a genre of lullaby not for babies, or that makes babies of all of us, binding the cowboy to the beasts of the field that clothe and feed us and keep us company in return. Country and western swing and honky-tonk roared in the brief defensive triumphalism following the war, as I was reading somewhere, followed by the unabashed optimism of postwar America in the songs of Bob Wills, Ernest Tubbs, Buck Owens, right around the time my parents got married, oblivious to the horns swaying behind the veil.

Back in Madrid, in our trailer that along with others encircled the shabby corral with the three neglected horses, I dismissed Frank and his New Testament with some inner indignance, and as soon as I got him away from the door of the trailer, along with his concern about my soul, pretended or real, and I threw supper together and drove it out to the field, I cornered Black Bart to ask what he knew about the hired hand Coyote, who, Frank had told me, was supposed to be tending the horses.

"Oh, Coy Boy," laughed Bart, so I knew he'd heard talk of him from the other crews or even met him somewhere, maybe at the bar. "He's a Dakota," Bart said. "Dakota Sioux."

"Why doesn't he clean the corral?" I asked.

"I don't know what's going on there," said Bart. He called Stan over, and he didn't know either.

But later that night, when they got back from the field and the bar, Bart and Stan came over and scratched on the side of my tent, where I'd already gone to bed. I opened the door flap, and we talked for a while down low. My tent was close to the screen door of the crew boss's trailer.

"What they're saying," said Stan, "is that Coy Boy is in trouble with the farmer for taking Hunter, the farmer's son, to a sweat lodge on the reserve up across the state line. And the farmer found out, and now he's refusing to pay Coy Boy his wages."

"Yeah, so Coy Boy is refusing to clean the corral and just keeps the horses fed and watered," said Black Bart. "Just doing minimum chores."

"Why would the farmer care about Hunter doing a sweat lodge?" I asked.

Bart said, "He says it's pagan, a pagan ceremony."

We all laughed.

"No, really, the farmer is born-again. Evangelical Christian. He thinks Coy Boy is corrupting Hunter."

We laughed some more—who was corrupting whom?—then went still when we heard the crew boss cough in his trailer, maybe his way of saying we should keep it down.

"But why doesn't the farmer just bawl Hunter out and get on with it?" I whispered. "I can't stand the neglect of those horses. The corral is stinking to high heaven. I can smell it in the trailer when I'm cooking."

Bart and Stan were kneeling down at the opened flap of my tent, and now they stood up to go to their beds in the crew trailer. Stan said they'd ask around, but it just seemed like something had gone pretty haywire up at the farmhouse, and the farmer was irate with Coy Boy.

Day by day, we learned a little more about Hunter, and I finally even saw him one time, about sixteen years old and a bit overweight. Or heavy, a bit rounded. More so than the usual, typically thin-to-wasting cowboy. Hunter was a reader, it turned out, and I thought, uh-oh, what is he reading? And it turned out he was reading conspiracy theories. He was just the kind of guy who would stay up all night listening to Art Bell and even phone in to ask a question about sighting a suspicious contrail or correct a fine point in somebody else's version of what happened in Roswell. Colorado Dave said he'd heard Hunter arguing with somebody that the landing had already begun. Then Dave said that wasn't the kind of thing, alien landings and conspiracies, that bothered the farmer. He might even believe in them. No, the farmer was jealous of Coyote and Hunter becoming so friendly, Dave thought, and the accusation about Coyote being a pagan was just an excuse to fire him and get him away from Hunter. Or maybe the farmer was downright racist, because Coy Boy was a full Dakota Sioux from the Pine Ridge Reserve, site of the massacre at Wounded Knee, and I would have liked to hear Coy Boy talk about that, but no opportunity arose that wouldn't be watched and speculated on by everyone around the camp, since Coyote was there only when all the crews were, very early in the morning or very late at night. He wore his hair in long braids under a pretty tall cowboy hat, a braid of sweetgrass dangled from his belt, and an enormous silver belt buckle that shielded his vitals from the bull's horns had the word *DAKOTA* engraved across it, eagle feathers etched around the lettering and a coyote howling down in one corner.

When Dave said his name, Coy Boy, with his Colorado drawl, I realized it might be a kind of pun, since it sounded from Dave's drawling mouth like Cowboy, but a little distorted, as if with a difference of some kind, or said with a smirk. Coyote was unmistakably Indigenous, so his nickname might have been ironic. He was an Indian, but at the same time more of a cowboy than anyone else there, the farmer, Hunter, or any of the combining crews, who only wished they were or saw themselves as cowboys but now rode machines, not horses. Maybe the farmer thought Coyote would contaminate Hunter, his politics, the politics the farmer thought he had learned for himself and then taught his son by example, but which weren't holding water, and maybe Hunter would switch sides and fight with the Indians, and that would torque the farmer's whole being. The farmer's more than Hunter's, I thought, for Hunter might have been ready for a complete historical change of allegiance. Or maybe, I thought much later, the farmer was afraid the friendship between Hunter and Coyote was homosexual, or maybe the farmer went that way and couldn't stand himself, so he tried to get it off his skin by accusing others of what he could not tolerate in himself. There was something in his manner, as if he was about to explode, that made me think that. And there was something girlish about Hunter's blond curly hair spilling out from under his hat and framing his plump and adorable Shirley Templish face. It all seemed to contradict his cowboy get-up, boots, and swagger, his eagerness to argue about all the conspiracies underfoot and in the sky, and then there was always a paperback stuffed in the bulging back pocket of his jeans that he'd pull out with a gesture like a cowboy drawing his gun, and he'd quote from the book to make a point. Kind of a sight to see, the three of them, as if the rage of the farmer, which maybe meant fear and vulnerability, or maybe meant guilt, made him like an action figure immobilized by indecision and inaction. Hunter had the appearance of both a girl and a cowboy, and Coyote a cowboy and an Indian, their costumes and postures that complemented or cancelled each other out, which could be put together and taken apart in different ways, dressed and undressed, funny or scary. Whoa, I thought, and maybe it was all too threatening to look at directly, so I didn't look any of them in the eye, not that I had occasion to, and kept watch from off to the side, my ears open, and the whole time I was expecting some kind of showdown, but it didn't happen while we were there. That's a whole story, I thought, and more than one.

A little before we finished that contract and pulled out of Madrid, Coyote was just gone one day, and a crew of noisy clean-cut cowboys came in with a front-end loader and a truck and cleaned the corral. They put down clean straw under the lean-to where the horses sheltered in storms, and then they loaded the small pony covered with sores into a trailer and drove off with him. At about that time, one of my leather sandals, which I had bought in Cheyenne on the way down, went missing in the night from outside my tent. The tent was so small that I always left them outside before crawling into my sleeping bag, since entering the tent and the sleeping bag was one and the same thing. Even though the sandals were outside, they were very close to my sleeping head inside, which made me shudder to think of a hand or toothy mouth, thief or animal, being that close while I was sleeping unawares. In the morning we were leaving, we hitched up the trailers and fastened down all the cupboards and things inside for the drive north, and I had to play my part wearing just one shoe. I looked everywhere and thought an animal must have found it good to chew on and made off with it. It slashed through my mind that the animal might have been a coyote, since we were on the edge of a very small town, close to the fields and coulees around, and the animals probably didn't distinguish much between our campground and their own territory. And since I thought of the thief as a coyote, I thought maybe it was Coyote, sending a signal he'd like to talk to me, and the lost sandal would lure me to wherever he was to ask for it back, and then he would explain everything I yearned to know about the horses and him and Hunter and the sweat lodge. I preferred this explanation of the missing sandal but couldn't approach Coyote because I didn't think I could maintain the rule of law if he turned out to be the thief. I didn't know what I could ask of him, especially if he did turn out to have my sandal, which seemed weighted with much greater significance than normally attaches to a shoe, and I didn't really care so much about it in comparison to the chance to talk with him. So we drove off about mid-morning without finding my sandal or anything more about how it all turned out, if Hunter ran away like his

mother had some years before, last seen working as a night
clerk at a roadside motel west of Omaha, as far as she got, and
the farmer too proud to go and get her back, or what became
of Coyote, or if he had my sandal, or where the cowboys had
taken the wounded pony, to the vet or the slaughterhouse, or
why the other horses were so closely corralled, without any
purpose I could see, and whose restless circling and pleading
at the burned-out fence, their long necks and scraggly manes
reaching and craning, all these many years, into my dreams,
and I still wish I had opened the gate and let them go free. It
was Hemingway who pointed out the strangeness of horses'
heads when he was lamenting their routine murder during the
bullfights in Madrid, Spain, the shape and size of their necks
in relation to the rest of their bodies, gored and disembowelled
without fail by the angry bulls, horses not protected or spared
despite foreknowledge and certainty of their sacrifice. Hemingway could only shake his own shaggy head in writing that's
just the way it is. The tragedy of the world is made up of two
kinds of characters, as I recall his words. "Those who accept
the fate of the horses and those who cannot bear it."

We drove north, keeping to the secondary highways. The
crew boss said over the radio it was too soon to stop at North
Platte just to get the cook a new pair of shoes, so we turned
west at Buffalo Bill's Ranch and followed along the river until
we circled around in a big, mostly empty parking lot at a strip
mall in Scottsbluff. I went in and got a new pair of cheap sandals, not leather, and picked up some takeout for lunch, and
we sat on the running boards of the vehicles and ate right there
on the asphalt. It would have been somewhere near there that
Coyote would turn straight north when he headed home to the
Pine Ridge Reserve in South Dakota and where he and Hunter
would have gone to the sweat lodge. Or they would have taken
the back roads Coyote would know well, and it was all I could
do to keep from leaving my crew right then and there, and
setting out to find him and my sandal, a more solid footing, I
thought. Coyote would know all the trails between the North

Platte River and Pine Ridge that William Cody would have followed to pick up the Hunkpapa Sioux Chief Sitting Bull when he joined Buffalo Bill's Wild West Show from 1885 to 1887, the much-beloved nature theatre that travelled all through the United States and Canada. Sitting Bull was the big draw, famous for being among the last of the resisters, much admired even by hecklers who shouted "Killer of Custer" when they saw him but who lined up like everyone else and pressed coins into his palms for an autograph afterward in all their imperial nostalgia. In the final year of performances, Cody invited Sitting Bull to accompany the theatre on a tour of a Europe awash in the pleasure of regret for all that was destroyed in its expansion west. Sitting Bull declined, preferring to stay put in the Dakotas to do what he could to prevent the taking back of yet more reserve lands for the settlers pouring off rail cars or rolling up in wagons and carts from points east. In Dee Brown's *Bury My Heart at Wounded Knee*, I read how Cody was one of the few white men Sitting Bull could tolerate. Their friendship was mutual, and when Sitting Bull left the little travelling theatre Cody gave him a parting gift of a white sombrero and a performing horse. The horse was "trained to sit down and raise one hoof at the crack of a gunshot," writes Brown. So when Sitting Bull, whose popularity for resisting the signing over of reserve lands was becoming more and more of a threat to the plans for settling the West, was awakened in his log cabin on the Standing Rock Reserve, which straddles the border between the Dakotas, early in the morning of December 15, 1890, by Lieutenant Bull Head, an Indian police officer hired to get his fellow Sioux to sign over the lands, who then herded Sitting Bull into a wagon surrounded by forty-three Indian police, backed up by a squadron of U.S. Cavalry three miles away, and when Sitting Bull's ally Catch-the-Bear raised a rifle he'd hidden under a blanket and fired at Bull Head, and Bull Head returned fire, the police bullet missed Catch-the-Bear and killed Sitting Bull instead, and his gift horse, at the sound of the shots, performed his routine of sitting down on his haunches and raising one front hoof to paw at the air, it seemed to all those present that the horse "was performing the Dance of the Ghosts," the dance that had spread north "like prairie fire" from the Paiute country near Pyramid Lake in Nevada and been performed as far away as Germany and elsewhere in Europe, an Amerindian reinterpretation of the coming of the Messiah, who turns out to be indigenous to the Americas, and whose arrival presages, in "the next springtime, when the grass was knee high, the earth would be covered with new soil which would bury all the white men," and all the dead Indians and the buffalo and wild horses will be resurrected, and they will live over the Great Plains as before, and it will all come to pass if the faithful dance the Ghost Dance, which they did, and which the U.S. authorities came to fear, failing to recognize its Christian underlay and deferral of the day of reckoning to the great hereafter, and feared it all the more at the fumbling, cock-eyed murder of Sitting Bull, since a crowd of Ghost Dancers, who outnumbered the Indian police "by four to one," had witnessed the killing, followed by the eerie performance of his gesturing show horse, which finally stood up on all fours and ambled away amid the wild gun-fight that then broke out, overwhelmed by too many gunshots to respond to each one, and the arrival of the cavalry, whose intervention alone "saved the Indian police from extinction" at the hands of the enraged Sioux. Who knows whether the dancers and Indian militiamen kept alive some small pockets of belief that Sitting Bull's power would return in some way, just as Sitting Bull had returned from Wood Mountain after six years there, a refugee on the run from the U.S. military after the victory over Custer at Little Big Horn. In 1878, the Canadian government of Prime Minister John A. Macdonald took criticism from the opposition in the House of Commons about the expense incurred by "the crossing of our frontier by Sitting Bull." No one wanted to spend money to provide Sitting Bull and his people with a reserve of land north of the forty-ninth parallel, or pay for any more than minimal rations for the band of about 3,000 Sioux who accompanied him, despite their willingness to pledge allegiance to the Queen. So every year during his stay at Wood Mountain, as the buffalo herds dwindled, small groups of Sioux drifted back across the Medicine Line, as the border was called, and by the time Sitting Bull decided to leave, too, he crossed into Montana with just 186 followers on July 19th, the significant Sandinista date of victory, but 100 years earlier, in the sweep and motion over all this vast territory, in time and space, in libraries of books and here in these few sentences.

In a few short hours, or a day, after we left Madrid, rolling north through Wyoming, crossing the Cheyenne River just west and over the hill from Wounded Knee, the thought of that battleground made me think of Coyote's forebears, his elders, Sitting Bull's friend Chief Red Cloud and the others at Pine Ridge, and how they figured out the link between writing on paper, of which they previously had no notion, and the taking of territory, coming to fear "touching the pen," to leave their marks on sheets pushed into their hands and then just as quickly snatched back by Washington or military men, a proceeding always followed by the loss of more and more land to settlement by newcomers. And how "touching the pen" presumed and reinforced the geometry of Palliser's survey, the southern line of his triangle tracing the forty-ninth parallel of latitude that demarcates the Canada-U.S. border. So when Sitting Bull left Wood Mountain, where for six years he had been the invited guest of his kinsmen, the Assiniboine, to return home to the Dakotas, he both crossed and erased the border imagined and drawn, leaving no mark but the hoofprints of his horse on the actual ground, his movements rejoining the northern plains from the apex of the Palliser Triangle to the Dakotas and far south, reclaiming the territorial continuity and extent of the Great Plains of North America. And to see it all from the perspective of Sitting Bull in the instant Lieutenant Bull Head fired, or in the instant before the trigger was pulled, or to see it from Coyote's point of view, in retrospect, is to see not only the shift of appearances but also in the substance of things, dissolution of the borderline so recently drawn, and a Buffalo Commons indeed appears, encompassing Johnny Bradley's lost bullfight, too, and Bern Morgan's misfortunes, descendants of settlers, catastrophes befalling alike Johnny's buffalo, King, the Assiniboine, Sitting Bull, all cast in the theatre of extinctions, peoples and beasts, migrants and settlers, hunters and gatherers no one wants to look at directly or account for on the scales of culpability and entitlement, grievous angels blowing their horns from all the thrown points of our origins, and what I reach for and despair over is a touch of the pen not lethal, not to conquer and steal, but to multiply and nourish the lives and stories that tarry and dwell at this our threshold.

COWBOYS OF THE AMERICAS

Around 1880 in Tombstone, Arizona, Richard Slatta, in *Cowboys of the Americas*, finds the word *cowboy* used only as an insult, cowboys dodging the law, smuggling tobacco and alcohol over the U.S.-Mexico border, horses and cattle over the U.S.-Canada border, just as the North West Mounted Police on the northern side equated all cowboys with outlaws, an Inspector Macdonnell reporting that "the American Cowboy (erroneously so called) or horse thief, is a desperado of the worst description, who holds the life of a man as cheaply as that of an animal, always being well-mounted and armed." Cowboys were considered rough stock, unbroken like the broncs they were famous for daring to ride, such as Bill Pickett when he invented steer wrestling, called bulldogging at first, when, with great theatricality, he leaned down to bite the upper lip of the steer whose back he had clambered onto, and hung on with his teeth to work the outraged, wincing animal to the ground with such intimacy and flair, his mouth open and teeth bared in just the right position, hands occupied in protecting himself from the puncturing horns, and you have to imagine Pickett's innovation came from the same place as his fear, the calculated recklessness of the rodeo rough rider, his cowboy act headlining the "travelling nature theatre of the Miller Brothers' 101 Ranch

Wild West Show," as the "Colored Hero of the Mexican Bull Ring in Death Defying Feats of Courage and Skill. Thrills! Laughs Too!"

Cowboys like Pickett worked first as slaves, of course, in the old Confederate states. Some escaped before the Civil War, others fled west only in the aftermath, finding paid work on ranches in the western states and up onto the northern plains, like Dan Williams, hired on as the cook for the Palliser Expedition and the only member the prickly Blakiston deemed capable of worthwhile conversation. The pool of vagabond ranch labour was made up of such men but also included Hispanics and whites from various ports in South America and Europe. On the northern Great Plains, especially on the U.S. side, they were mostly from Mexico and worked seasonally for low wages, owning nothing more than a saddle, a bedroll, and their boots until they could catch a wild pony or rustle a horse already broken. Vagrant, unfettered cowboys claimed to prefer topping up their sporadic wages, writes Slatta, with the proceeds of their entrepreneurial efforts, casual or opportunistic, such as smuggling but also by following the rodeo circuits to compete for cash prizes between cattle drives.

Cowboys were sometimes forced by a shortage of funds to operate on both sides of the law, which gave them a glimpse of freedom on the open range of communally owned land, no man's land and every man's, that meant freedom to dwell in solitude, what was longed for and lamented in the country and western world, day to day, acutely aware as we are of how much we need each other and the animals, habitat and home, and the cowboy personifies that contentious crux of individual and social life. All through and around the Big Muddy Valley, east of Wood Mountain and south of Assiniboia, everybody knows the name Dutch Henry, renowned horseman, and Marjorie Mason, born on the Rohde Ranch, wrote his story in *One Hundred Years of Grasslands*, her oversized book crammed with facts and photos and lore that came down to me, with her autographed inscription, along with the rest of my mother's library. Dutch Henry was known to be one of the best cowboys around and worked on the Bonneau Ranch near Willow Bunch. A revolver belted to his hip, he commanded respect and was unfailingly polite, cowboy-style, while employed, yet found he could earn a better living stealing horses, making regular trips across the narrows of Big Muddy Lake, a dried-up lake bottom most of the year, to deliver stock on either side of the border. By the turn of the twentieth century, he had built a solid reputation among the local ranchers, who had to know he was all the while crossing to the other side of the law, buying his own ranch with the proceeds of robbery and horse theft on that dark side. Local ranchers came to fear as well as respect him and his gang, which included the cruel Sam Kelly, "cold as a fish," and Frank Carlyle, a former North West Mountie who failed to show up for work one day when he was supposed to slip south across the border and blow up a train bridge to stop a train the gang lay in wait to rob west of Plentywood, Montana. Carlyle instead rode to the bunkhouse of the Marshall Ranch to sleep off his hangover from a night of drinking, and he holed up there until two members of Dutch Henry's gang picked him up and took him out into the badlands and shot him, as the story goes, his body later turning up in a coulee in the Big Muddy Valley.

Dutch Henry and the gang were among the sometimes jobless, homeless cowpunchers drifting north to the Big Muddy Badlands, where they took over and enlarged caves that had been wolf dens, even hosting in Castle Butte the Wild Bunch, Butch Cassidy, and the Sundance Kid, so nicknamed for the eighteen months he spent in jail for train robbery in Sundance, Wyoming. On his release, the Kid went to work helping Cassidy organize an outlaw escape route patterned on the Pony Express, with relays of horses placed at friendly or adequately bribed ranches along the way from the Big Muddy in the Palliser Triangle to Mexico and beyond. The Big Muddy hideout was Station Number One of the Outlaw Trail. Once the border patrols were on to his switches of allegiance, now inside, now outside, the law, Dutch Henry stayed mostly on the U.S. side and used disguised innocents such as Jenny Sallet, the Wood Mountain milkmaid, supplier of butter and milk to the Mounted Police post, when she suddenly took up the sideline of selling horses at Dutch Henry's behest. No one inquired too deeply at first about where the ponies came from. She sold some thirty-five stolen ponies, possibly an appaloosa among them, grandsire or -dam of the horse I rode named Princess, to William Ogle, Lord Ogle, the English aristocrat who married a Lakota woman when he began ranching at Wood Mountain, the ancestor of Lizzie and Roy and Harold and all the Ogles thereabouts ever since. Jenny found many local customers eager to help her out and none who suspected her of stealing the horses or consorting with thieves. Eventually, though, she tried selling stock to a rancher suspicious enough to look into the horses' brands, and that led to rustling charges laid against Jenny and her son-in-law, Ed Shufelt, a Montana saloon owner who had gone into partnership with Dutch Henry on the underside. Shufelt died in prison, but the charges against Jenny were dropped, just as she dropped out of the historical record.

Whatever happened to Dutch Henry remains unknown, no matter what the locals try to tell you they know for sure. One report, no more than a rumour, has him shot by Mounted Police south of Moose Jaw. Another records him shot in Minnesota, and a third has him convicted of counterfeiting in Montana as late as 1905. Most say he fled after Butch and the Kid led the way, jumping the falls and extending the Outlaw Trail as far south as the pampas of Argentina. Dutch Henry and the Wild Bunch would find their claim to freedom from the law and their disregard for border restrictions aligned them with the gaucho, the Argentinian cowboy feared and disparaged before he was tamed and domesticated, the cowboy cousin or ancestor of the southern cone, where natural plenty—food, water, shelter—meant he had no need to go into town or become part of anything so abstract as the town or nation, with their drawing of borders, rural against urban, since independence from those very borders was the source of the enormous political power the gaucho began to wield, north and south, and attempts to rein him in took the form in Argentina especially of civil strife and partisan political violence.

Juan Facundo Quiroga, known as Facundo, was the name that came to stand for the combined resourcefulness and coal-black heart of the cowboy, north and south, his freedom from social bonds that made him sometimes the good guy, sometimes the bad. In Argentina, gauchos were nomadic, rambling over all the Pampas, their world defined by the lack of fences, superior horsemanship, and radical self-reliance. The gaucho revels in his "defiant solitude" and like the North American cowboy wants only to be left alone, according to Roberto González Echevarría in his introduction to the famous book called *Facundo* by Domingo Faustino Sarmiento. Facundo first headed a band of gauchos who controlled the western regions of San Juan and La Rioja. After Argentina won its independence from Spain, by 1829 the political faction aligned with the gauchos had become powerful enough to install one of its own in Buenos Aires, Juan Manuel de Rosas, who became "ruler of the whole country." But Rosas, like William Walker in Nicaragua, soon turned on the party that had brought him to power. He feared the political muscle wielded by the gauchos, their casual strength, so he set up an ambush to have Facundo assassinated.

Facundo had started out as a hired hand on a hacienda in the Plumerillo area. For a year, he stood out for his punctuality at work, showing up on time. My dad's slight lateness for work, like poor Frank Carlyle's, sleeping it off on the Marshall Ranch, was more the cowboy norm. Facundo was known, too, for the control he exercised over the other cowboys, as Sarmiento tells it in *Facundo*, the book and the cowboy so popular that the author himself was later elected president of Argentina! When a gaucho wanted to skip work and spend the day getting drunk, as who wouldn't if they could, he would discuss it first with Facundo, who would immediately report it to the señora and offer to take responsibility for the gaucho to show up for work the next day. The grateful cowboys called him "the Padre." After a year or so spent disciplining less powerful cowboys while retaining their loyal allegiance, as well as that of the range bosses, Facundo asked for his wages, amounting to seventy pesos. He laid them down on the gambling table, lost them all in one bad hand, mounted his horse, and wandered off until he met a judge along the road who asked to see his "working papers." Seeming to fumble in his pocket for them, Facundo produced a knife instead that the judge scarcely glimpsed before it cut him down, and the gaucho rode off with a sneer.

Was Facundo "avenging his recent loss on the judge?" asks Sarmiento. Or did he only want to indulge his hatred of civil authority and add "this new deed to the luster of his growing fame? Both," Sarmiento writes. Acts of ruthless vengeance were frequent in Facundo's life. Sarmiento gives several examples, to the extent that the highly moralistic and initially critical author betrays his awe, even begrudging admiration, of the purity of Facundo's resolve in savagery, the way we admire outlaws, always secretly rooting for their success in escaping laws and constraints we might also wish to escape but would never dare attempt ourselves. Facundo's worst deed, surely, though Sarmiento prefers to avert his eyes even while retelling it, eager to accept the slim evidence of its contrary, was the gaucho's reaction to his father's refusal to give over a sum of money Facundo had requested. On being turned down, the gaucho waited "for the moment when both his father and mother were sleeping the siesta" so he could block the door of their room before setting fire to the thatched roof of their house and watch impassively as his parents burned to death. The harrowing story of severing ties to his parents, in Sarmiento's telling, along with a story of Facundo's leading a prison break seen as the Argentine version of "Samson's jawbone, the Hebrew Hercules," becomes, on the national scale, the paradigm of the severance of ties to the colonial parent nations of Europe, and there Sarmiento begins to take the full measure of the gaucho and the cowboy, the power of his fascination and hold on settler descendants of the Americas to this day. Sarmiento then offers up a contrasting account to display Facundo's respect for his father and for the law in a previous exchange that emphasizes the gaucho's ambiguous nature, now good guy, now bad guy. The gaucho begs forgiveness for his crimes and acquiesces as his father turns him over to the law for his transgressions.

Sarmiento and his readers display typically mixed feelings for the gaucho, admiring his disregard for the law while damning him for it, with an ambivalence also evident in the Borges poem about the assassination of Facundo, "General Quiroga Rides to His Death in a Carriage," which is at pains to name and lay blame not on the gaucho for his crimes but on his killer, Rosas, in keeping with popular sentiment. "To ride to your death in a carriage—what a splendid thing to do!" Borges sets out in his poem. "[F]our black horses with a tinge of death in their dark coats" carry the man "whose name alone is enough to set the lances quivering." Now riding in his carriage, now cut down and dead, now alive on his feet, and "now immortal, now a ghost," in the poem by Borges, Facundo reports to the section of "hell marked out for him by God." The poet Borges himself stands equally admired and accused and in writing this poem perhaps recognizes his own fate, descended as he is, like the gaucho, from European settlers. In recounting the death of the gaucho, Borges confronts his own impending extinction, imminent disappearance, in the mestizo-Métis borderlines, gaucho and cowboy personifying the point of colonial contact, at once the perpetrator and legacy, the remnant of its glory and bearer of its criminality.

Voices were raised until they became a clamour against the bloody dictator de Rosas for ordering the death of the gaucho! After the publication of *Facundo*, outbursts of national indignation and protest appeared in short stories, novels, whole newspapers such as *La Nación*, the Salón Literario, and the Association of May. In what became the most enduring of literary works, *Facundo* cast Argentina as engaged in a kind of mythic steer wrestling or rodeo, a life-and-death struggle between Facundo's savagery, necessary for survival, and his promise of freedom from Europe, its strictures and constraints, freedom from our parents and the past, while counting on their provision for the cultural transmission of Europe through the library and the law.

In the wake of *Facundo*, another Argentine writer, José Hernández, wrote the most famous of epic gaucho poems in books called *Martín Fierro* and *The Return of Martín Fierro*, in the 1870s, around the same time Treaty 4 was signed and Sitting Bull and his Lakota band rode into Wood Mountain. The gaucho speaks there as the *criollo*, the Argentine-born son of European immigrant settler parents who—like me, my dad, Johnny Bradley, my brother, and my mom—knows the truth of his condition. The word *criollo*, something like the "pioneer" of North American English, is a compliment and sympathetic to complaints about the law and how it cuts right through the gaucho, law/outlaw, ruling mostly in favour of the few and against the poor, especially the rural poor, in the words of the translator, C.E. Ward. So gaucho and cowboy personify the settler/Indigenous and the rural/urban divide that rends the Americas, North and South, perhaps fatally, to this day.

> I can tell you that in my part of the land
> There's hardly a real *criollo* left—
> They've been swallowed by the grave,
> or run off, or been killed in the war—
> because in this country, friend,
> there's no end to the struggle.

In six-line stanzas that rhyme in the original Spanish, and whose last lines often form a proverb that lies ready on the tip

of the Argentine tongue, *Martín Fierro* runs to over 7,000 lines
meant to be accompanied by the gaucho strumming his guitar. The gaucho is "a man kept from sleep / by an uncommon
sorrow" that pursues him:

> And listen to the story told
> by a gaucho who's hunted by the law;
> who's been a father and husband
> hard-working and willing—
> and in spite of that, people take him
> to be a criminal.

Only horse breaking and rodeo and branding time yield songs
of joy and wit, the gaucho always landing on his feet, drinking
and eating over open fires, yet with the foreboding that the
days of heaven are numbered.

Martín Fierro is the cowboy masterpiece in any language,
it is agreed by all, though it's hard to say from English if the
criollo completely displaces or, alternatively, joins forces with
the nomadic Indigenous riders of the pampas. Sarmiento's
Facundo, in contrast, is much further away from perfection,
divided against itself carelessly or tragically, and stylistically
flawed, even apart from its self-contradiction on the significance of the gaucho, good guy or bad guy, that animates the
writing, now for him, now against him. Riven with contradictions and hobbled by flaws, *Facundo* makes "cavalier" use
of sources and is rife with outright factual errors. Over the
whole work there hangs an air of "improvisation," according to
González Echevarría. Yet all these faults serve only to enhance
"the work's vitality" and "the reader's sense that the book is
alive, making itself even as he or she turns the pages," with
a startled sense of recognition and discovery of far-reaching
and even fantastical connections suddenly made visible in episodes revealing bravery, selflessness, and wonderment amid
all the shameful failures because of tragic but all too predictable miscalculations by mere creatures, lone cowboys, their

pitiless testing and shattering of dreams in the shambles of myth, gods, greater and lesser, falling from the sky, awakening to themselves as their own betrayers. "It is mostly Sarmiento's powerful voice . . . infused by the sublimity of the boundless Pampas that rings through and true in *Facundo*," writes González Echevarría, a voice that echoes through all Spanish American literature right down to García Marquéz's *One Hundred Years of Solitude* and the many works of the Americas that belong "to many genres and to none"—lament, diatribe, tragedy, novel, essay, autobiography, epic, memoir, confession, eulogy, travelogue—drawing on all of them, and "untrammeled by the demands of form," Sarmiento straddles fiction and non-fiction, the boundaries between them never quite clear, with only a sideways glance at historical truth in places, more a manual for how to shape the truth than the truth itself, how to patrol the borders of fact amid certain seepages of fiction, necessary and enlivening, the whole nevertheless true, where life meets the law, the open range is fenced, and those fences are then laid down or breached.

The word *cowboy* used as an insult began to give way to its opposite, a compliment, as private property displaced communal land use in the Americas. Conflict—class conflict—between the politically powerful ranchers and the cowboys whose labour they depended on increased, writes Slatta, and that's where the cowboy rode into the realms of fiction and myth. Ranchers needed the casual labour of cowboys, and to avoid paying the full compensation for a cowboy's work, what it actually was worth, or to avoid becoming too obviously beholden to the cowboy's labour, they romanticized the cowboy as a free spirit, but at the same time they engaged cowboys to police their privately owned lands, territory now property, ruthlessly, not least by branding cattle with the sign of ownership and by riding fences against predators and rustlers, but then they let the cowboys go without pay when the seasonal work was done. This was how the cowboy was transformed from the violent, untrustworthy, frontier smuggler, hunter, dreamer, opportunist, loafer, into the figure of true manly courage, according to the *Texas Livestock Journal* of October 21, 1882. The western cowboy was "as chivalrous as the famed knights of old," the *Journal* waxed poetic, with a clear and distinct sense of the cowboy's ancestry in the fiction and fantasies of Don Quixote and in that Spanish cowboy-knight's inability to distinguish between fact and fiction.

> Rough he may be, and it may be that he is not a master in ballroom etiquette, but no set of men have loftier reverence for women and no set of men would risk more in defense of their person or their honor. Another and most notable of his characteristics is his entire devotion to the interests of his employer. We are certain no more faithful employee ever breathed than he; and when we assert that he is, *par excellence*, a model in this respect, we know that we will be sustained by every man who has had experience in this matter.

Likewise, John Baumann, writing in the *Fortnightly Review* in 1887, quoting his own sources, carefully cited in Slatta, dismissed the myth of the cowboy as a "long-haired" ruffian. Baumann wrote that the cowboy was "in the main a loyal, long-enduring, hard-working fellow, grit to the backbone, and tough as a whipcord; performing his arduous and often dangerous duties, and living his comfortless life, without a word of complaint about the many privations he has to undergo."

"How can we account for such sharply conflicting visions of the cowboy?" asks Professor Slatta. To ask that question is to ask how we account for the change from communal to private ownership of land. And to know how much pivots on that. As Slatta knows, no contradiction is resolved or resolvable in logic or life. We live with them, the contradictions, and they with us, and they are always doing something to us and for us and against us. In the case of the cowboy, what's kept him alive and kicking for so long despite the loss of habitat, the open range replaced by feedlots that make him an industrial worker like any other, just another link in the food chain, and the rodeo prize money claimed by TV dudes who never rode a horse, all the richly knotted conflicts that he embodies and that nourish the belief, dearly and widely held, is that we can have it both ways: private property for the few, dream of a Buffalo Commons for all. The cowboy makes attractive and desirable all our grounding contradictions, removing any need to choose between veneration and repudiation of our settler grandparents. Between obeying the law and murdering the judge. Between allegiance to Europe and commitment to the renewal of Indigenous life.

U.S. President Theodore Roosevelt stumbled onto the cowboy myth and quickly harnessed it to his country's apparent benefit. Writing in 1913 about the few years he spent on a ranch in the Dakota Badlands as a young man, he reported that the experience taught him self-reliance, hardihood, and the value of the instant decision, like his sudden decision to invade Gran Colombia and create Panama to sever the isthmus and open a passage by way of a canal. Writing in the May 24th issue of *The Outlook*, Roosevelt titled his article "In Cowboy Land." He enthusiastically described Buffalo Bill's Wild West Show and the Congress of Rough Riders of the World, then still travelling and performing on both sides of the forty-ninth parallel, though with only the alluring memory, not the star attraction, of Sitting Bull. The president's embrace of cowboy land was further propagated among the reading public by penny press and dime novels. Prentiss Ingraham's 1877 potboiler *Buck Taylor, King of the Cowboys* made exciting cowboy stories available to a mass audience, and like all cowboy literature it "extolled the virtues of courage, honour, chivalry, individualism, and the triumph of right over wrong. Wild west shows, circuses, films," the pulp fictions of Zane Grey and Louis l'Amour, "radio, and finally television perpetuated cowboy mythology," the cowboy even lifted out of the West to represent a certain strain of Americanism in all its newfound imperial reach through the twentieth century, embrace of all things new and forward looking, the sunny side of colonialism, while yearning for a mythical past when the good guys won, all those contradictions I've been lining up here to disentangle once and for all in my essay, perennially forthcoming, "On Long Guns and Rural Life."

The class conflict buried in the suddenly corporate-approved cowboy is documented by Slatta in a rancher's complaint of 1888 about the scarcity of unhorsed labour around Macleod, Alberta. No one could be found to dig a well, the complainant said, because "a man cannot dig a well from a horse's back." In Mexico, it was considered too dangerous to allow mestizos, considered non-white or non-European, to ride horses at all, too "dangerous and democratic," because their rise to the heights of horseback might put ideas in their heads about rising to the level of the landowner more generally. Conflict among the conquistadors, Spanish and English, also persisted in the general whitewashing of the cowboy of North America. Hispanic origins were erased or aligned with the racialized mestizo, Indian, Métis as they became the enemy, when in fact cowboys, English and Spanish, and so-called half-breeds and Indians were natural allies in defending communal land use against the narrow class interests and forces that stamped it out in favour of private property, the privatizations corralled for narrowly private *bonanzas*, that Spanish-become-English word naming the law-abiding ponderosa of Ben Cartwright and his cowboy sons on the TV show *Bonanza* that we watched religiously on Sunday nights without fail throughout the Great Plains and beyond.

The Spanish conquistadors brought the horses and wild cattle to the New World in the first place, and the first cowboys, north and south, recognized only communal land use. They were hunter-gatherers, hunting the cattle for food and clothing, making leather goods for their own use and trade. A few of the wild cattle roaming the northern continent went farther north and then west from Florida, but most went from Mexico and the western coast, from various points along the isthmus of Central America and from California, as far north as Vancouver Island, some hundreds of animals ranging into the foothills of Alberta and entering the Palliser Triangle probably around Manitou Lake and down to the Cypress Hills and grasslands around Maple Creek, Swift Current, Wood Mountain, the Assiniboia plains, and ranging over the strange empire that might have been envisioned by Louis Riel and the Métis at the headwaters of the Red River near St. Paul, Minnesota, and on up to Winnipeg, where the Red meets the Assiniboine, itself fed by confluence with the Qu'Appelle at the border of what is now Saskatchewan. So much of this languishes on old maps and in books because of the corralling of English speakers inside the linguistic fence to keep out the Amerindian languages, and likewise the French of Willow Bunch, St. Boniface, Quebec, the reduction and expulsion of Spanish to the language of minstrels in sombreros strumming guitars at hot chili pepper restaurants.

The great cattle drives north and west from Texas, beginning in 1866, according to Slatta, were all about rounding up the wild cattle still out there by that late date. English round-ups and Spanish rodeos spread over the continent alongside the diminishing indigenous stock, buffalo herds and their Indigenous hunters triggering stampedes into the pounds. Cowboys befriended the Plains Indians at first out of necessity, depending on them to get the lay of the land, the knack of surviving the harsh weather, overwhelming sky, and stark solitude. But then the cowboys became the good guys, white guys, European descendants, and that's when bad guys were called for to distinguish one from the other. Indigenous rough riders and other-skinned hombres were recast as bad guys, savages, killers of Custer, horse thieves, in cruel displacement of what actually undermined the cowboys and Indians of the Great Plains, the private enclosures of land. Yet the colonial languages, English and Spanish at least, preserve our common origins and interests, since it is not possible to speak of cattle ranching, of Johnny Bradley's corral and nostalgia for the open range and reintroduction of the buffalo, without the Spanish vocabulary as it is brought into English: the *corral* where the waltz of fate took place and Johnny took the horns is Spanish for "ring," as also in the Ring of Fire, although the word now used instead of *corral* in Spanish America, curiously, is the English *cowpen*, according to Slatta, the two languages, in these words, exchanging glances in a mirror without seeing each other.

In "The Bullfight as Mirror," Michel Leiris, now writing as an anthropologist and not an autobiographer, defines God according to the definition given by Nicolas of Cusa, as "the coincidence of contraries," which other writers, notably the absurdist Alfred Jarry, have described as a geometric line where it touches on a curve. Leiris works out this idea in writing about the Spanish bullfight as the drama of our reaching for that point of contact, toward those places where we feel in touch with both our community and ourselves as individual members, the point of contradiction personified in the tragedy of Antigone, torn between loyalty to her dead brother and conformity to the law of the land prohibiting his burial. In common with all the arts and religions of tragedy, writes Leiris, the matador swerves to avoid the bull's horns, which he also draws toward him with the swish of the *muleta*, the red cloth "creating a void that the bull immediately fills, giving us an acute and . . . searing perception of the reality of space," in particular that space or place where we feel most profoundly the point of our connection to life, at once individual and social, and so contradictory, the essence of the conflict that is life itself. The bullfight is the performance on demand of this geometry and deviance from it, the line that is the trajectory of a life, and our deviation from it caused by misfortune, the channel formed in each of us by the entrance of trouble and sorrow. There is no form, nothing beautiful, no perfection or its idealization, no heaven, without this "drop of poison, hint of incoherence, grain of sand" or dirt that "derails" the whole act, its composition and disruption of extending the line to the infinitude of its projection.

What surprised me, though in retrospect I should not have been surprised, is how, in the case of the bullfight, the deviation is not the bull or made by the bull, or not only by the bull, which, after all, is only being a bull, sticking exactly to his line, the trajectory of his individual existence as a member of his species. Neither does the bull nor his horn, in isolation or on its own, represent the cause of deviation in a life, the disruptive element or flaw. Instead, it is the bullfighter who is the "tempted angel" playing with fire, engaging the agon of our interplay at the intersection of our distinctly social and individual natures, condition of existence. For Leiris, it is the matador who deviates, not the bull. The repeated turning of the tables in the bullfight, in which now the matador waves the red flag, now the bull charges, horns first, mimics for the spectator, in safety and for pleasure, the continual see-saw motion of perception, now and then, of "what lies at the real heart of our emotional life." "The *muleta* is the flaw in becoming," for Leiris, a mere "red rag," the "blemish on the matador's sumptuous costume, a fleck of dirt spoiling his fastidious grooming—slicked hair, trimmed mustache, over-built muscles of the torso and slim hips beneath the short, sequined bolero." The *muleta* is shown to be "like the veil of an illusionist or the glittery get-up of a showman," a trick of his trade, and, as a trick, the sign of corruption in place of what you "might have thought . . . was nothing but pure courage." The red rag is so puny in comparison to the threat of the gouging horns it rouses to rage that it points to the scale of heaven as not infinitely great, that extreme extension of height Nimrod built toward with his Tower of Babel. Rather, the red rag aligns heaven's scale with the tiniest detail, decisive particle, drop of water that makes the cup runneth over, single grain of sand or slightest breath of wind that triggers the landslide, what separates us from the abyss between here and hereafter where space and time are indistinguish-ably fused.

The bullfight is among those theatres of life in which we strive to feel, for however brief a time, our material connection to the world, whose sum and summit, heaven, is our existence, each as a single living creature whose incapacity, otherwise, to join utterly and be at one with that world, "except in death's fusion," is equivalent to the presence of the flaw, our condition that makes life itself the necessary flaw, red rag taunting the bull. Along the "channel formed by the entrance of misfortune," our individual and unique trajectory opens up, and that's life, its arc and curve, "the price of a fresh departure," deviation, swerve, "gust of air igniting a flame" by whose light each single life appears as a revelation, is a revelation. The entire action of the bullfighter, writer, mirror maker, reader, lonesome trav-eller is founded upon the tiny but tragic flaw by which "our unfinished condition shows itself." Everything depends on the material possibility of our wounding, on spatializing our infinite incompletion, our comprehension and measure of it, however momentarily, in space, and hence the profundity of geometry over all the other sciences, starting point and inter-section in my story of cowboys, corrals, triangles, and rings that are cracked, broken, gored, shot, and damned.

"The left! The left! *La izquierda! La izquierda!*" With those words, the crowd at the Spanish bullfight urges the matador to make increasingly risky provocations of the bull, inciting him to dare left-handed passes that pose "the gravest risks." And the crowd will not be satisfied until the matador has taken upon himself "the entire sinister aspect of the drama . . . drunk the poison almost to the last mortal drop," Leiris says—before the kill, when a sacramental lightning flash of justice restores the law and order of our vital incompletion to the ring. It's all "finally played out in the hazardous area of a threshold as narrow as a razor blade," the line of the watershed, domain of the sacred, where a river flows one way or another, north or south, the boundary itself without language. On either side, things abandon their shapeless, any-which-waywardness on the line, take on configuration and form, Spanish or English, south or north. What we've caught in the mirror is a glimpse of our "ambiguous strife" on the edge of the blade, the marriage of the rule and its glorious exception that is life, our obligatory incompletion, void that we seek in vain to fill, gap opened up in our surrender to formlessness. Just so are the pathways and revelations that glance and wink from Spanish to English in the north and in the south, vocabularies of reflection, back and forth, mirror images, especially in domains of the cowboy and corral I'm speaking of here. So when I am asked on an exam or at the border what is the difference and what is the bond between Spanish and English America, I shout out my answer: "They say *cowpen*, we say *corral*!"

Inside that corral, what we call *broncs* in English comes from the Spanish *broncos*, meaning "rough" or "rude," Englished in the bucking animal, the bucking bronc, combined with the rough rider trying to stay on its back for those enlivening seconds on the edge of the blade. The word *cowboy* fuses two words in English to sound very like the Spanish word for horse, *caballo*, in which the double *l* is pronounced as a *y*, but the word in English is more ploddingly credited to Jonathan Swift in the 1720s writing the two-word form of *cow boys* to refer to boys herding cattle, as distinct from shepherds tending sheep. Had my dad shown up for work on time on that day in early March 1979, he might have thrown a *lariat*, from the French word taken from the Spanish *la reata*, later settled into English as *lasso*, and from a safe distance slipping a noose over at least one of the thrashing horns of the bull, when the slightest tug or even the swish of the rope overhead could have distracted King for the second or two Johnny needed to run up the corral fence to safety, and we'd be talking about a close call for the surprised matador, probably nursing complacency about the certainty of the restoration of cosmic justice right now. Of course, if my dad were a gaucho, he would have had the ingenious remedy of the bolas, *las bolas*, to trip up

King and stop him in his tracks. Now a weapon used by urban street gangs, the original bolas of the gauchos was two or three stones, each wrapped in a leather pouch and strung together with leather ties. The gaucho throws the bolas into the stampeding front feet of the charging animal, and it is tripped into helplessness. The bull becomes confused and usually goes down headfirst, instantly disarmed but without serious injury to gaucho or animal. In one passage I read, a gaucho calls the bolas "Tres Marías," the three Marys, as if the non-lethal, life-saving tool evokes the blessing of the Mother of God herself, as well as the Virgin and the Magdalene, goddesses to aid the bullfighter in battles against the forces of fate he confronts in every ring. Now I see the *Tres Marías* and *las bolas* everywhere in Spanish and wonder if they are not indispensable to that language well beyond the rodeo, though I can just barely fathom the range of their reference from within the borders of English. "Enough!" shout the anti-austerity crowds in Buenos Aires, "Hasta las bolas!" as if to say, "we've had it up to our balls" (Spanish) or "our ears" (English)! How many tyrants and enraged bulls could be stopped by the timely throwing of the bolas to just that spot where it trips them up before the damage is done, horns gashing, triggers pulled, justice denied? The beauty of the bolas, too, is that it does not make a murderer of the matador, cowboy, gaucho, or dissident. The beast, deliberately provoked or not, need not be killed.

His social position as ranch owner gave Johnny Bradley the authority to prohibit drinking on his ranch, and the word for that is *caporal* in Spanish, meaning "range boss," as in the enticingly named Sweet Caporal cigarettes, or Sweet Caps, Dad's brand and my own when I first took up smoking. In Johnny's bachelor porch that time Dad took us to see the stuffed buffalo head that came up to my chin, an enormous pair of leather chaps hung on a hook by the back door, ready to be strapped on like an apron to protect the legs of the cowboy while riding on horseback through rough bush or cactus to round up strays or unbranded cattle, and the English word *chaps* comes from the Spanish word *chappererras*, with the same meaning as in English. *Rodeo* is Spanish for round-up, and in English it refers to the New World imitation of equestrian displays beloved by the conquistadors and the English upper class alike, whereas in Spanish America the rodeo is the *charreadas*. At the rodeo, the cowboy, like the conquistador, preens and performs expert horsemanship, mastery over the beasts of the field, with a pronounced disregard for the danger and difficulty of the ride, as exaggerated and celebrated in Bill Pickett's kissing the horned steer. And like the bullfight and the circus, the rodeo enthralls more without a net beneath the high wire, so at every stampede cowboys are thrown and mangled, injured horses have to be put down, especially in the chuckwagon races, in which horses race in teams tied together and to the wagon with complicated hardware and tack, with so much to become entangled and go wrong that it often does, ratcheting up the tension and threat of violence, the sought-after renewal of the perception of space with the special cruelty that the Romans also enjoyed, and seems essential, the vital nutrient or addictive drug, to inhabitants of vast prairie lands spreading to infinity beneath sublimely overarching skies.

Wallace Stegner in *Wolf Willow*, his memoir of the Palliser Triangle, its southern part where the Milk River flows toward the Missouri River in Montana, draws attention to how the cowboy blood sport is called the rodeo mostly in the United States, whereas in Canada it usually goes by the name of stampede. Wood Mountain is typically on the borderline in alternating both names. The word *stampede* is from the Spanish *estampedia*, "to stamp," linking the word to both the charging of the animals and their branding with the stamp of ownership, the rodeo's working function beyond the show-offmanship with horses and cattle. This difference between the United States and Canada in naming the gory games stands out and calls for more explanation than Stegner offers, since the rodeo refers to the round-up, the gathering in and together, the corralling of the herd to the law and orderliness of the loading chutes or the containment of fenced pastures, whereas the stampede suggests the opposite, the alarmed and dangerous scattering and dispersal of the herd. I would have guessed the word choice would be the other way around, if you go by national character stereotypes, with the Canadians, whose motto is the mild-mannered "Peace, Order, and Good Government," selecting the round-up and rodeo as their metaphor, as if to summon Her Majesty's loyal subjects to gather round our crown and sovereign centre, as we all agree, whereas the Americans, with their motto of "Life, Liberty, and the Pursuit of Happiness," are more plausibly envisioned in a stampede, every head going its own way in general abhorrence of a gathering centre of any kind, the notion of a round-up toward a centralized state anathema to Republican and Democrat alike.

On reflection, though, the Englished words *rodeo* and *stampede* fit better in the territories where they are used when you consider what I have called Geometry Absurd, which brings together the contradictory ideas of geometric form and absurd formlessness for enumerating the extent to which there is a plan at work in the universe and in the stories we tell about it. The idea of a manifest destiny or, negatively put, a conspiracy at work is pronounced in the United States, whereas the lack of pretence of any such overarching idea, and embrace of a loose confederation, originating as a French expansion then subsumed by British collateral conquest in wars centred elsewhere, the whole bound together most recently by the dream of universal health care, is more typical of the Canadian sprawl across distinct regions, hither and yon, a place first linked by Aboriginal and buffalo migrations, then by fur-bearing creatures chased by voyageurs along rivers, then by railways, whose ties were then thoughtlessly dismantled and gave way to highways now left to the vagaries of provincial finances, then by pipelines that take up all the political oxygen, provincial and federal, and on and on to produce the absurdity that seems to hang together, though not yet fairly for all. However it is, north and south of the forty-ninth parallel, *stampede* turns out to be the right word for what happened in the corral I'm speaking of, the charging of the bull, the goring, gunshots reverberating and sending all of us flying, smashing I don't know how many families to smithereens, bits and pieces flung to the four corners of the Earth, even language dismembered and discomposed, which, after all, might be what saves us in the end to write a new day. Johnny Bradley must have known the risk he was taking that morning, and, calculating, he took it anyway. He and King had known each other a long time, and surely the risk was no greater than the bovine kiss that brought Pickett cowboy glory inside and outside the rodeo ring and could just as well have killed him. So in the cold spring morning of that final stampede, in that sacrifice of the cowboys and the bull, King and Johnny and then my dad three weeks later, that was the hewing of the channels of misfortune that opened up all the pathways I'm travelling on, all my deviations to the points charted on the maps for writing a story of settlement now profoundly unsettled, the tale that unravels even as I weave it together.

How far I had to stray on land and sea, in the air and across all these pages, in the library, map in hand, and how studiously I looked away from what I could not bear, or peered sideways at what my dad could not bear, until he faced it at the end of his gun on April Fool's Day, his death and Johnny's now keeping alive the dream of tearing down the fences to restore the buffalo, of resurrection of the Assiniboine and restoration of the prairie to precolonial conditions before the maps and borders were drawn (all those fictions), before the horns were taken in the guts, triggers pulled. Who does not long to redress the crimes, resurrect the dead, and return the land to its original inhabitants, but that calls for the overthrow of the settler parents, most of whom could scarcely conceive of themselves as guilty given what they were fleeing and the hardships endured in getting here.

Suknaski found the words in Wood Mountain for what I encountered on the pathways of my misfortune when he wrote of "vaguely divided guilt; guilt for what happened to the Indian (his land taken) imprisoned on his reserve; and guilt because to feel this guilt is a betrayal of what you ethnically are—the son of a homesteader and his wife who must be rightfully honoured" in their turn. In Wood Mountain, in the library, at Borges's knee, Suknaski was tracking the way to some kind of alliance or fusion between settler and Aboriginal in the mixed, Métis guises of cowboy and gaucho in his poetry and in our searching through all the graveyards of literature and art and their ruins. And on the morning of my mother's death that would finally free up the story and me for its telling, such as I have been able to do, I stood at her bedside and found her fitful. The skin of her cheeks had hardened to the shells they would be once the last of her vital spirits passed out of the corpse she was already becoming. Teardrops exploded from her eyes. They bounced and slid, and when they touched they formed rivulets pouring down her death mask as it hardened before my eyes. Clutching at my arms, she seemed to be trying to tell me something, her lips moving, but they were as flimsy and crisp as dried leaves and only rustled feebly. I reached over to offer her a sip of water from a straw, but she brushed it away, reinforcing my sense she had something to say to me, and what could that be? Blood rushed to my head, my own mouth trying to speak but also trying not to so I could hear any words that might escape on her breath.

Flailing about in my mind, I glanced down toward the foot of her bed and there caught a vision of what I thought she motioned toward, the Great Plains spreading south in a tremendous golden oval sweep from the northern point of the Palliser Triangle to the Rio Grande and beyond in the distant mists of the isthmus. Voices and words wafted in the air, and I thought they came from the Assiniboine camps around the Old Post at Wood Mountain or the coulee south of Willow Bunch, or from Standing Rock, Madrid, Dodge City, from all through the panhandles, Oklahoma and Texas, down through Chihuahua, farther and farther, leaping the Panama Canal and south to the plains of Colombia, the pampas of Argentina. Spanish, English, Métis French, Nakoda, Dakota, Lakota, Siksika, nēhiyawēwin, how those languages are resurging and reclaiming their proper names.

Mom's hands softened on my arms and fell to her sides, and I thought she was at rest. Still I looked away from her and toward what startled me, what I saw from the vantage point of her dying out, what her death was opening up for my life. I saw myself crouched over a low fire. Ancient women were teaching me, among many others, how to cook with hot stones. For dwelling in Assiniboia and on the Great Plains, I thought. I reached for some ingredient—paprika, cumin, or cayenne—from the mess box behind me and saw our wagon was emblazoned with "Great Plains Story Theatre Company" on its side, the letters entwined with real willow whips braided ingeniously to shape the stretched and elongated faces of coyotes howling from tall grasses that appeared to grow out of the wheel wells. We were camped atop the petroglyphs at St. Victor, the prairie spreading before and all around us. Actors were milling about mouthing new words, their lines in Métis French and what I took to be Lakota mixed into English for gathering the stories they would make into scenes, like the one just ended, called "Last Seen," about sightings by witnesses of people who'd gone quiet or missing, their cries and stories not heard exactly but wafting on the wind and awakening memories to recover the clues about where to find them in the darkening theatre of the world.

Afterward, while clearing Mom's desk with my sisters, I found an envelope with a list in Mom's handwriting of all the destinations and jobs I'd held in my wayward life up to 1990, when I picked up my interrupted university studies at Carleton University and she lost much of the sway she'd had over me as I escaped into the library and formal education, her overbearingness backing me up the ladder of social mobility, higher and higher. What? My first reaction on reading that list, her outline of my life, was disbelief. Then alarm. My life in her hand. Was it the outline for her next book? I became acutely aware of the lack of any boundary between us, the way it is with our mothers and fathers. After prohibiting my writing and shutting me up all these years, had she been planning to colonize and write my story too? Or, as I thought more generously on reflection, was it the outline for my own book that could only be written after she died, and she had helpfully left its outline there for me to find? Did it mean she passed away resigned or even contented she could no longer prevent me from writing what I would? One or the other might have been what she had been trying to say, or so I thought.

My life in her hand begins with Wampum Day. How could I have forgotten the family legend that I was born on Wampum Day, which pinpointed my birth on a Wednesday, Wampum Day always on Wednesdays in Assiniboia, when the descendants of the Assiniboine were paid the small amounts, one or two dollars a year, allotted to each by Treaty 4, the payments that pretended to compensate as it cleared them from what became farmland for families like mine and made us the instruments of colonization, glad yet wearied, indignant and sorry, for which shortfall we did not and never could make up or rectify. "Wednesday's child is full of woe," said one of the sisters' tea towels embroidered by my mother's hand. As far as Mom was concerned, Wampum Day marked the beginning of my story, and so it has, though I never thought to ask while she was alive about the significance she apparently attributed to that coincidence and connection. Was she now prompting me with her list to make something of it, my life, to somehow write the story in a way that wouldn't compound the losses of those crowded out and displaced by our settlement? An acknowledgement, an apology, a rendering of accounts for debts that can be repaid only by answering the call of history, the calls to action, and finding the words to answer, the ways to proceed, neighbour by neighbour, in recovery of the Indigenous names and lands returned?

I pored over Mom's crabbed handwriting, marvelling at the headings of my life in her hand, the trespassing and caring intrusiveness of it all. Her dying and my dad's washed over me, and I felt more than heard the stirrings of the Buffalo God, high overhead, now turning to peer under the parlour table on which it was so precariously perched. I thought it was about to step down and cause a real commotion, toppling the table in what would be a tumultuous levelling, a reckoning and revaluation of land and kin and community, its huge wet nose nudging and about to sink that puny ship on the lower shelf, beneath an indifferent moon.

AFTERWORD

In July 2015, fully thirty-six years after the events in Johnny Bradley's corral, one of my Swift Current cousins, who grew up on a farm near Cantuar and is like a sister to me, told me out of the blue that it wasn't a buffalo bull that gored Johnny but an Italian Chianina bull, bred for its gentleness and docility. She told me Johnny intended to cross-breed the Chianina with his buffalo to produce "beefalo," a hybrid he hoped would be safer to handle, part of a North American breeding program now widely considered a failure, not only in Johnny's corral but also in the Grand Canyon and elsewhere, where it has had unintended and undesirable consequences that my cousin did not specify. More recently, that cousin's sister, a writer herself, wrote to me to correct the record yet again. She had it from Johnny Bradley's nephew, the same one who shot the bull in the corral in my reconstruction of that scene and found Dad on the morning of April 2. He told her that it was a Marchigiana bull, yet another Italian breed, docile or wild she did not say. And whether Johnny was loading or unloading the bull, neither cousin has confirmed, though I forgot to ask in what seems an endless pile-up of conflicting details and sources on bloodied and perpetually shifting ground.

Perhaps even more damaging to the factual status of the story is that my cousin said her brother-in-law Jack had looked in on Dad sometime during the day on Sunday, April 1, 1979, and reported he found Uncle Bern, as Dad was to him, cleaning his gun. He seemed to be in good spirits despite the loss of his friend Johnny just a few weeks earlier. So Dad was cleaning his gun, and later drinking, as the coroner's report attests, all of which raises the possibility that he accidentally shot himself, though no one, to my knowledge, thought or said this at the time, his pain at the loss of Johnny assuring everyone he had taken responsibility by shooting himself that night on purpose.

On hearing of these corrections regarding the nature of the bull, not necessarily entirely reliable or unreliable, and the report of Jack's account of that April Fool's Day, I wondered if the species and breed of the goring bull matter to the story as it finally unfolds, or if the death as either suicide or accident makes a difference, if I would have carried the corpses around all these years or been haunted by and worried about the writing without the motivating romance of the buffalo, the pathos of two old cowboys, and cruel displacements of the Assiniboine, all those deaths and obliterations from the record that burn at the centre of life within the Palliser Triangle and beyond to this day. Whether it was a Chianina or a Marchigiana bull that gored Johnny, killing him when it was meant to lower that very risk through cross-breeding for the reintroduction of the buffalo in the form of a new hybrid, the historical irony is only intensified. Johnny's death by a bull supposedly more docile yet more dangerous than the buffalo he was reintroducing to the prairie, as the story is revised by my Swift Current cousins, even more decisively locates the violence and destructiveness of the colonial encounter at the feet of the imported, immigrant European party.

Fortunately, we have a greater capacity to intervene in matters of culture than in biology through the stories we tell about the near extinction of the buffalo and their restoration

to the Great Plains, the displacement of the Assiniboine, and now the fate of some few descendants of settlers who crowded them out. In the end, I decided the stunning assertions of my cousins if true—and who is to say at this far remove?—introduce just more uncertainties that threaten to further delay all reckoning by obstructing the telling of the story that could not be uttered aloud or looked at directly until now.

ACKNOWLEDGEMENTS

With this book, I acknowledge the losses suffered by Indigenous peoples of the territory covered by Treaty 4 as the precondition of my origins there. I do not claim to tell their stories but find grounds for solidarity with Indigenous peoples in recovering and telling my own. In acknowledging their losses, I seek to share the burdens of reconciliation between settler descendants and Indigenous people.

I would like to thank St. Thomas University in Fredericton, New Brunswick, and our faculty union for the provision of sabbatical leaves and other supportive working conditions from which I have benefited. Departmental Assistant Barb Haines cheerfully helped with seemingly endless photocopying and distributing of drafts. I thank also the editors at the University of Regina Press. David McLennan, Daniel Lockhart, managing editor Kelly Laycock, designer Duncan Campbell, and copyeditor Dallas Harrison have helped to make my book more accessible.

I thank writers Erín Moure and Kathleen McConnell for several incisive suggestions for improving the manuscript. My friend Jill Spelliscy, now of Charlottetown, listened to many of these stories and took them seriously as I first began to piece them together. Her validation of my experience has been critical for my ability to communicate my story to others. Dennis Gruending and Martha Wiebe hosted a memorable supper in

Ottawa that became a storytelling occasion for me to say some things out loud for the first time and spurred the writing. Marike Finlay, on the eastern shore of Nova Scotia, made helpful suggestions for revision of an earlier version. Karin Cope invited me into her class on "Strategic Fictions" at NSCAD University in Halifax, which helped me to hear what the story sounds like to others. I thank also the composer Martin Kutnowski of St. Thomas University, who wrote a score for my country song, "Now That I Been to Nashville," that we sang with a pick-up choir at the Art Bar in Halifax in October 2016.

Many others assisted in the writing of this book without knowing of its existence. My many brothers and sisters have been my anchors in time and space. Our Morgan cousin Connie Leibel, of Unity, Saskatchewan, extended warm hospitality when I was tracing the Palliser Triangle to its apex there. Cabri cousins Grant and Louise McLeod offered bed and board when I was hanging around or passing through that small town that looms so large in our lives to this day. Meryl Colpitts welcomed me like a sister when I needed to retrace steps on the sunken Morgan place across the road from her farm, and we all thank Meryl's brother John Colpitts for his care and concern for our lost brother during his last days in and around Cabri. Swift Current cousins Bonnie Dunlop and Lexie Lines corrected some crucial points of fact, for which I am thankful. All remaining uncertainties are just the way the story remains in a perpetual state of unfolding and ongoing revision.

Finally, I thank my husband, Michael Kamen. He acquires the name Chase in my account of chasing him to Nashville, where he caused the heartbreak that inspired me to write my country song as recounted in Chapter 5. The names of some others are similarly changed or suppressed to emphasize their social roles or relationships to me, such as crew boss, wife, and farmer.

Dawn Morgan
Fredericton, New Brunswick
October 3, 2021

PLAYLIST

(songs quoted or referred to, in order of appearance)

"Sunday Morning Coming Down" (Kris Kristofferson)

"Four Strong Winds" (Ian Tyson)

"Wayfaring Stranger" (Traditional)

"Lake Charles" (Lucinda Williams)

"Starwalker" and "Indian Cowboy of the Rodeo" (Buffy Sainte-Marie)

"Singin' the Blues" (Marty Robbins)

"Don Quixote" (Gordon Lightfoot)

"Paprika Plains" (Joni Mitchell)

"When a Ration Book Is Just a Souvenir" (Jule Syne and Samuel Cahn)

"Watch Your Step Polka" (kd lang)

"What Goes Around (Comes Around)" (Laura Smith)

"Lost Highway" (Hank Williams)

"Don't It Make My Brown Eyes Blue" (Crystal Gayle)

"River Road" (Sylvia Tyson)

"Luckenbach, Texas (Back to the Basics of Love)" (Waylon Jennings)

"Outskirts" (Blue Rodeo)

"Kansas City" (Jerry Leiber and Mike Stoller)

"Ring of Fire" (June Carter Cash/Merle Kilgore)

"Return of the Grievous Angels" (Gram Parsons)

"Desperado" (Glenn Frey and Don Henley)

"I'm So Lonesome I Could Cry" (Hank Williams)

"Brass Buttons" (Gram Parsons)

"Hickory Wind" (Gram Parsons)

"Wild Horses" (Mick Jagger/Keith Richards)

"Motherless Child" (Traditional and Blind Willie Johnson)

"Never Been to Spain" (Hoyt Axton)

"Guitars, Cadillacs" (Dwight Yoakam)

"Girl from the North Country" (Bob Dylan)

"Heartaches by the Number" (Harlan Howard)

"Now that I Been to Nashville" (Dawn Morgan)

"Fairytale" (Anita and Bonnie Pointer)

"Still Haven't Found What I'm Looking For" (Bono and U2)

"In My Hour of Darkness" (Gram Parsons and Emmylou Harris)

"Love Will Come Again" (Michael L. Kamen)

"Water for My Horses" (Hoyt Axton)

SOURCES AND
SELECTED REFERENCES

Adorno, Theodor W. *Minima Moralia: Reflections from Damaged Life.* Translated by E.F.N. Jephcott. London: Verso, 2020.

Andrews, Nigel. "The Cowboy Rides Again. . . ." *Financial Times* [London, UK], (December 3, 2005): 34.

Atwood, Margaret. *You Are Happy.* Toronto: Oxford University Press, 1974.

Bandlamudi, Lakshmi. *Dialogics of the Self, The Mahabharata, and Culture.* London: Anthem Press, 2010.

Bastos, Wilson, and Sidney J. Levy. "A History of the Concept of Branding: Practice and Theory." *Journal of Historical Research in Marketing* 4, no. 3 (2012): 347–68.

Bataille, Georges. *The Story of the Eye by Lord Auch.* Translated by Joachim Neugroschel. San Francisco: City Lights, 1987.

Benjamin, Walter. *The Origin of German Tragic Drama.* Translated by John Osborne. Brooklyn: Verso Books, 1998.

Billington, James H. *The Icon and the Axe: An Interpretive History of Russian Culture.* Vintage, 1970.

Böhme, Jacob. *Aurora, That Is, the Day-Spring, or Dawning of the Day in the Orient, or Morning-Rednesse in the Rising of the Sun, That Is, the Root or Mother of Philosophie Astrologie, and*

Theologie from the True Ground, or a Description of Nature. . . . Translated by John Sparrow. London: n.p., 1656.

Borges, Jorge Luis. *Borges: A Reader*. Edited by Emir Rodríguez Monegal and Alastair Reid. Works quoted are translated by N.T. di Giovanni and Alastair Reid respectively. New York: Dutton, 1981. Excerpts from "Dawn" and "General Quiroga Rides to His Death in a Carriage" reprinted with permission.

———. *Ficciones*. Edited by Anthony Kerrigan. Translated by Anthony Bonner and Alastair Reid. New York: Grove Press, 1962.

Brown, Dee. *Bury My Heart at Wounded Knee*. 1970; reprinted, New York: Washington Square Press, 1981.

Browne, Thomas. "Hydriotaphia: Urne Buriall; Or, A Discourse of the Sepulchrall Urnes Lately Found in Norfolk." In *Religio Medici and Other Writings*, by Thomas Browne, 91–139. London: Everyman's Library, 1965.

Butala, Sharon. *Wild Stone Heart: An Apprentice in the Fields*. Toronto: Harper Flamingo Books, 2000.

Butler, Judith. "Who Owns Kafka?" *London Review of Books* (March 3, 2011): 3-8.

Cardenal, Ernesto. *With Walker in Nicaragua and Other Early Poems, 1949–1954*. Translated by Jonathan Cohen. Middletown, CT: Wesleyan University Press, 1984.

———. *Zero Hour and Other Documentary Poems*. Edited by Donald D. Walsh. Translated by Paul W. Borgeson, Jr., Jonathan Cohen, Robert Pring-Mill, and Donald D. Walsh. New York: New Directions Press, 1980.

Cervantes, Miguel. *The Adventures of Don Quixote*. Translated by J.M. Cohen. London: Penguin, 1950.

Crozier, Lorna. *Inventing the Hawk*. Toronto: McClelland and Stewart, 1992. Excerpt from "Hemingway in Spain," reproduced by permission of the author.

Daschuk, James. *Clearing the Plains: Disease, Politics of Starvation, and the Loss of Aboriginal Life*. Regina: University of Regina Press, 2013.

Deleuze, Gilles, and Félix Guattari. "Kafka: Toward a Minor Literature: The Components of Expression." Translated by Marie Maclean. *New Literary History* 16, no. 3 (1985): 591–608. https://doi.org/10.2307/468842.

Erasmus, Peter. *Buffalo Days and Nights*. As told to Henry Thompson. Calgary: Glenbow Institute, 1999.

Fabini, Luis, with text by Wade Davis. *Cowboys of the Americas*. Vancouver: Greystone Books, 2016.

Fernández Retamar, Roberto. *Caliban and Other Essays*. Translated by Edward Baker. Minneapolis: University of Minnesota Press, 1989.

Galchen, Rivka. "Wild West Germany: Why Do Cowboys and Indians So Captivate the Country?" *The New Yorker* (April 9, 2012) www.newyorker.com/magazine/2012/04/09.

Hayek, Friedrich. *The Road to Serfdom*. London: Routledge, 1944.

Hemingway, Ernest. *Death in the Afternoon*. New York: Charles Scribner and Sons, 1932.

Henighan, Stephen. *Sandino's Nation: Ernesto Cardenal and Sergio Ramírez Writing Nicaragua, 1940–2012*. Montreal and Kingston: McGill-Queen's University Press, 2014.

Hernández, José. *The Gaucho Martín Fierro*. Translated by C.E. Ward. New York: SUNY Press, 1967.

Herriot, Trevor. *Towards a Prairie Atonement*. Regina: University of Regina Press, 2016.

Hutton, Patrick H. *History as an Art of Memory*. Hanover, VT: University Press of New England, 1993.

Kafka, Franz. *Amerika*. Translated by Willa and Edwin Muir. New York: Schocken Books, 1962. (First published in German in 1927.) Excerpts copyright 1946 by Penguin Random House LLC, copyright renewed 1974 by Penguin Random House LLC. Used by permission of Schocken Books, an imprint of the Knopf Doubleday Publishing Group, a division of Penguin Random House LLC. All rights reserved.

———. *The Castle*. Translated by Mark Harman. New York: Schocken Books, 1998. (First published in German in 1926.)

Kinsey Howard, Joseph. *Strange Empire: The Story of Louis Riel*. Toronto: Swan Publishing, 1952.

Klossowski De Rola, Stanislas. *The Golden Game: Alchemical Engravings of the Seventeenth Century*. London: Thames and Hudson, 1997.

Leiris, Michel. "The Bullfight as Mirror." Translated by Ann Smock. *October Magazine* 63, (1993): 21–40.

———. "Literature Considered as a Bullfight" (later retitled "Afterword: The Autobiographer as *Torero*"). In *Manhood: A Journey from Childhood into the Fierce Order of Virility*, translated by Richard Howard, 153–64. Chicago: University of Chicago Press, 1992.

Malick, Terrence, dir. *Days of Heaven*. Paramount Pictures, 1978.

Mason, Marjorie Rohde. *One Hundred Years of Grasslands*. North Battleford, SK: Turner-Warwick Publishing, 1993.

McCarthy, Tom. "Writing Machines: Tom McCarthy on Realism and the Real." *London Review of Books* (December 18, 2014): 21–22.

Narasimhan, Chakravarthi V. *The Mahabharata: An English Version Based on Selected Verses*. Edited by William Theodore de Bary. New York: Columbia University Press, 1965.

Newlove, John. "Not Swimming, but Drowning." In *Addicted: Notes from the Belly of the Beast*, 2nd ed., edited by Lorna Crozier and Patrick Lane, 169–85. Vancouver: Douglas and McIntyre, 2001.

Palliser, John. *Solitary Rambles, and Adventures of a Hunter in the Prairies*. British Library, Historical Print Editions. London: John Murray, 1853.

Popper, Deborah E., and Frank J. Popper. "The Buffalo Commons: Metaphor as Method." *Geographical Review* 89, no. 4 (1999): 491–510.

Randall, Margaret. *Sandino's Daughters: Testimonies of Nicaraguan Women in Struggle*. Edited by Lynda Yanz. London: ZED Books; Vancouver: New Star Books, 1981.

Rickard, Paul M., dir. *Ring of Fire.* Six-part documentary series. Mushkeg Media and APTN, 2015.

Robertson, William. *k.d. lang: Carrying the Torch.* Toronto: ECW Press, 1992.

Sarmiento, Domingo Faustino. *Facundo: Civilization and Barbarism.* Translated by Kathleen Ross. Introduction by Roberto González Echevarría. Berkeley: University of California Press, 2003. (Originally published in Spanish in 1845.)

Savage, Candace. *A Geography of Blood.* Vancouver: Greystone Books, 2012.

Shepard, Sam. *Buried Child.* In *Sam Shepard: Seven Plays,* introduced by Richard Gilman, 61–132. Toronto: Bantam Books, 1981.

Slatta, Richard W. *Cowboys of the Americas.* New Haven, CT: Yale University Press, 1990.

Spak, Harvey, dir. *Wood Mountain Poems.* National Film Board of Canada, 1978.

Spry, Irene M., ed. *The Palliser Papers 1857–60.* Toronto: The Champlain Society, 1968.

Stegner, Wallace. *Wolf Willow: A History, a Story, and a Memory of the Last Prairie Frontier.* Toronto: Macmillan, 1955.

Suknaski, Andrew. "borges and i; mandel and me." Review-article of Emir Rodríquez Monegal, *Borges: A Literary Biography* (New York: Dutton, 1978). In *Brick: A Literary Journal* 9 (Spring 1980): 16–24.

——. *The Ghosts Call You Poor.* Toronto: Macmillan, 1978.

——. *Silk Trail.* Toronto: Nightwood Editions, 1985.

——. *Wood Mountain Poems.* Toronto: Macmillan, 1976.

Tressell, Robert (a.k.a. Robert Noonan). *The Ragged Trousered Philanthropists: Being the Story of Twelve Months in Hell, Told by One of the Damned and Written Down by Robert Tressell.* 1914; reprinted, London: Monthly Review Press, 1962.

Born and raised in Assiniboia, Saskatchewan, DAWN MORGAN is currently Associate Professor of English at St. Thomas University in Fredericton, New Brunswick.